PONDERING
POSTINTERNATIONALISM

SUNY series in Global Politics
James N. Rosenau, editor

PONDERING POSTINTERNATIONALISM

A Paradigm For The Twenty-First Century?

Edited by

HEIDI H. HOBBS

State University
of New York
Press

Published by
State University of New York Press, Albany

© 2000 State University of New York

For information, address State University of New York Press,
State University Plaza, Albany, N.Y., 12246

Production by Michael Haggett
Marketing by Fran Keneston

Library of Congress Cataloging-in-Publication Data

Pondering postinternationalism : a paradigm for the twenty-first
  century? / edited by Heidi H. Hobbs.
        p.   cm. — (SUNY series in global politics)
    Includes bibliographical references and index.
    ISBN 0-7914-4507-0 (hc. : alk. paper). — ISBN 0-7914-4508-9 (pb.
: alk. paper)
    1. International relations.   2. World politics.   I. Hobbs, Heidi
H.   II. Series.
JZ1242.P66   2000
327.1'01—dc21   99-39747
                                                              CIP

10 9 8 7 6 5 4 3 2 1

To the Rosenau in all of us who looks for patterns in a chaotic world from the highest rungs on "the ladder of abstraction" and contemplates the question—"Of what is this an instance?"

CONTENTS

TABLES

ACKNOWLEDGMENTS

I am very fortunate to have been a part of this project. This volume grew out of a panel entitled "Pondering Postinternationalism: A Rosenau Retrospective" at the American Political Science Association annual meeting in San Francisco in 1996. The idea for the panel came from two of my former colleagues at Florida International University, Dario Moreno and Nick Onuf. Dario was serving as the program chair for the Foreign Policy Section at the time and he and Nick came upon the idea for the panel over lunch. Dario enlisted me to chair the panel and as they say, "the rest is history." Even before the panel actually met, several of the participants and I saw the potential for an edited volume and proceeded accordingly. Six of the seven panel participants have chapters here, as well as six others who were interested in the project.

The editing process has been delightful, given the insightfulness of the essay themselves and the professionalism of the contributors, who have gotten their chapters to me in a timely manner and followed my requests. There is a lesson for new scholars in the field to learn from these authors!

I am most thankful for the assistance I have received in this project, first and foremost, from the Department of Political Science at Florida International University. I am also grateful to the Department of Political Science and Public Administration at North Carolina State where I have been visiting while finishing the manuscript.

Several individuals stand out in this process. From an intellectual point, the contributors and especially Joe Lepgold, Dario Moreno, Nick Onuf, and Jim Rosenau have been most helpful. Computer support from Carmen De Jesus and Barbara Herrera at Florida International, and Carol Apperson and Terri Dinse at North Carolina State has been critical. Finally, my husband, Steve Fishler, and children, Perry Hobbs Fishler and Madison Hobbs Fishler, must also be recognized for their unconditional love and patience. Academics, and especially authors with a deadline, can be quite difficult at times!

INTRODUCTION

Pondering Postinternationalism

Heidi H. Hobbs

There is widespread agreement that the dynamics of international relations have changed since World War II. The postwar period has seen
a tremendous growth in the number of actors in the international
system, including both newly created and independent nation-states,
as well as a growing subnational presence. These new actors have
been confronted with unprecedented challenges and have risen to the
occasion. Yet, the study of these forces in international relations theory
remains rooted in traditional debates (realists versus transnationalists)
and familiar discourses (sovereignty and states' interests).

James N. Rosenau has responded to these changes by breaking
out of what he calls the "conceptual jails in which the study of world
politics is deemed to be incarcerated."[1] He has fashioned a paradigm
for the study of these diverse phenomenon—the postinternational
paradigm or turbulence theory (used interchangeably)—that can simultaneously cope with both state and "nonstate" actors and the
changes experienced by them in an ever evolving international order.
He has added a new lexicon to our ordering of world affairs, and
continues to push us to "think theory thoroughly."

The postinternational paradigm is the culmination of Rosenau's
many years of hard work. Steve Smith, of the University of Wales,
Aberystwyth, in speaking at an International Studies Association panel
honoring Rosenau in 1991, most eloquently pointed out the way in
which the many stages of Rosenau's work has led to postinternationalism,
most notably, linkage theory, adaptation, and the pretheory of foreign
policy.[2] Rosenau has distinguished himself in the field of international
relations as a leader. He has championed the cause of social science and
directed his colleagues to look closely at their discipline. While not a
methodologist himself, he has urged scholars to proceed carefully and

in a methodologically correct manner in their attempts at understanding the complexities of global life.

But what about content and contribution? Rosenau's forte has been in the marriage of the discipline to the complexities of everyday life—in understanding "global patterns" when many were unsure there was such a thing beyond a traditional state-centric, realist-dominated point of view. Rosenau was one of the first to elaborate on the linkages between domestic and foreign policy. The pretheory of foreign policy offered a reasoned way to understand similarities in the way in which states behaved, at a time when there was little attention beyond very cursory comparative analysis. He recognized the important points his colleagues were making at the time—such as David Easton, J. David Singer, and Bruck, Snyder, and Sapin—and brought them into a broader frame of reference in his subsequent work.[3]

In his theory of adaptation he argued that the contradictions of complexity did not spell disaster for the nation-state, but instead pushed the state to rise to the occasion and adapt accordingly.[4] He incorporated these abilities in his review of the pretheory on its twentieth anniversary, bringing together the increasing ability of individuals to influence the nature of international relations while relying on the adaptability of the state to respond to this challenge.[5] These ideas precipitated many of the changes that would emerge in the next few years, as the bipolar system eroded, and the Cold War came to an end. Was Rosenau a visionary in this regard? Perhaps, but Rosenau's work never focused on the constraints of the existing system, which has tied the hands of so many of international relations theorists. Instead, Rosenau was always looking beyond those constraints, and the fact that they ultimately broke down just offered greater evidence for his contentions.

Rosenau captures these contradictions in the turbulence model, in which he notes the prolific global changes experienced in the world today.[6] Identifying three parameters of global change—the micro, the micro-macro and macro parameters—Rosenau argues that at each level individuals are becoming more skilled in their ability to deal with the world around them while, simultaneously, their world is less able to provide them the authority structures that once governed their environment. The result is a bifurcation of global structures, where individuals and states may often find themselves as odds. These changes require a new terminology and better tools of analysis to understand the dynamics at work.

The central question remains, however, the extent to which the postinternational paradigm constitutes a coherent research program. The purpose of this volume is to explore both the strengths and weaknesses of the postinternational paradigm as a model for studying international relations in the twenty-first century. It provides an opportunity not only for the critics to have their say, but for those who espouse this perspective to refine their views toward a more workable paradigm that allows for clear specification of research parameters, empirical testing of hypotheses, and ultimately, true theory building.

Toward that end, the chapters in Part 1, "Postinternationalism in Perspective," explore the paradigm from other points of view in the field. In the opening chapter, Richard Mansbach explores the underlying arguments of the postinternational paradigm and their relationship to historical trends. Dario Moreno follows with an examination of the role of sovereignty in the paradigm. In the third chapter, Margaret Karns explores the postinternational paradigm from the context of governance, while Spike Peterson concludes this part with a feminist point of view.

A critical dimension of the turbulence model is the unique role of individuals. Part 2, "The Role of Citizens in a Postinternational World," examines the individual from three different perspectives. First, Ronnie Lipschutz compares the growing literature on global civil society and the way in which postinternationalism both informs and is informed by this view. Nicholas Onuf then adopts a more postmodern perspective as he looks for traditional writings on the role of individuals and their habits, specifically Hume, and how that might relate to Rosenau's conceptualization. Finally, Ole Holsti explores public opinion and its impact on postinternationalism, comparing both realist and liberal worldviews.

The third part, "Postinternationalism: A Paradigm for the Twenty-First Century?", offers some methods for operationalizing the paradigm for future research. Mary Durfee clarifies the meaning of complex systems in her chapter and how they might be examined. Joseph Lepgold places postinternationalism in the liberal tradition and identifies ways to move forward. Ralph DiMuccio and Eric Cooper take a more methodical approach, first giving an in-depth history of Rosenau's personal evolution to postinternationalism, then doing a citation comparison with Waltz's, *Theory of International Politics*, to chart the movement of postinternationalism into the mainstream of international relations discourse. Yale Ferguson concludes this part with a call to arms for those interested in postinternationalism to take up their pens and test hypotheses, chart a new course, and create new structures.

The final part, "A Postinternationationalist's Response," gives Rosenau his say. Rosenau responds to his colleagues, complementing their insights and looking to the future.

The contributors to this volume share an interest in the postinternational paradigm and a respect not only for James N. Rosenau, the scholar, but for the person as well. They have all known Rosenau either as students, colleagues, or both. I myself have been fortunate enough to be both student and colleague, and both my academic and personal life have been enriched by this association. Therefore, this volume serves not only as an exploration of the enormous intellectual contribution Rosenau has made to the field of international relations, but as an example of the personal touch he has extended to students and colleagues all over the world. The dedication and enthusiasm Rosenau brings to his work is an inspiration for us all.

There can be no doubt that the international system has changed in profound ways. While some would argue that the forces of history simply repeat themselves, the ways in which we have studied those forces have been limited by the narrow focus international relations scholars have employed. The postinternational paradigm suggests an alternate view that may enable us to be more effective in our theorizing. It is a useful starting point for reevaluating our theoretical limitations as we move into the future.

NOTES

1. James N. Rosenau, *Turbulence in World Politics: A Theory of Change and Continuity* (Princeton, N.J.: Princeton University Press, 1990), p. 22.

2. Steve Smith, University of Wales, Aberstywyth, speaking at the International Studies Association, Vancouver, B.C., 1991.

3. James N. Rosenau, *The Scientific Study of Foreign Policy* (London: Frances Pinter Publishers Ltd., 1981).

4. James N. Rosenau, *The Study of Political Adaptation* (London: Frances Pinter Publishers Ltd., 1981).

5. James N. Rosenau, "A Pre-Theory Revisited: World Politics in an Era of Cascading Interdependence," *International Studies Quarterly* 28 (September 1984): 245–305.

6. James N. Rosenau and Mary Durfee, *Thinking Theory thoroughly: Coherent Approaches to an Incoherent World* (Boulder, Colo.: Westview Press, 1995).

PART 1

Postinternationalism in Perspective

The subtitle of this book asks the question of whether postinternationalism is indeed "a paradigm for the twenty-first century." To answer that question, we must first put the paradigm in perspective, particularly as it relates to the broader field of international relations. The chapters in this part are designed with that purpose in mind.

The study of international relations historically has been fairly circumspect in delineating its heritage. Richard Mansbach explores this history by carefully defining what postinternationalism is and what it is not.

Dario Moreno follows with an examination of postinternationalism from the more prevailing view of relations between states—sovereignty. Rosenau acknowledges sovereignty as a defining concept in the international arena, but is not constrained by it, arguing some of the most interesting relations that develop are not bound by the demands of sovereignty.

Margaret Karns takes us further in this journey as she looks at the patterns of global governance, so relevant today, and the comfortable relationship postinternationalism can enjoy with this view.

Finally, Spike Peterson employs the innovative approaches developing in feminist international relations theory to critique the "political correctness" of postinternationalism. Despite Rosenau's attention to individuality, Peterson argues his perspective still suffers from a masculine-dominated structure.

CHAPTER 1

Changing Understandings of Global Politics: Preinternationalism, Internationalism, and Postinternationalism

Richard W. Mansbach

In my salad days when I was green of judgment, I was fortunate to work with and learn from three of the field's most distinguished theorists—Kenneth N. Waltz, Robert O. Keohane, and James N. Rosenau. The first, my undergraduate mentor, persuaded me of the centrality of power, the virtues of neorealism, and the pleasures of parsimony. The second, with whom I taught at Swarthmore College, persuaded me that structural explanations only explained part of the world around us, omitting the complex and growing interdependence among societies that facilitate cooperation and the mechanisms, both formal and informal, that were proliferating in global politics in response to demands for collective goods. The third, who, wisely or not, hired me at Rutgers University, persuaded me of the virtues of combining reason and science to understanding global politics and of wedding rigorous theoretical and empirical analysis.

ROSENAU: CONTINUITY AND CHANGE

In the ensuing decades, these three theorists towered over their peers as theorists of international relations, but their ideas about global politics evolved in very different directions. Waltz became, if anything, increasingly associated with a highly parsimonious version of generalizable, system-level, and deductive theory that we label "structural realism."

Keohane has been immersed in global institutions and ideas that serve as intervening variables between the state and its capabilities, on the one hand, and emergent properties of the global system, on the other. He too is a neorealist, but only sometimes. Rosenau's thinking about global politics has evolved more dramatically than the others' and is, therefore, the hardest to categorize. It has also had a deeper and more enduring impact on me. For this reason, what follows is something of a personal response to the issues raised in this volume. Postinternationalism, in any event, only has meaning in the context of the evolution of Rosenau's ideas.

I first met Jim Rosenau about the time that *Contending Approaches to International Politics* and the revised edition of *International Politics and Foreign Policy* made their appearance. (For those of you who have ever wondered about Rosenau the teacher, you should look at the dedication to his introductory undergraduate students in *International Politics and Foreign Policy*.) The appearance of these books was something of a high-water mark of Rosenau the prophet of science. Still, despite his attachment to the scientific method, Rosenau, for better or worse, was never preoccupied with parsimony. Although he virtually invented the subfield of the comparative study of foreign policy, he remained basically catholic in approach and was never wedded either to a particular methodology or theoretical prism.

At first glance, the distance traveled from the rigorous state-centric empiricist to the advocate of a somewhat less robust "potential observability"[1] and occasionally reflexive postinternationalist seems immense. As an advocate of science, Rosenau confidently declared that "the nation-state is no different from the atom or the single cell organism." The patterns of behavior of any human institution were, he believed, as susceptible to empiricism as "the characteristics of the electron or the molecule."[2] Contrast this with the later Rosenau, who argues that "postinternationalist politics" are the result of dramatic changes in global politics just as the social sciences more generally are "marked by analyses of postcapitalist society, postcivilized era, postcollectivist politics, posteconomic society, posthistoric man, postideological society, postliberal era, postliterature culture, postmarket society, post-Marxists, postmaterialist value system, postmaturity economy, postmodernism, postorganization society, post-Christian era, postscarcity society, postsocialist society, posttraditional society, and postwelfare society, as well as postindustrial society."[3]

At first blush, the postinternational enterprise seems light-years away from the concerns of Rosenau the scientist. Such a conclusion would be mistaken. In fact, there is much continuity in the evolution of Rosenau's thinking and, throughout his career, he kept returning to many of the same key puzzles, notably the relationship of wholes and parts, the relationship of domestic and international factors (and, therefore, necessarily, the role and nature of the state in global politics), and the interdependence and linked fates of individuals and communities.

The Relationship of Wholes and Parts

Rosenau was never an advocate of structural determinism, and "black boxes," "billiards," and similar metaphors never attracted him. Instead, much of his work revolved around the problem of how parts and wholes interact and are related to one another. In *Turbulence*, this takes the form of "mixing micro-macro."[4] The most important aspect of "mixing micro-macro" is the role of individuals in the political universe and their relationship to the collectivities of which they are a part. In a very real way, then, Rosenau was wrestling with the "agent-structure" question long before that term became fashionable. "[I]ndividual actions," he declared, "can cumulate into system-wide outcomes," and "people are becoming ever more powerful as galvanizers of global change."[5]

Do individuals qua individuals matter, or are they only relevant as subjects of the state? For Rosenau, this is not merely a theoretical question but one with profound normative implications, and he repeatedly returns to the tension created by the juxtaposition of human beings as autonomous and moral beings, and as the pawns of larger structural forces. As spokesperson for the application of science to international phenomena, Rosenau depicted individuals less as self-motivated actors than as acted upon. In this context, theory was at once instrumental and utilitarian, providing the means to control human behavior and directing it into less destructive channels than in the past. Even while urging scholars to be alert to any confusion of facts and values and, in R. K. Ashley's words, inhabiting "the domain of the 'is' rather than the domain of the 'ought'," where no "normative defense" of truth was necessary,[6] scientists implicitly disparaged the capacity of human beings to alter their own fate.

In his pretheory, Rosenau brought human agents in with individual and role factors. Already one could sense a tension between the individual as a cog in a larger system and the individual as an autonomous being: On the one hand, "the potency of an individual factor is assumed to be greater in less developed economies (there being fewer of restraints which bureaucracy and large-scale organization impose in more developed economies)."[7] On the other, "[o]ur values stress the dignity of the person, the inviolability of the human spirit, and normative responsibility for one's own actions," yet "[i]ndividuals need to be treated . . . as complexes of roles and statuses" so that there is little scope for the "unique person."[8] Writing of the impact of race in global politics, Rosenau warned readers not "to exaggerate the potency of individual variables" because of the "limits set by role, governmental, societal, and systemic variables." Yet, the particular experience and personality traits of officials produce different reactions "to the fact and symbolism of skin color."[9] Finally, in his conception of the postinternational world, Rosenau has placed citizens squarely at the heart of the analysis; it is their growing skills and escalating participation in world politics, whether as users of e-mail or as demonstrators in Leipzig or Beijing that have brought an end to the Westphalian world.

The Relationship between Domestic and International Politics

Related to the puzzle of parts and wholes is another of Rosenau's enduring concerns—the linkages between what takes place within and between states. His 1967 edited volume, *The Domestic Sources of Foreign Policy*, marked a sharp break with the state-centric premises of realism. "Perhaps never before," he declared, "have the domestic sources of foreign policy seemed so important."[10] The notion that domestic and international events can be shielded from one another or that states can be treated "as an actor whose nature, motives, and conduct are so self-evident as to obviate any need for precise conceptualizing" is alien to Rosenau. "Such a usage takes macro analysis back to unitary actors and reified collectivities."[11]

Initially, Rosenau's examination of the links between the internal and external realms took the form of efforts to explore the ways in which domestic political processes and structures condition foreign policy. In the course of this exploration, the concepts of national interest and state sovereignty received critical scrutiny. Inevitably, this stream of analysis led Rosenau to question more generally the nature and role of the sovereign state in global politics.

Linkages and Linked Fates

Rosenau's early recognition that sovereign frontiers had become porous was associated with his interest in the way in which peoples, even those geographically remote from one another, shared common fates. In a frequently cited passage, he declared: "Almost every day incidents are reported that defy the principles of sovereignty. Politics everywhere, it would seem, are related to politics everywhere else." He then proposed a research agenda that would subject "national-international linkages" to "systematic, sustained, and comparative inquiry."[12] He viewed this topic as part of his larger project on the relationship between parts and wholes, in particular his effort "to develop theoretical constructs for explaining the relations between the units it [political science] investigates and their environments."[13]

Rosenau's effort to analyze domestic-international linkages did not initially move him to abandon the sovereign state as his principal unit of analysis. "Transnational polities," he argued, "are a long way from supplanting national politics and, if anything, the world may well be passing through a paradoxical stage in which *both* the linkages and the boundaries among polities are becoming more central to their daily lives."[14] He was still a "foreign-policy" theorist. Only later, with postinternationalism, did he decide "to break out of the conceptual jails in which the study of world politics is deemed to be incarcerated."[15] This meant recognizing that making "states" equivalent to the "parts" of the global system was only partly justifiable.

POSTINTERNATIONALISM

But what is "postinternationalism"? To date, it has been less a coherent theoretical position than a rejection of "internationalism"; that is, the European state-centric tradition and the model of global politics derived from this tradition that have dominated international relations (IR) thinking in recent centuries. While the vocabulary and conceptual elements of postinternationalism perform the critical function of "pointing to" a different set of factors in order to understand global politics, it has not yet acquired an explanatory or predictive capacity. Nor is postinternationalism a "paradigm" in the Kuhnian sense any more than was realism or neorealism, even though it reflects a subject marked by intellectual discontinuity and dramatic shifts in cognitive evolution. The absence of dominant research areas that generate puzzle-solving normal science makes it difficult to apply Kuhn's analysis of paradigms and paradigm shifts to social science.[16] This is less a criticism of Rosenau than a comment on the nondisciplinary nature of global politics, as well as other social sciences.

Postinternationalism represents an attractive (even seductive) break with the dominant "neos" of our field and is a highly promising first step to account for anomalies unexplained by the various theoretical islets into which international relations, like an amoeba, has divided and subdivided. In this sense, postinternationalism is another "pretheory" that, far more than its predecessor, takes account of the dynamic side of global politics. Like Rosenau's earlier pretheory, the postinternationalist enterprise seeks to encourage communication among these isolated and incommensurable islets in order to recommence the quest for grand (or at least grander) theory.

Happily, Rosenau, unlike many other IR theorists, never abandoned the possibility of "grand" theory. His determination to develop both a vocabulary and analytic framework to account for a dramatically changed reality is especially welcome in light of the proliferation of "dissident" and "guerrilla" analyses that reject objectivity, lionize relativism, and obfuscate by the felicitous misapplication of words and ideas. Happily, too, even as Rosenau was being influenced by reflexivity, he refused to descend into relativism or retreat from the effort to make sense of the world around us and thereby reduce the dangers to human well-being and survival.

The concept of postinternationalism enabled Rosenau to focus on the dynamic element in global politics "because it suggests flux and transition" and "allows for chaos."[17] Older formulations would not suffice because change "is so pervasive in both the internal and external lives of communities and nation-states."[18] Postinternational politics, as Rosenau conceptualized it, was the product of the emergence of a "multicentric" world in which individuals with increased analytic skills no longer unquestioningly complied with authority.[19]

The most important feature of the postinternational world is that it is no longer only a system of sovereign states, each enjoying exclusive control over a defined territory and with no authority above it. "Postinternational" reflects Rosenau's recognition that the parsimonious model of a state system is no longer adequate to describe or explain the complexities of contemporary global life. Instead, the state is treated as only one of several types of collective "macro actors"—subgroups, transnational organizations, leaderless publics, and movements—and has itself become "less coherent and effective." Rosenau's analysis "self-consciously breaks with . . . the 'state-is-still-predominant' tendency."[20]

There are at least six key features of a postinternational world that distinguish it from an international world.

The Skills and Participation Explosion

For Rosenau, the acquisition of new skills and orientations by individuals, accompanied by a growing sense of self-efficacy, is of fundamental importance. No longer is it possible to declare, as does Waltz, that "Domestic systems are centralized and hierarchic."[21] Hierarchy breaks down as people's "ability to employ, articulate, direct, and implement whatever their attitudes may be" and as they come to "believe they have the skills and orientations to participate in the processes of aggregation."[22] No longer can we understand global politics by limiting our field of vision to official foreign-policy elites. Global politics has become a participant sport. Whether as consumers, activists, or protesters, individual citizens collectively create global constraints and opportunities.

At the same time as the fates of people everywhere have become linked, citizens' expectations are expanding, and the demands they place on states and on the global system more generally are multiplying. No longer do people meekly accept the status and destiny that come with birth. Expanding claims tax national and international institutions, pressuring them to find new ways to cope with burgeoning pressures from below. Modern citizens enjoy advantages that were unavailable to their ancestors, but their expectations have risen even faster. As a result, their *relative* satisfaction may decline even as their absolute well-being grows.

Rosenau argues that the "printing press, telephone, radio, television, and personal computer have created conditions for skill development among citizenries that governments could not totally control and that have helped make citizenries more effective in relation to the centers of authority."[23] There is a strong democratic implication to this observation.

There is, however, another side to this that tends to work against democratic norms. Skills and knowledge acquisition is uneven. Although everyone acquires *some* additional skills, a managerial and technocratic class is emerging that is linked globally by language (English and "techno-jargon"), the Concorde, and e-mail. In the words of Susan Strange, "the nature of the technology meant that almost all [new users] were employees of big business, government or universities," and the privileges of these " 'knowledge workers' were greatly enhanced by comparison with those of manual workers in agriculture or industrial manufacturing."[24] Democracy is actually eroded by the fact that new communications technologies make it easier to maintain closed epistemic communities.

The Changing Nature of Security

National and global security are merging, because in a complexly interdependent world the conditions for well-being and happiness for most people require a high degree of collective action. Just as most individuals cannot by their own effort meet their needs for food, shelter, health, and old age, as their ancestors did, individual states can neither shield citizens from all threats, nor cope with global environmental and economic trends. Overall, as interdependent individuals caught up in a variety of authority patterns, we are probably less secure in our collective existence than in earlier epochs when our survival depended on our own exertion and imagination.

As individuals diversify and specialize their occupation and role in society, the world mimics them, and we have increasingly specialized collective actors to deal with threats. As states fail to cope by themselves, we get global and regional organizations and regimes to coordinate economic policies.

The Decline of Inside/Outside and its Consequences for the State

As we noted earlier, Rosenau never regarded state frontiers as impermeable, and, as he came to recognize the growing irrelevance of sovereign borders, he began to question the state itself and the role that it could play in global politics.

By the early 1980s, Rosenau was struck by the inadequate attention he had paid to "the onset of global changes that may amount to a *world crisis of authority*."[25] Since his "Pre-Theory was a static product of a static era," he recognized that "we need to return to fundamentals"[26] to achieve theoretical breakthroughs. In a dramatic break with the prevailing Eurocentric conception of the international system, Rosenau turned upon the Westphalian state itself, blaming the "static conception of authority structures, both within and between societies" that "treated the world as frozen into a structure comprised of nation-states"[27] for shortcomings in the original pretheory. He pointed to six "macro changes" in global politics—resource scarcities, demands for redistributing global wealth, breakdown of authority in nation-states, fragmentation of ties among states, the growing importance of "unfamiliar" socioeconomic issues, and the microelectronics revolution—as having fundamentally altered global politics and as having made obsolete the Eurocentric model of a state system.[28] In consequence, "the worldwide crisis of authority can be viewed as having so thoroughly undermined the prevailing distribution of global power as to alter the significance of the State as a causal agent in the course of events." So profound was the impact of "skillful publics" and "subgroupism," that "it no longer seems compelling to refer to the world as a State system."[29]

These changes, Rosenau believed, heralded the emergence of new authority structures and the growing importance of forms of "governance" other than that of "sovereignty-bound" actors. The latter he distinguished from an increasingly important cast of "sovereignty-free actors"—"multinational corporations, ethnic groups, bureaucratic agencies, political parties, subnational governments, transnational societies, international organizations, and a host of other types of collectivities."[30] No longer was the Westphalian state system the only game in town. Now there were two political worlds, one "state-centric" and consisting of "fewer than 200" "sovereignty-bound" states, and the other "multi-centric," with "hundreds of thousands" of "sovereignty-free" actors.[31] The second world, he admits, does not entail "a thoroughgoing jailbreak," but only "an escape hatch through which to beat a hasty retreat back to the neorealist paradigm in the event the multicentric world proves too chaotic for incisive theorizing."[32]

The Revolutions in Time and Space

Postinternationalism takes account of revolutions in time and space. Technology such as e-mail and facsimile machines have made it possible to move ideas and funds almost instantaneously. Such technologies have reduced the gap between "short-term" and "long-term." The French historian Fernand Braudel distinguishes three types of change. The fastest encompasses daily events in individual lives; the second, which is slower, entails economic and political change that is the result of aggregating daily events; and the slowest, which was almost imperceptible in past centuries, includes basic changes in the way people live.[33] These three types have begun to merge in the modern world.

The meaning of space has changed too. As opposed to postinternational politics, international politics has what Jonathan Boyarin calls "close genealogical links between the 'Cartesian coordinates' of space and time and the discrete, sovereign state." However, technology has redefined "our possible experiences of 'proximity' and 'simultaneity'."[34] A postinternational map takes account of the fact that polities may share the political and geographic space.

The phenomenon by which some polities are encapsulated by others and embedded within them, Yale Ferguson and I call *nesting*. In the process a dominant polity is modified and may assume some of the characteristics of the polity it has partly "digested." In the process, old identities and loyalties do not vanish, however. Instead, they lie dormant, ready to be triggered perhaps centuries later. The post–Cold War explosion of tribal, ethnic, religious, and racial identities entails the revival of ancient identities and memories, often mobilized against state institutions imposed by colonial authorities. Thus, in Guatemala ancient Mayan identities are challenging the primacy of the Westphalian state. "It is not that someone is speaking on our behalf, defending us," declared Demetrio Cojtí, a Maya social scientist, "but that we ourselves are developing visions of our own identity, from a colonialist church to our relationship with the state."[35]

Fragmegration

Rosenau's postinternational world features simultaneous "centralizing and decentralizing" processes that together he calls "fragmegration."[36] Some societies are falling apart even as others come together; "some norms are spreading and others are receding; some multilateral projects are utter failures and others are remarkable successes."[37] Here Rosenau commits himself forcefully to a dynamic orientation toward global politics. These processes, largely ignored by IR specialists in recent decades, are the engines of political change, and he commends research agendas to focus on "[t]he seeming contradictions between the forces spreading people, goods, and ideas around the world and those that are impelling the contraction of people, goods, and ideas within narrowed or heightened geographic boundaries."[38]

Some clues are emerging that may help us make sense of these "contradictions." On the one hand, the growth of political institutions create problems of control,[39] the "crisis of authority" to which Rosenau alludes. Alone, the issue of control is largely mechanistic. Clearly, we must also identify why people reject authority and seek to insulate themselves from larger political institutions. Here, a combination of technological change and the skills revolution can be combined with insights from "clash-of-civilization"[40] arguments to yield a first approximation.

As new authorities utilize changing technology to expand (whether stirrups "about the turn of the fifth–sixth centuries A.D."[41] or the microelectronics revolution in recent years), they overwhelm old local political structures and cultures and the accompanying norms that had anchored identities and provided clear and powerful normative and prescriptive guidance. These local structures and institutions—for example, the extended family, the tribal clan, or the church to mention a few—provided individuals with a sense of who they were and of their "proper" place in the world, and served as filters for mediating and interpreting "external" information and ideas.

As these structures and institutions are swamped by "modern" images and homogenized ethics and aesthetics, there is nothing to buffer and regulate excessive individualism and heightened anomie. Old identities are eroded and muddled, and the well-being of human beings is determined by remote forces about which little is known or understood. Instead of a world of distinctive cultures, there has emerged a globalized culture that places a premium on individual choice and market forces. This process is most visible among urban elites, integrated in the global economy, whose tastes and norms—whether in Caracas, New York, or Karachi—are the same. The psychological distance between these elites and the much larger and poorer underclass has grown in many countries even as geographic distance between these classes has narrowed owing to massive urbanization.

One consequence of these processes is the search for new identities or the revival of old ones that can provide coherent norms. Another is the proliferation of horizontal cleavages in societies that undermine the unity of Westphalian states. It is in this context that religious fundamentalism—whether the efforts of Islamists in Algeria, Orthodox Jews in Israel, Hindu militants in India, or the Christian Coalition in the United States—begins to make sense. Fragmegration, then, implies growing instability in human loyalties, and the movement "away from loyalties focused on nation-states and toward variable foci."[42]

Global Governance

The combination of individuals' greater analytic skills and cathectic capacities, the revolutions in space and time, market globalization, the breakdown of authority structures and sovereign boundaries, the incapacity of states to cope with challenges to citizens' welfare and survival, and the proliferation of nonstate identities led Rosenau to distinguish between government ("activities that are backed by formal authority") and governance ("activities backed by shared goals that may or may not derive from legal and formally prescribed responsibilities").[43] He conceives of governance as the "numerous patterns that sustain global order" unfolding "at three basic levels of activity"—intersubjective, behavioral, and "the aggregate or political level where . . . rule-oriented institutions and regimes enact and implement the policies" produced at the other levels.[44] Thus, governance includes phenomena from individual market decisions to "world civic politics"[45] and international regimes and customary law. As a result, despite the growing incapacity of many states, things still get done, often efficiently and effectively, in our postinternational world.

Rosenau views the characteristics of the postinternational world as unique. So dramatic has the world changed in his view "that the lessons of history may no longer be very helpful," and this leaves "observers without any paradigms or theories that adequately explain the course of events."[46] Here we part company with Rosenau, because this view implies, mistakenly in our view, that the features of the postinternational world are novel. As we shall see, it is not that history is less relevant, but just the opposite: that a richer understanding of history that acknowledges that there is more to global politics than a few centuries of European experience can open new vistas for theorizing about what is happening today.

Just as we must examine the "international" world to make sense of postinternationalism, so we must go further back and examine the preinternational world. What we shall find is that that world has more in common with postinternationalism than with the relatively brief epoch in which European states dominated the world in which we live.

CONCLUSION: POSTINTERNATIONALISM AND HISTORY

Until recently, most IR theorists have universalized the Westphalian state and its ideological baggage of state sovereignty. For example, although Waltz recognizes that "[s]tates are not and never have been the only international actors," he never describes either a "prestate" or "poststate" era.[47] And, even though "[s]tates vary widely in size, wealth, power, and form," they "perform . . . tasks, most of which are common to all of them."[48] In other words, states differ but not so much as to matter. For Rosenau, who does recognize changes that diminish the potency of an interstate model, failure to consider what went before leads to a rather linear view of history as "going somewhere."

There are a few exceptions to the universalizing of the Westphalian state. Over three decades ago, George Modelski hypothesized two distinct models of social and economic organization—Agraria and Industria—that he believed formed different types of international system.[49] So different were the actors in the two systems that they produced different systemic outcomes, for example different kinds of warfare. Agraria consisted of polities in which land was the key source of power and wealth and sovereignty resided with a small elite selected by ascription. By contrast, Industria featured nation-states with large populations and plural elites chosen for merit, enjoying access to vast new resources and a greater capacity to mobilize such resources, but with sovereignty residing with the citizens as a whole.

Another exception was Adda Bozeman's brilliant analysis of pre-Westphalian and non-Western civilizations.[50] Bozeman sought to show the variety in political organization, political ideas, and "international" behavior prior to Europe's ascendancy and the spread of European institutions and ideas into other regions. "Most of these indigenous patterns of life and thought became blurred during the centuries of European supremacy, when they were being integrated in the Occidental scheme of things," but "it became increasingly apparent that the Western ideas were not the exclusive mainsprings of their political attitudes and actions." [51] Then, in a remarkably prescient rejection of "the end of history," she observed:

> One of the basic concepts in modern international politics is the sovereign democratic nation-state which acquired its connotations in the histories of Western Europe and America. Since groups of people in all continents have willingly identified their collective aspirations with this norm of organization by claiming the right to self-determination . . . , it was generally understood that the modern state had actually superseded older, local forms of government. In the prevailing climate of egalitarian thinking, it is easy to forget that most communities in the Balkan and Black Sea regions had matured under the political tutelage of the monolithic Byzantine Empire, whose tenets of rule were quite at variance with those developed in the West.[52]

Bozeman pointed out that neither Indian nor Chinese political history had analogues to modern democracy. Islam lacked the secular legal experience necessary to derive civic rights, and West African history in today's Ghana lacked both the common culture and language necessary for a European-type state.

Finally, among IR specialists, John Gerard Ruggie is something of an exception. Ruggie turns to medieval Europe—" 'a patchwork of overlapping and incomplete rights of government,' which were 'inextricably superimposed and tangled'[53]—to make sense of a world in which polities overlap and share the same space, and he uses the same language to describe the European Community and its "transnational microeconomic links." "Perhaps the best way to describe it . . . is that these links have created a nonterritorial 'region' in the world economy—a decentered yet integrated space-of-flows, operating in real time, which exists alongside the space-of-places that we call national economies. . . . In the nonterritorial global region . . . the conventional distinctions between internal and external . . . are exceedingly problematic, and any given state is but one constraint in corporate global strategic calculations."[54]

In some measure, both Rosenau the scientist and Rosenau the postinternationalist lack historical perspective. However, in recognizing the impact of change, his approach is light-years in advance of realists with their "1066-and-all-that" outlook. Few have cared to consider the world before 1648 or in a non-European context, a significant omissions at a time when old historical political forms and ideas, especially non-European ones, are being resurrected around the world. Moreover, in recent decades, political science and international relations have been dominated by scholars from a sociological tradition, with little sympathy for those with roots in history. For Rosenau, a deeper historical analysis would reveal dark currents that might erode his liberal conviction that history is headed in some discernibly positive direction.

To choose one example, consider fragmegration—the simultaneous processes of political fragmentation and integration that characterize Rosenau's postinternational world. These simultaneous processes are hardly unique to contemporary global politics. Indeed, they have been present in virtually all epochs and places and reflect an apparently continuous and universal cycle of political organization and reorganization brought about by changing human identities and loyalties. It is only by turning to history that we can discern how fragmentation and integration are related to each other.

So critical is the role of history that today, as in past epochs, practitioners and theorists are engaged in a contest for control of historical meaning. In practice, this requires shaping the meaning of the past to legitimate policies for and interpretations of the present.[55] The dominance of statist internationalist theory reflected the dominance of Europe's control over historical meaning and the forgetting of rival forms of identity. Rosenau's postinternational framework contributes to eroding this dominance and frees us to look beyond Westphalian Europe in order to make sense of the world around us.

NOTES

1. James N. Rosenau, *Turbulence in World Politics* (Princeton, N.J.: Princeton University Press, 1990), pp. 27–33.

2. James N. Rosenau, *The Scientific Study of Foreign Policy* (New York: Free Press, 1971), p. 21.

3. James N. Rosenau, "Global Changes and Theoretical Challenges: Toward a Postinternational Politics for the 1990s," in Ernst-Otto Czempiel and Rosenau, eds., *Global Changes and Theoretical Challenges: Approaches to World Politics for the 1990s* (Lexington, Mass.: Lexington Books, 1989), pp. 2–3.

4. Rosenau, *Turbulence in World Politics*, pp. 141–77.

5. Ibid., p. 142.

6. R. K. Ashley, "The Poverty of Neorealism," in Robert O. Keohane, ed., *Neorealism and Its Critics* (New York: Columbia University Press, 1984), p. 250.

7. Rosenau, *The Scientific Study of Foreign Policy*, p. 112 n. 45.

8. Rosenau, *Turbulence in World Politics*, pp. 115, 117.

9. Rosenau, *The Scientific Study of Foreign Policy*, pp. 359, 360.

10. James N. Rosenau, "Introduction," in Rosenau ed., *The Domestic Sources of Foreign Policy* (New York: Free Press, 1967), p. 2.

11. Rosenau, *Turbulence in World Politics*, p. 117.

12. James N. Rosenau, "Introduction: Political Science in a Shrinking World," in Rosenau, ed., *Linkage Politics* (New York: Free Press, 1969), p. 2. Rosenau's analysis of linkages anticipated the growing interest in the 1970s in "transnational politics" and "international regimes."

13. Ibid., p. 4. See also James N. Rosenau, "The External Environment as a Variable in Foreign Policy Analysis," in Rosenau, Vincent Davis, and Maurice A. East, eds., *The Analysis of International Politics* (New York: Free Press, 1972), pp. 145–65.

14. James N. Rosenau, "Toward the Study of National-International Linkages," in Rosenau, ed., *Linkage Politics*, p. 47.

15. Rosenau, *Turbulence in World Politics*, p. 22.

16. Thomas S. Kuhn, "Reflections on My Critics," in Imre Lakatos and Alan Musgrave, eds., *Criticism and the Growth of Knowledge*, (Cambridge: Cambridge University Press, 1970) p. 245. Rosenau himself retains the language of paradigms but makes fewer demands of those instruments than does Kuhn. "The world is too murky and uncertain for . . . knowledge claims to approach irrefutable truth. . . . [T]here is no magic to the paradigms we employ to comprehend the course of events." "Multilateral Governance and the Nation-State System: A Post–Cold War Assessment," (paper for the first meeting of a study group of the Inter-American Dialogue, Washington, D.C., April 24–25, 1995), p. 5.

17. Rosenau, "Global Changes and Theoretical Challenges," p. 3.

18. James N. Rosenau, "Before Cooperation; Hegemons, Regimes, and Habit-driven Actors in World Politics," *International Organization* 40 (autumn 1986): pp. 849–50.

19. Rosenau, *Turbulence in World Politics*, p. 11.

20. Ibid., p. 97.

21. Kenneth N. Waltz, *Theory of International Politics* (Reading, Mass.: Addison-Wesley, 1979), p. 88.

22. Rosenau, *Turbulence in World Politics*, p. 334.

23. Ibid., p. 239.

24. Susan Strange, *The Retreat of the State: The Diffusion of Power in the World Economy* (New York: Cambridge University Press, 1996), p. 102. See also Robert B. Reich, *The Work of Nations: Preparing Ourselves for Twenty-First-Century Capitalism* (New York: Alfred A. Knopf, 1991), pp. 177–80.

25. Rosenau, "A Pre-Theory Revisited: World Politics in an Era of Cascading Interdependence," *International Studies Quarterly* 28, 3 (September 1984): 246. Emphasis in original.

26. Ibid., pp. 246, 247.

27. Ibid., p. 251.

28. Ibid., pp. 253–55.

29. Ibid., p. 263–64.

30. Rosenau, *Turbulence in World Politics*, p. 36.

31. Ibid., pp. 249–53.

32. Ibid., p. 247.

33. Fernand Braudel *On History*, trans. Sarah Matthews (Chicago: University of Chicago Press, 1980), p. 3ff.

34. Jonathan Boyarin, "Space, Time, and the Politics of Memory," in Boyarin, ed., *Remapping Memory: The Politics of TimeSpace* (Minneapolis: University of Minnesota Press, 1994), pp. 4, 13.

35. Cited in Larry Rohter, "Maya Renaissance in Guatemala Turns Political," *New York Times*, August 12, 1996, p. A5.

36. James N. Rosenau, "New Dimensions of Security: The Interaction of Globalizing and Localizing Dynamics," *Security Dialogue* 25 (September 1994): 256, and Rosenau, "Multilateral Governance," p. 10.

37. Rosenau, "Multilateral Governance," p. 3.

38. Ibid.

39. Yale H. Ferguson and Richard W. Mansbach, *Polities: Authorities, Identities, and Change* (Columbia: University of South Carolina Press, 1996, pp. 39–40.

40. Samuel P. Huntington, "The Clash of Civilizations?" *Foreign Affairs* 72, 3 (summer 1993): 22–49.

41. William H. McNeill, *The Pursuit of Power* (Chicago: The University of Chicago Press, 1982), p. 20.

42. Rosenau, *Turbulence in World Politics*, p. 335.

43. James N. Rosenau, "Governance, Order, and Change in World Politics," in Rosenau and Ernst-Otto Czempiel, eds., *Governance without Government: Order and Change in World Politics* (Cambridge: Cambridge University Press, 1992), p. 4.

44. Ibid., p. 14.

45. See Paul Wapner, "Politics beyond the State: Environmental Activism and World Civic Politics," *World Politics* 47, 3 (April 1995): 311–40.

46. Rosenau, *Turbulence in World Politics*, p. 5.

47. Waltz, *Theory of International Politics*, p. 93.

48. Ibid., p. 96.

49. George Modelski, "Agraria and Industria: Two Models of the International System," in Klaus Knorr and Sidney Verba, eds., *The International System: Theoretical Essays* (Princeton, N.J.: Princeton University Press, 1961).

50. Adda B. Bozeman, *Politics and Culture in International History* (Princeton, N.J.: Princeton University Press, 1960).

51. Ibid., p. 5.

52. Ibid., p. 6.

53. John Gerard Ruggie, "Continuity and Transformation in the World Polity: Toward a Neorealist Synthesis." *World Politics* 35, 2 (January 1983): 274. He is citing Perry Anderson *Lineages of the Absolutist State* (London: New Left Books, 1974), pp. 37–38. Rosenau, too, compares his "bifurcated global sys-

tem" to "the decentralized structures of the medieval era." ("Multilateral Governance," p. 9).

54. John Gerard Ruggie, "Territoriality and Beyond: Problematizing Modernity in International Relations," *International Organization* 47, 1 (winter 1993): 172.

55. Boyarin describes this as "the question of who controls the archives" ("Space, Time, and the Politics of Memory," p. 15). Acts of remembering, such as national pageants, ceremonies, or parades are part of the contest over the meaning of history.

CHAPTER 2

The Limits of Sovereignty in a Bifurcated World

Dario Moreno

Writing about James N. Rosenau's views on sovereignty is akin to writing about the United States Supreme Court's view on pornography. You know they are against it, but you are not sure why, and you are not convinced they know what it is. Rosenau's fuzziness on sovereignty is understandable given that the centerpiece of his scholarship is the prominence of nonstate actors in world politics. Sovereignty, on the other hand, defines the rights and powers of the nation-state both domestically and internationally. Yet, it is precisely because Rosenau rejects the traditional state-centric approach to international relations, that his view on sovereignty is critical to understanding his contribution to international relations theory and the postinternational paradigm.

Postinternationalism accepts the notion that states possess sovereignty. This accords them the exclusive rights to employ coercive force at home and renders them free of higher authority abroad.[1] Postinternationalists differ with traditional scholars, however, on the extent to which sovereignty is practiced and on its durability. Rosenau was among the first scholars to argue that world politics is in the midst of a profound authority crisis in which traditional conceptions of state sovereignty are everywhere under siege. State sovereignty, according to the postinternationalists, is "diffusing," "shifting," "diminishing," "maturing," "pooling," leaking—and all this is happening, it would seem, at once."[2]

The argument that the concept of sovereignty is undergoing a fundamental change is in sharp contrast with traditional formulations of sovereignty. Realists view sovereignty as empowering states to "develop their own strategies, chart their own courses, making their own decisions".[3] International politics are consequently the relations between these sovereign entities dedicated to their own self-preservation, ultimately able to depend only on themselves, and prepared to resort to force. Realists use "anarchy" as a metaphor to describe the international system resulting from nation-states making independent choices to maximize their power and preserve themselves. Further, realists argue that sovereignty enables political scientists to distinguish between domestic and international politics. Hierarchy characterizes domestic politics where the state has a monopoly over the legitimate use of force. Anarchy, on the other hand, characterizes international politics where every sovereign state has the independent authority to use force. Realists presume that states jealously guard their prerogative for independent actions and will not knowingly accept any diminution in their sovereign rights. Consequently, the importance of sovereignty has traditionally rested in its serving as a boundary marker between domestic and world politics. As one scholar put it, sovereignty "simultaneously provides an ordering principle for what is 'internal' to states and what is 'external' to them".[4] Thus, one of the classic definitions of sovereignty is that it is *the supreme legitimate authority within a territory*. Supreme authority within a territory implies both undisputed supremacy over the land's inhabitants and independence from unwanted intervention by an outside authority.[5]

POSTINTERNATIONALISM AND SOVEREIGNTY

The endurance and relevancy of such an absolute view of sovereign authority is questioned by many modern scholars. The postinternational paradigm rejects such a clear-cut and simplistic model of the domestic-foreign distinction. Rosenau argues that such an absolute concept of sovereignty ignores and obscures the fact that state authority is weakening. "It dismisses the problem of system-subsystem relations by collecting all authority under the rubric of sovereignty instead of focusing attention on the conditions whereby authority is created, legitimacy sustained, and compliance achieved".[6] Rosenau maintains that in an age of complex interdependence the boundaries between foreign and domestic politics has become increasingly blurred. Unitary states simply lack the authority, resources, and legitimacy to deal with the problems besetting them. Environmental, economic, and technological issues are increasingly beyond the competency of individual states.

The complexity of these issues and the interdependence that they necessitate have resulted in states losing authority. States are interpreting fewer and fewer situations as posing a challenge to their sovereign privileges. Interdependency has forced states to relinquish control over functions that traditionally have been viewed as part of their sovereign rights. The propagation of international regimes and other informal arrangements in the postwar era stand as testimony to the eroding effects that complex interdependency has had on sovereignty.

This authority crisis is due to the modern state's inability to adequately address some of the most critical issues facing humanity. Postinternationalism argues that as citizens' analytic skills expand, the source of authority has shifted from traditional to performance criteria of legitimacy. Individuals' readiness to comply with government directives is dependent on their assessment of the performance of the authorities. The less they approve of the performance record, the more likely they are to withhold their compliance or otherwise resist state authority. States and government have consequently become less effective in confronting challenges and implementing policies than they were in the past.

The result of this pervasive authority crisis has been the relocation of legitimacy away from the state and in the direction of nonstate actors. This transfer of authority toward these new groups is determined, according to Rosenau and Durfee, "in good part on the scope of the enterprises people perceive as more receptive to their concerns and thus more capable of meeting their increased preoccupation with the adequacy of performance".[7] In some circumstances, this process has involved "downward" relocation to subnational or domestic groups—toward ethnic minorities, local government, single-issue organizations, religious and linguistic groupings, political factions, trade unions, and others, while under other circumstances, there has been an "upward" realignment of authority toward groups and organizations that transcend national boundaries. The beneficiaries of this "upward" realignment range from supranational organizations such as the European Union and the North American Free Trade Association, to intergovernmental agencies such as the International Labor Organizations; from international citizens groups such as Greenpeace and Amnesty International to professional groups such as Medecins sans Frontiers; from multinational corporations such as IBM to social movements that join together environmentalists or women in different countries, from informal to formal associations of political parties such as those that share conservative or socialist ideologies. These entities are all competing with the nation-state for legitimacy, authority, and the loyalty of the individual.

The postinternational paradigm holds that this proliferation of nonstate actors is undermining the principle of national sovereignty.

These new actors are challenging the legitimacy of the state at both the supranational and subnational level. The new actors may even demonstrate autonomy within their jurisdictions without also possessing sovereign power. Rosenau claims that while "there is no obvious relationship between the location of authority and sovereignty, [n]evertheless, trends toward the relocation of authority are bound to contribute to the erosion of sovereignty."[8] As a result, sovereignty is under siege everywhere.

> If a state is thwarted in its effort to mobilize effective armed forces then its sovereignty is hardly a conspicuous feature of its existence as an independent collective. If a state cannot prevent outside actors from calling attention to its human rights record and thereby intervening on behalf of political prisoners, then the reach of sovereignty is certainly reduced.[9]

The blurring of the foreign-domestic distinction has resulted in the proliferation of actors in world politics. Domestic interest groups, growing increasingly dissatisfied with large-scale collectives and existing state authorities, are reconstituting themselves as international pressure groups. No longer satisfied with just trying to persuade their home governments, nongovernment entities are increasingly organizing across national boundaries to influence global politics. The dramatic increase in nongovernment organizations (NGOs) illustrates, from the postinternational perspective, the authority crisis that has weakened the state-centric world during the last decades.

The rise of new groupings organized along issue areas instead of the territorial state, underscores the erosion of the traditional foreign-domestic demarcation. David Elkind argues that the extraordinary effects of contemporary technological and economic processes strain the conventional controls available to the sovereign state. It is the "decoupling of governance from its territorial roots" that fosters, indeed necessitates, new nonterritorial political and social configurations throughout the globe.[10] The globalization of the world economy has led to a radical change in international politics. As more and more people experience globalization, that is, become aware that new worldwide interaction allows the creation of a previously undreamed-of variety of relations: the "citizen" is "unbundled." Individuals can enter an "à la carte" global society, selection participation and membership from a wide variety of electronic communications groups, international groupings, new political processes and organizations, and perhaps citizenship.[11]

The postinternational argument that it is becoming progressively more difficult to distinguish between domestic and international politics is substantiated by current events. For example, in the United States, issues that were traditionally treated as exclusively foreign-affairs matters such as human rights in China, the economic boycott of Cuba, and trade relations with Japan, are increasingly being shaped by domestic constituencies.

This phenomenon of linkage between internal and external politics is found throughout the international system. Rosenau postulates that in an age of interdependency the traditional distinction between domestic and international politics is no longer applicable. The complicated nature of the linkage between international and domestic politics is due to two historic processes that have shaped today's world. They consist of those dynamics that are conducive to integration on the one hand, and disintegration on the other. Rosenau named the twin processes, formed by the disintegration of longstanding authority relations and the advent of complex interdependence, "cascading interdependence."[12] He describes the process in these terms: "Today, precisely because scarcities are greater, subgroups stronger, and governments weaker, these tensions can spread and interlock with comparable tensions in other systems, thereby producing changes which cascade endlessly upon each other across the global system."[13]

Although the principle of sovereignty is being weakened by unprecedented pressures, the postinternational paradigm concedes that nation-states continue to be bound by the doctrine. Instead of claiming that sovereignty and the state are obsolete, it postulates that alongside the traditional state-centric world, a complex multicentric world of diverse actors has emerged, replete with structures, processes, and decision rules of its own. Rosenau proposes a "bifurcated global structure" to explain the coexistence of these two increasingly autonomous worlds.

> These two worlds embrace the same actors, but they have distinctive structures and processes that require the actors to employ very different decision rules as they move back and forth between them. . . . To be sure, these two worlds are interactive and overlapping, but each nevertheless retains its identity as a separate sphere of activity because of the different structures and processes through which its actors relate to each other.[14]

While accepting the continuous existence of sovereignty, the postinternational paradigm differs sharply with traditional paradigms because it rejects the predominance of the state-centric world. Instead, Rosenau goes so far as to suggest that entities not constrained by sovereignty might enjoy greater freedom of action in world politics than those burdened by the requirements of state sovereignty. He conceives of states to be *sovereignty-bound* actors, while multinational corporations, ethnic groups, bureaucratic agencies, political parties, subnational governments, transnational societies, international organizations, and a host of other actors he calls *sovereignty-free* actors.

Rosenau adopts this terminology to call attention to "the ways in which states are limited by the very considerations that are usually regarded as the source of their strengths."[15] States are compelled by their sovereign responsibilities to engage in a vast array of activities and allocate resources among those issues to preserve and enhance their integrity and welfare. The very size of the global agenda and the complexity of issues that states must confront underscore their vulnerabilities and their inability to concentrate prerogatives and energies upon a few selective goals. As Rosenau observes,

> The responsibilities of sovereignty-free collectivities, on the other hand, are not so dispersed. They can pursue limited objectives, and they can move forward without diverting their resources to a wide range of other obligations. Thus, the new terminology serves as a continual reminder that the differences between state and other collectivities may not be as one-sided as they are usually assumed to be.[16]

While the bifurcation of international relations has not rendered the doctrine of sovereignty obsolete, it has reduced its stature. States are interpreting fewer and fewer situations as posing a challenge to their sovereignty. "Indeed, one cannot help but be struck by the extent to which claims of sovereignty have waned in the discourse of states. The peremptory declaration that 'this is strictly an internal matter' no longer commands global assent."[17]

THE STATIST TRADITION IN INTERNATIONAL POLITICS

Rosenau's thinking on sovereignty postulates a bifurcated world in which states face the new task of coping with disparate rivals from the multicentric world as well as the traditional challenges emanating from the state system. This view that states are no longer the key actors in world politics and that sovereignty has been seriously undermined is not new to international relations theory. Robert Keohane and Joseph Nye pointed out the importance of nonstate actors in international relations almost three decades ago in *Transnational Relations and World Politics*.[18] However, Rosenau was among the first modern scholars to systematically explore the link between domestic and international politics.[19] His seminal article "Pre-Theories and Theories of Foreign

Policy" focused on the sources of foreign policy, demonstrating how the internal structure of states influence their external behavior.[20] Pretheory's lasting contribution to the field rests in its classification of the external behavior of states as the dependent variable and its treatment of the individual, role, governmental, societal, and systemic antecedents of such behavior as independent variables.

The claim that the boundary between domestic and international politics is blurred and undefined has gained general acceptance in the field. Even realist scholars concede that the domestic structure of the states influences their foreign policy. Henry Kissinger, for example, has argued that the ideologies, historical experience, and shared values of states have a significant influence on foreign-policy behavior. He wrote, "When the domestic structures are based on fundamentally different conceptions of what is just, the conduct of international affairs grows more complex. Then it becomes difficult even to define the nature of the disagreement because what seems most obvious to one side appears most problematic to the other."[21]

The controversy over Rosenau's view and postinternationalism, generally, lies in the significance he gives to the role of non-state *(sovereignty-free)* actors in the global system. This view is clearly at odds with traditional international relations scholarship. Realists point out that domestic pressure groups have always had some influence in international politics. Hence, Rosenau's claim that we have entered a new epoch in international politics where subnational and supranational actors are playing a major role in international politics, is highly suspect. For example, Hedley Bull pointed out that, "the multinational corporation is not a new phenomenon in world politics, and no present day corporation has yet had an impact comparable with that of the English East India Company, which employed its own armed forces and controlled territory."[22]

Traditional statists are unconvinced by the evidence that Rosenau uses to argue that states have willingly surrendered a major portion of their sovereign rights to subnational and supranational actors. They argue that he is confusing the weakness of some states with the general breakdown of the concept. Realists point out that sovereignty has always been dependent on the capability of states. Sovereignty has never been very effective in protecting the autonomy and independence of weak states. The Polish partition, at the end of the eighteenth century, is a spectacular example of the failure of the doctrine of sovereignty to preserve the independence of an individual state. In other words, strong states have always had more latitude in international politics than weak states. Nations that lack the capacity to maintain internal order or the integrity of their national territory are at the mercy of stronger states.

Traditional scholars have also taken issue with Rosenau's suggestion that the multicentric world of nonstate actors is equally as important as the traditional state-centric world. They contend that Rosenau overstates the influence of nonstate actors; for statists, it is not at all clear that these subnational and supranational organizations are undermining sovereignty. Waltz reasserts the preeminence of the state as he argues,

> Though they may choose to interfere little in the affairs of nonstate actors for long period of time, states nevertheless set the terms of the intercourse, whether by passively permitting informal rules to develop or by actively intervening to change rules that no longer suit them. When the crunch comes, states remake the rules by which other actors operate.[23]

Robert Gilpin shares in the view that states determine the rules and conditions under which nonstate actors operate in world politics. He notes that sovereign states in both the developing and the developed world have the capacity, able as they are in most cases to command the predominant loyalties of their citizens, to lay down their own terms under what basis corporations will be given access to national territory. "Whether one is talking about the merchant adventures of the sixteenth century, nineteenth-century finance capitalists, or twentieth-century multinational corporations, transnational actors have been able to play an important role in world affairs because it has been in the interest of the predominant power(s) for them to do so."[24]

The conviction that states are still the key actors in international politics is also shared by a new generation of scholars. These theorists' primary concern is with the origins and process of change that institutions and social and power relations go through over time. Instead of taking concepts such as sovereignty for granted, critical scholars are committed to explaining what they view as the most "important contextual change in international politics in this millennium: the shift from the medieval to the modern international system."[25] This shift was based on the transformation of the basic organizing principle of global politics—from heteronomy to sovereignty. Janice Thomson refers to this paradigm as institutionalist. This theoretical approach focuses on the historical development and evolution of sovereignty as an institution that defines and empowers the state.[26] Thus, for critical scholars, sovereignty is not a static attribute of world politics; it is unique to the modern state system. "It is socially constituted and reproduced through practices of state rulers. Sovereignty organizes global political space and is territorially bound."[27]

Institutionalists, in sharp contrast to postinternationalists, claim that the doctrine of sovereignty has actually been strengthened over the last two centuries. Thomson points out that nonstate actors actually played a larger role in international politics before the nineteenth century. She postulates that the boundaries between domestic and international, the economic and political, and the state and nonstate realms of authority were redrawn to eliminate nonstate violence from the international system. Thomson holds that "boundaries before the nineteenth century were unclear. So long as non-state violence persisted, the boundaries between the state and non-state realms of authority, between the political and economic, and between the domestic and international realms were blurred or did not exist. . . . What the institutional change in sovereignty produced was a clarification of the boundaries—both authoritative and territorial—that characterize the modern national-state system."[28]

Other theorists, while agreeing with neorealists that sovereignty is still the organizing principle of world politics, disagree with the notion that sovereignty is a timeless attribute. They reject traditional notions of sovereignty because they claim that its assumptions about sovereignty make it incapable of explaining change. They hold that the concept of sovereignty is not fixed, and that there is nothing natural about it. On the contrary sovereignty is arbitrary, contested, and ever changing. It is nothing more than an artifact of human behavior. The notion that sovereignty has changed over time has been articulated by Jens Bartelson among others.[29] Exploring the development of sovereignty during three different periods—the Renaissance, the classical age, and modernity, he concluded that sovereignty means different things during different times, functions differently within different epistemic arrangement, and that it is something altogether different from time to time. Bartelson in providing a genealogy of sovereignty argues that sovereignty is not something that should be thought of as having an ontological context. Rather, it has a function. In international relations, sovereignty's function is to demarcate the international from the domestic, so that the boundaries of the discipline appear to be self-evident. Currently sovereignty is in crisis because it has ceased to function in representational logic, when its parergonal (framing) qualities no longer sustain domestic/international boundaries. Bartelson concludes that, no longer able to fulfill its function, sovereignty is in crisis.[30]

Bartelson's theoretical construct does not contradict the post-international view that we are currently in the midst of a fundamental change in world politics. Rosenau's turbulence model postulates an international system being overwhelmed by dynamics that foster intense conflict, unexpected developments, pervasive uncertainties, and swift changes. The disagreement between postinternationalists and institutionalists does not lie with the theoretical question of whether change in the institution of sovereignty is possible but with the empirical question of whether that change has or has not occurred. Thomson herself asks, "How much can practices change and yet remain consistent with the institution of sovereignty? If this book's arguments are correct, a shift away from sovereignty to heteronomy or something else would require a fundamental change in the identity of the nation-state. This would entail an end to or at least a significant erosion of the state's monopoly on the authority to deploy violence beyond its border. It is not at all clear to me that this is occurring."[31]

CONCLUSION

There is some evidence to suggest that states are defining sovereignty differently today than in the past. This supports Rosenau's contentions that states are viewing fewer and fewer situations as a challenge to their sovereignty. He maintains that claims of sovereignty are becoming rarer in international politics. International consensus on global standards of human rights, democratization, and the war on drugs have significantly reduced the ability of unitary states to claim sovereign privileges. Moreover, the increasing authority of the European Union has created a notable exception to traditional conceptions of absolute state sovereignty.

It seems clear that the meaning of sovereignty has altered over time to reflect changes in the global agenda. At the beginning of the twentieth century, it would have been inconceivable for a state to interfere in how another sovereign state treated its citizens. The doctrine of sovereignty clearly allowed each state to treat its citizens as it pleased. By the middle of this century this principle had been severely eroded by the Nuremberg War Crimes Trials and the Universal Declaration of Human Rights. Today, human rights are a major component of the global agenda. While some governments might assert that the human-rights situation in their country is strictly an internal matter, these claims are rarely recognized by the global community. Human rights have now gained wide recognition as a legitimate issue in the relationship between sovereign states. States as powerful as the

People's Republic of China and the former Soviet Union have been forced to accept "human rights" as part of their bilateral relationships with the United States and the European community. States that refuse to accept human rights as a legitimate global concern are often reduced to the status of "rogue" states (Cuba, Libya, and the Sudan).

The international effort to stop the flow of illegal drugs has also led to the redefinition of the principle of sovereignty. Drug-producing countries find themselves under immense pressure from the international community to comply with the efforts of the great powers to reduce drug cultivation. This had led to unprecedented interference in these states' internal affairs. U.S. diplomats, for example, now view as part of their legitimate diplomatic duties the monitoring of the judicial systems of these countries. Issues that have always been the exclusive domain of sovereign states, such as who is appointed attorney general in Colombia and who is the police chief of Mexico City, are now subject to external pressure.

These changes in sovereignty reflect the fact that states hold other principles and goals in international politics as more important than sovereignty. Janet Reno, the U.S. attorney general, speaking on the drug war warned the states of the Caribbean that "outmoded notions of sovereignty" should not be permitted to interfere with interdiction efforts to bring drug-related criminals to justice. Similarly, during the crisis in Central America, Assistant Secretary of State Elliot Abrams declared that the process of democratization was more important that the obsolete principles of sovereignty.

However, the most dramatic indication of the weakening of sovereignty is the increasing authority of the European Union. As Daniel Philpott pointed out, "For the first time since the demise of the Holy Roman Empire, a significant political authority other than the state, one with formal sovereign prerogatives, has become legitimate."[32] The European Union (EU) now shares many of the privileges of sovereignty with its member states. The Union's constitution carefully accords prerogatives to both members states and the EU bureaucracy itself. While, EU law itself is still sovereign in only a limited number of areas, the authority of the Union continues to expand. The Maastrict Treaty (1991), which called for the further integration of monetary policy and the introduction of a common currency in 1998, illustrates the continuous expansion of the European Union's authority.

Rosenau, by refusing to treat sovereignty as an uncontested concept, is able to successfully offer an alternative model for world politics. Postinternationalism postulates a bifurcated international system where sovereignty is no longer the ordering principle in international politics. In this paradigm the state-centric and multicentric world coexist and the nation-state is no longer the most important actor in global politics. While neorealist and critical scholars reject Rosenau's view that nonstate actors are equally as important as states, critical scholars accept the notion that sovereignty is an ever changing concept.

As such, the postinternational view of sovereignty offers an intriguing paradigm for theorists who prefer to look beyond the nation-state as the principle actor in world politics. The erosion of sovereignty is but one aspect of the systemwide authority crisis that is transforming the current state-centric system into a bifurcated system. Rosenau is able to offer an impressive body of empirical evidence indicating that sovereignty has eroded during the last decades. However, he has yet to show that sovereignty has been reduced to the point that there has been a contextual change in the international system.

NOTES

1. James N. Rosenau and Mary Durfee, *Thinking Theory Thoroughly: Coherent Approaches to an Incoherent World* (Boulder, Colo.: Westview, 1995), p. 59.

2. Sohail H. Hashmi, ed. *State Sovereignty: Change and Persistence in International Relations* (University Park, PA: The Pennsylvania State University Press, 1997), p. 3.

3. Kenneth W. Waltz, *Theory of International Politics* (New York: McGraw-Hill, 1979) p. 96.

4. A. Giddens, *A Contemporary Critique of Historical Materialism*, vol 2 of *The Nation State and Violence* (Berkeley: University of California Press, 1985), p. 281.

5. Daniel Philpott, "Sovereignty: An Introduction and a Brief History," *Journal of International Affairs* 48, 2 (winter, 1995): 357.

6. James N. Rosenau, *Turbulence in World Politics: A Theory of Change and Continuity* (Princeton, N.J.: Princeton University Press, 1990), p.117.

7. Rosenau and Durfee, *Thinking Theory Thoroughly*, p. 39.

8. Ibid., p. 39–40.

9. Ibid., p. 40.

10. David Elkind, *Beyond Sovereignty: Territory and Political Economy in the Twenty-First Century* (Toronto: Toronto University Press), p. viii.

11. Ibid.

12. James N. Rosenau, "A Pre-Theory Revisited: World Politics in an Era of Cascading Interdependence," *International Studies Quarterly* 28 (September, 1984): 256.

13. Ibid., p. 257.

14. Rosenau, *Turbulence in World Politics*, p. 100.

15. Ibid., p. 36.

16. Ibid.

17. Ibid., p. 436.

18. Robert Keohane and Joseph S. Nye, eds., *Transnational Relations and World Politics* (Cambridge, Mass.: Harvard University Press, 1972).

19. James N. Rosenau, ed. *Linkage Politics:* (New York: The Free Press, 1969).

20. James N. Rosenau, "Pre-Theories and Theories of Foreign Policy," in R. Barry Farrell, ed., *Approaches to Comparative and International Politics* (Evanston, Ill.: Northwestern University Press, 1966), pp. 27–93.

21. Henry Kissinger, "Conditions of World Order," *Dedalus* 95 (spring 1966): 504.

22. Hedley Bull, *The Anarchical Society: A Study of Order in World Politics* (New York: Columbia University Press, 1977), p. 271.

23. Waltz, *Theory of International Politics*, p. 94.

24. Robert Gilpin, "The Politics of Transnational Economic Relations," in Robert O. Keohane and Joseph S. Nye, eds., *Transnational Relations and World Politics* (Cambridge: Harvard University Press), p. 54.

25. John Gerard Ruggie, "Continuity and Transformation in the World Polity: Toward a Neorealist Synthesis," *World Politics* 35 (January 1983): 273.

26. Janice Thomson, *Mercenaries, Pirates, and Sovereigns: State Building and Extraterritorial Violence in Early Modern Europe* (Princeton, N.J.: Princeton University Press, 1994), p. 14.

27. Ibid., pp. 13–14.

28. Ibid., p. 19.

29. Jens Bartelson, *A Genealogy of Sovereignty* (Cambridge: Cambridge University Press, 1995).

30. Ibid., p. 246.

31. Thomson, *Mercenaries, Pirates, and Sovereigns*, p. 153.

32. Philpott, "Sovereignty: An Introduction and a Brief History," p. 367.

CHAPTER 3

Postinternational Politics and the Growing Glomerations of Global Governance

Margaret P. Karns

International relations theory has traditionally ignored questions of governance and treated international law and organizations as activities of marginal importance. The governments of states governed. International rules were different from other rules—less lawlike because of the absence of international enforcement and, hence, less legitimate. International organizations had no authority over states. Only states' power and interests mattered. And, the dominant state(s) determined the norms, principles, and rules, that is, the order or pattern of relationships and activities.

The postinternational paradigm James Rosenau articulates in his book *Turbulence in World Politics: A Theory of Change and Continuity*, challenges the dominant international relations theories and puts the global politics of governance in a central position.[1] With good reason. What previously was described as inter*national* governance must now more accurately be analyzed in terms that account for the influence and interactions of state and nonstate actors, powerful social movements and emerging civil societies, proliferating transnational and global interdependence issues associated with technological change, globalization of capital, markets, production, and labor, as well as environmental degradation, evolving norms, and conflicting value systems.[2]

Less than a theory, however, postinternationalism offers a new paradigm for thinking about global politics, including what may more accurately be termed the global politics of governance rather than the politics of global governance since the rule systems and activities are not all global in scope. Postinternationalism guides us into looking at macro, micro/macro, and micro parameters of underlying change, indeed, into thinking in terms of the dynamics and effects of on-going patterns of change as well as the forces of simultaneous integration and fragmentation. In many ways, then, the postinternational paradigm is another of Rosenau's pretheoretical contributions to the field. The very term "postinternational" connotes its temporariness: international clearly referring to the Westphalian interstate system; and post implying the passing of that system. One of us will have to invent a new dominant cliché.

This essay focuses first on the evidence of global governance, considering whether all the recent interest in the subject constitutes a fad, fantasy, or basis for a new academic field of study. Secondly, I examine the driving forces behind the expansion of global governance and how these mesh with the postinternational paradigm. The third section outlines an analytical framework for studying the politics of governance, including the questions of scope, domain, and who gets what, when, how, at what cost, and with what degree of effectiveness. Finally, I suggest a research agenda utilizing the postinternational framework to frame the questions to be asked and the empirical evidence sought.

GLOBAL GOVERNANCE: FAD, FANTASY, OR FIELD?

The "tribes" of academe are notoriously subject to fads. We invent new words to show our uniqueness, as well as to overcome what we regard as the inadequacies of existing language to express what we mean. Rosenau's term "fragmegration," designed to capture the simultaneous phenomena of integration and fragmentation in late-twentieth-century international politics, is a good example. We should ask ourselves, then, is the phrase "global governance" just another such fad? With all of the literature on international organizations, regimes, and multilateral institutions, what does the phrase "global governance" connote that these other terms do not? Or, is it just today's catchphrase among the up-to-date, aspiring cognoscenti?

Undoubtedly, there is an element of faddishness to the explosion of writing on global governance, but the phrase also captures some significant recent developments in world politics, particularly when qualified as "governance without government." Indeed, governance has traditionally been the focus of what politics concerned: the *activities associated with exercising influence or control* over people, space (not just territory), resources, and issue outcomes. In other words, it is the activities associated with the *allocation of values* such as security, wealth, access to markets, or human dignity. Those activities may occur *with or without government, that is, with or without the constitutionally, ascriptively, or sovereignty-based authority* to use force to secure compliance.[3]

What has increasingly given these activities *legitimacy* in the global community of what Rosenau terms sovereignty-bound and sovereignty-free actors, is the *consent of the governed*. Whether through majority- (or qualified majority–) rule decision processes in intergovernmental organizations (IGOs), consensus rules, concurrence with multilateral treaties, or provisions for participation of nongovernmental organizations (NGOs) and other interested parties, global-governance activities increasingly have a consent base. Indicative of a postinternational paradigm shift for conceptualizing world politics is Thomas Franck's assertion that international law need no longer concern itself with the old question of its legitimacy, but should now focus on questions of fairness.[4] That very statement emphasizes the politics of governance: the contest over *which* values shape outcomes.

Global governance, then, is more than a system (or systems) of rules. As Lawrence Finkelstein has put it, we need to think of "governance as activity."[5] It is also more than what international organizations and legal regimes do. They are a means of achieving governance. Some areas of global governance, such as the pursuit of cooperative security in Asia Pacific, are handled by ad hoc and informal groups of public or private actors, in this instance CSCAP—the nonofficial Conference on Security Cooperation in Asia Pacific. The informal governance of prices by markets illustrates a further deviation from the association of governance activities with formal organizations.[6]

Beyond rule and norm creation, the range of activities includes information gathering, analysis and dissemination, standard setting, dispute settlement and adjudication, negotiations and consultations aimed at coordinating actors' policies and actions affecting global climate change, prevention of terrorism, international drug traffic, and nuclear proliferation. It also encompasses programs from humanitarian relief, women in development, human rights education and promotion, peacekeeping, and managing the Global Environmental Facility, to privatization of state-owned enterprises and informal planning allocation of satellite orbits.

Global governance is a bit like swiss cheese, an important characteristic of which is its holes. In some cases, they are quite large, leaving the consumer with narrow "bridges" of cheese itself. There are many significant, irregularly shaped holes in the "cheese." Yet, there is definitely a cheese, or a continuum that is made up of the activities of public and private, governmental, intergovernmental, transnational, and supranational actors directed at controlling or steering relationships, interactions, and transactions on the broadening range of issues affecting people, societies, corporations, governments, markets, economies, the physical environment, and other species of planet Earth and its atmosphere. The irregularly shaped holes of this swiss cheese are the gaps in governance: those issues or interactions for which there are no operative rules and "steering activities" as yet.

The globe is a single, bounded entity, but there is no single system of global governance. Rather there are *pieces of governance* at the global, regional, subregional, national, provincial, local, and individual "levels" of human societies worldwide, many of which are linked, some of which are not.

The process of international organization described so lucidly almost forty years ago by Inis Claude in his now classic book *Swords into Plowshares*[7] has accelerated in the interim with the further proliferation of international organizations and the expansion of international law. As Ruggie put it, "multilateralism matters."[8] It has become a major practice of late-twentieth-century diplomacy and international relations with much of that multilateral activity (but by no means all) taking place within the UN system, regional, and subregional organizations. Hence, states have become increasingly enmeshed in networks of regulatory and collaborative organizations from which "exit is generally not a feasible option."[9] In the process, they have also shifted to varying degrees from unilateral to multilateral orientations, from concern for narrowly defined national interests pursued alone, to recognition of interdependence and how some collective interests require coordination and cooperation with others to secure desired outcomes that benefit both, although not necessarily equally.

International law, which once applied only to states, now governs relations between international organizations, between states and persons, persons of states, and between states and multinational corporations. Consensus is also growing in the international legal community (and among governments) on the need for an international criminal-law code to deal with terrorism, drug trafficking, as well as war crimes and crimes against humanity. Clearly, the expanding scope of international law has played an important role in constructing pieces of global governance.[10] While much of that construction since the 1960s has taken place through conventions and treaties in which the newer Third World states have been able to participate (hence widening its acceptance and legitimacy), customary practice continues to be a major source of law, particularly its evolution in new areas.

The proliferation of international nongovernmental organizations (NGOs) and NGO networks, however, is one of the most striking phenomena of the last thirty years. Although the UN Charter made provision for NGO representation within the Economic and Social Council (ECOSOC), their demands for greater "say" beyond the parallel fora held in conjunction with global conferences is one of the major issues of UN reform. Although many scholars paid lip service to NGOs as nonstate actors, only recently has there been a burgeoning literature of case studies analyzing NGOs' roles in promoting human rights, environmental regime building, humanitarian relief, and other aspects of global governance.[11]

The analytical construct of international regimes has greatly aided scholarly efforts since the early 1980s to probe the evolving dimensions of international institutionalization—of formal and informal sets of rules, practices, and decision-making processes. In one sense, this approach has "contextualized" particular pieces of international law and specific international organizations, thereby facilitating an understanding of these pieces of global governance. We understand a great deal more about issue-area differences and various types of cooperation and coordination "problems" and the effects of both on regime requirements. Still, relatively little attention has been paid to more informal patterns, although the international law literature contains some interesting recent treatments of customary practice as a primary means of expanding the scope of law in a world of rapidly changing technologies, expanding economic activities, environmental degradation, shared natural resources, and evolving norms of human rights.[12]

What might be labeled a Western tendency to think in terms of formal organizations and structures, formal rules, and agreements has confronted a major challenge, however, in the Asia-Pacific context. Led by Malaysian Prime Minister Mahathir Mohamad and bolstered by the work of Malaysian and Singaporian think tanks, proponents of an "Asian Way" have opposed North American suggestions to formalize structures and rules for promoting economic cooperation in the region.[13] The Asia-Pacific enterprise is the first effort to construct regional economic cooperation encompassing developed, industrialized, capitalist, and democratic countries as well as developing, authoritarian, formerly colonized, and, communist states. Within this "emerging" region of the world, second-track diplomacy has involved business leaders, economists and security specialists from university centers and think tanks, and governmental officials "acting in their private capacity" in the effort to develop both economic and security cooperation through the Pacific Economic Cooperation Council (PECC), the Pacific Trade and Development Conference (PAFTAD), the Council for Security Cooperation in the Asia Pacific (CSCAP), and, most recently, the APEC Business Advisory Council (ABAC).[14] What is happening in Asia-Pacific illustrates the proliferating players, playing fields, and policy processes of the postinternational, multicentric world.

There are also ad hoc multilateral initiatives. From the initial experiment with a Western Contact Group seeking a negotiated settlement of the Namibian problem in the late 1970s, Latin American states formed the Contadora Group to facilitate peacemaking in Central America in the 1980s.[15] More recently, another "contact group" attempted to broker peace in the former Yugoslavia.

These various developments have all contributed to the sense that traditional international relations theory is inadequate for explaining a world in which governance activities have expanded (which is not to overlook the demise of IGOs or breakdown of governance arrangements—the creation or enlargement of holes in the cheese). In other words, the evidence of governance has accumulated to the point where it is noticeable—a just noticeable difference (JND) in Rosenau's terminology. At the same time, the nature and exercise of power, influence, and leadership are changing with respect to many issue areas and domains of governance. Analysis of that evidence, however, requires us to put on new "lenses" in order to sharpen our understanding, to adopt new discourses to describe the emerging phenomena, and to utilize multi- and inter-level analyses, much as Rosenau has never confined himself to a single level of analysis. And, even as we reformulate the central questions of world politics to accommodate the evidence of growing glomerations of global governance, we must ask whether Rosenau's postinternationalist paradigm with its focus on changes in three parameters provides a sufficient analytical framework.

Should we constitute a new field to study the phenomenon of global governance? Hardly! Rather we need to reframe the field of world politics and draw from many fields, subfields, and strands of literature: from political and legal theory on the subjects of rules, authority, and legitimacy; from public policy and administration as well as international organizations on structures, procedures, processes, implementation, and evaluation; from comparative politics on the dynamics of politics in different systems (but not only those of sovereign states), the formation and functioning of "policy communities," and the interactions of the international, transnational, and domestic environments; as well as from those in international relations who are exploring the politics, the emergence of a global "civil society," the dynamics and power of social movements, the influence of ideas and "epistemic communities," transnational networks and transgovernmental coalitions, or the evolution of new norms. There is also much to be learned from other disciplines including from economists on the dynamics of markets, different economic sectors, and the private governance of firms.

The very notion of a "field" in academe, like that of the discipline itself, creates a set of boundaries around areas of inquiry and knowledge that tend to inhibit the search for insights and methodologies to answer our most important questions. Reframing how we think about the field of international relations, however, to place governance at the center of our conceptualization of what *world* politics is all about will enable us to fit together pieces of inquiry from disparate fields in ways that will significantly enhance our understanding of the turbulent, postinternational world.

DRIVING FORCES

The historical process of international organization that Inis Claude described was closely linked to major power wars (the Napoleonic Wars, World Wars I and II) and power transitions, technological innovation, economic growth and rising interdependence, expansion of the state system, and the actions of IGOs themselves. It was largely a state-driven process. Clearly, the end of the Cold War marked a transition every bit as significant as a major power war, without the fighting.

Far more significant, however, than the end of the bipolar superpower rivalry for the evolution of global governance are the various underlying or *deep* trends about which Rosenau and others have written. These include: globalization of labor, capital, production, markets, and culture; the revolution in communications; the accumulating evidence of environmental degradation and species loss; the growth of civil society through the effects of education, technology, urbanization, and information on individuals and nongovernmental groups; increased demand for democratization; greater economic and cultural interdependencies as well as wealth; and migration of peoples as refugees and workers. In short, three interactive sets of factors: environmental degradation, global socioeconomic changes, and technological revolutions—are changing the actors, issues, and stakes in the global politics of governance. They have contributed to a very different type of power transition: from a state-centric to a multicentric world wherein the patterns of conflict and cooperation, integration and fragmentation, are driving the phenomenon of multiple layers and pieces of governance with overlapping geographic and issue jurisdictions (and holes of "ungovernance"). The result is an emerging global order that we might term "complex governance."[16]

The expansion of global governance is also driven by changes in thinking and understanding often shaped by new visual images and crisis situations. Recall for a moment the images of Earth from outer space—that small, spinning sphere, with swirling clouds and glimpses of the shapes of continents, the polar ice caps, and oceans. Nary a boundary line in sight. One small planet shared by 6 billion-plus human beings, several million plant, animal, fish, and insect species, and countless bacteria. For the first time, we have a visual image that gives meaning to the word "global" and to feelings of commonness among the humans living in different parts of that globe, the feeling of being part of what Marshall McLuhan (based on different phenomena to be sure) called the "global village" and what the Commission on Global Governance, composed of twenty-eight world leaders, has more recently termed, "Our Global Neighborhood." History is replete with events and images that emphasize difference as today's revived ethnic conflicts remind us. The image of Earth from space has simultaneously given meaning to our common interest and heritage.

Consider a crisis situation: the report in 1985 of a hole in the Earth's ozone layer over Antarctica. Scientists had been warning of depletion in stratospheric ozone for more than a decade. International negotiations prompted by the United Nations Environment Programme (UNEP) had resulted in the 1985 framework convention (Vienna Convention on the Protection of the Ozone Layer) for reducing use of the chlorofluorocarbons (CFCs) thought to be the highest contributor to ozone depletion. The 1985 report, however, provided critical impetus for negotiating the supplementary Montreal Protocol concluded in 1987 that mandates reductions in CFC use. Clearly, the evidence of environmental degradation that if continued would threaten human well-being provided enough sense of common threat to galvanize the global scientific community, the director of UNEP, national governments of many states, and the chemical industries of major developed countries to reach agreement in almost record time on steps to reduce CFC use.[17] The threat gave meaning to the common interest of humankind (and other species that have already suffered harm as a result of ozone depletion).

Both the image of Earth from space and the scientific evidence of ozone depletion provide fuel for a paradigm shift that can encompass concepts of common security and a common future. For many people, security has become far more than protecting national territorial spaces and the people who inhabit them or exercise power within them. The Report of the Commission on Global Governance endeavored to articulate a new discourse of shared responsibility for the planet and its inhabitants.[18]

The politics of global governance is not just about emerging global issues and thinking globally. Technological revolutions, environmental degradation, global socioeconomic changes, and paradigm shifts in human beings' understanding of their world are driving the phenomenon of multiple layers of complex governance. The piecemeal nature of that complexity, however, combined with the disorderly nature of the contradictory tendencies currently at work in the world, make prediction of a single direction impossible. New governance arrangements for security in Europe, trade in South America's Southern Cone, or tropical timber may encompass societies, regions, or sectors not previously linked. Simultaneously, English, Norwegian, and Danish voters have all expressed their opposition to closer European integration, and regions from Lombardy to Scotland are demanding greater local authority. Subsidiarity is as much an issue within the European Union as its democratic deficit and monetary union. As we have learned with respect to the older discourse on modernization and development, we must be wary of a tendency to think in linear, progressive terms. Where there may be evidence now of enlarging cheese and shrinking holes in that piece of swiss cheese, mold could well set in.

Rosenau's postinternational paradigm forces us to think about such changes and to consider the interactions among the three parameters of underlying change. Is it an adequate analytical framework, however, for answering the questions of scope, domain, and who gets what, when, how, at what cost, and with what degree of effectiveness that make up Lasswell's classic definition of politics whether we are considering the postinternational politics of a piece of global governance or local politics in Dayton, Ohio?

ANALYZING THE POLITICS OF GLOBAL GOVERNANCE: OR, ALL IS NOT MECHANICS (OR JUST, FAIR, WISE, OR EFFECTIVE)

Much of the global-governance literature to date has been devoid of any real sense of politics. There is an almost mechanistic tone to many discussions of managing problems of massive human migrations, developing country indebtedness, species depletion, rainforest destruction, international shipping, or global capital markets. Often lost are the realities (and messiness) of politics, the potential for ineffective governance (or "dysgovernance"), and the ungovernable.[19]

Who Governs?

Who governs international shipping, for example? Who governs the global financial markets that have developed? Who governs the rapidly expanding global telecommunications field? Who or what is providing security if the authority of all states is eroding? What governance functions have the European states effectively ceded to the EU or NATO, TNCs, or global financial markets? In Africa, what domains are effectively governed now by the International Monetary Fund (IMF), humanitarian agencies, or subnational groups? As Strange notes, the marketplace has emerged as perhaps the most powerful "actor" governing the world economy, generating outcomes that affect the choices of states large and small. Yet most political scientists are poorly equipped to analyze how and why that may be.

There is no simple answer to the question of who governs. The phenomenon of complex governance means multiple types of authorities and arrangements affecting outcomes in different domains, with varying degrees of effectiveness. No single state, coalition of states, or set of nonstate actors governs the political, social, economic, and environmental issues that make up the broad scope of what governments and governance encompass in the late twentieth century.

We must link our analysis of who exercises power over particular types of outcomes, and how, with what effects, and at what costs, to specific types of issues and domains of interaction whether those are inter- or transnational relations, market sectors, social groups, or ecosystems. The range of actors we must consider includes states and subnational governmental authorities such as port authorities, provinces, and municipal governments; transnational corporations (TNCs) and cartels—whether single firms or associations of firms; groups like the Mafia controlling international criminal activity; the international bureaucrats of IGOs such as the IMF, World Bank, European Commission, United Nations Environment Programme, or World Health Organization; religious authorities in major transnational religions; and also markets.[20]

The actors also include NGOs and the social movements to which many are linked that may be sources of opposition to governments, corporations, and IGOs, or sources of information, ideas, expertise, and impetus for new policies and programs, new rules, norms, and activities. NGOs often function as the interest aggregators, demanders, legitimizers, and supporters for governance, monitors of the consequences of new rules and policies (especially important for compliance and enforcement of environmental rules or human rights), for assisting in implementation itself through grassroots links. Hence, through organizations such as Amnesty International, the World Wildlife Fund, or Development Alternatives with Women for a New Era (DAWN) larger issues of human rights, environmental protection, and women's roles in development have been shaped and situations in specific countries affected.

As the complexity of global, transnational, subregional, or sectoral issues rises, the need for expert input clearly does too. NGOs are one potential source, but "epistemic communities"—informal groupings of individuals providing consensual knowledge and advice for policy-making and regime building—are yet another.[21] In grappling with problems of environmental degradation such as in the Great Lakes, the Mediterranean and Baltic Seas, stratospheric ozone, Antarctica, tropical rainforests, and deserts, we increasingly confront, however, the limits of scientists' knowledge of how particular ecosystems "work." The solutions devised for cleaning up the Mediterranean, for example, were based on then prevailing understandings of currents and the circulation of effluents that have since proven flawed. In other cases, such as global warming and climate change, there is sharp disagreement within the scientific community on evidence and its interpretation. Playing the politics of environmental risk, determining what is known (and unknown), and assessing its significance are important dimensions then of global environmental governance. In these domains and others, epistemic communities are likely to be important players.

For all the dogma among international relations scholars about the state, the billiard balls have been permeated and constrained, the black boxes opened; the state is not what it once (if ever) was. In considering the role of states in complex governance, we must take cognizance of the realities of weak, quasi- and failed states as well as states that are more powerful or effective in the politics of particular domains of governance. Rosenau's postinternational paradigm posits a bifurcated world. In answering the question "who governs," we must adjust our analytical frameworks to deal with politics in domains where governance processes are still largely state-centered as well as those where states play little or no role and yet others with a variety of actors. Conceptually, I believe, we have one world with many governance domains and a changing mix of state and nonstate actors exercising or sharing power over outcomes.

The Scope and Domains of Governance

The range of security, socioeconomic, and environmental matters that governance in today's world encompasses is virtually unlimited. Likewise, in conceptualizing the domains of governance, we face a range of territorial and geographical as well as nonterritorial "spaces," sectors, "imagined" communities, issues, activities, interactions, and relationships in which links are forged by mutual interest, shared identity, and need.[22]

With the development of telecommunications networks, financial markets, and capital flows that reach all parts of the world and with the accumulating knowledge of planetary climate patterns, some governance domains clearly need to be truly global, in the sense of controlling or steering actors and outcomes anywhere on the Earth. Some domains are linked to a geographically or functionally delimited set of actors and activities, for example polar species, the Mediterranean Sea, security in the South China Sea, or the global shipping industry. There are also the "spaces" of Internet, satellite orbits, high frequency radio transmissions, and intellectual property rights.

The postinternationalist paradigm's three parameters roughly correspond to the systemic, national/societal, and individual levels of analysis. The politics of global governance spans many levels, many "spaces." Studies of global governance, then, need to analyze *multi-* or *N-level* as well as *interlevel* games and domains to analyze who gets access to which markets, to which telecommunications technologies, or to renegotiated debt and credit packages; which countries' civil wars become the object of international attention, humanitarian intervention, or peacemaking efforts; or which environmental problems become agendas for action.

One analytical question pertaining to domains of governance concerns the loyalty or identity people may have with those who govern. Scholarly literature on the subject of identity affirms the ability of human beings to hold multiple and even overlapping identities simultaneously, let alone over time. Hence, there is little difficulty in conceptualizing nested and overlapping communities composed of people and groups (including states) who identify with one another in some way. More important, is the meaning people attach to those identities and communities and the consequences, then, of their "imaginings."[23] Thus, even if we can gather the empirical evidence that certain groups of people believe there is an "international community" or an "Asia-Pacific community," or a "Europe," what difference does that make in the actions they take or are willing to have others take on their behalf? What form does that then give to "community?"

Answers to these questions about how communities are imagined and formed and to what ends, are important to any study of governance for they tell us who are the governed—that is, what are the domains of governance. Rhetoric and symbols matter in politics, and discourse about community (or the absence thereof) will shape political actions that give substance and form to beliefs. So, the study of global governance needs to consider the imagined community or communities and the politics that surrounds the creation of those domains whether they are territorially or geographically, functionally or sectorally, or otherwise defined.

The "How" of Global Governance

Power exercised directly in relationships through bargaining or other means or indirectly through resources and "structural" position is an essential ingredient in who gets what. Yet political scientists seldom analyze nonstate or nongovernmental power. Indeed international relations scholars have had far more difficulty with power analysis as the utility of military force in determining outcomes of interstate relations has declined.[24] How much more complicated the analytical task becomes with the proliferation of nonstate actors, the suggestion of markets as "governors," and the expansion of complex governance.

The postinternational politics of global governance requires renewed attention to power analysis and to paradoxes of power where outcomes diverge from expectations based on assumptions about who or what has either positional or instrumental means to get what they want. Likewise, in addressing the "how" of global governance, we must examine the various means state and nonstate actors use to secure desired outcomes. In this respect, we face the problem that IGOs, for example, are both actors and arenas, agents and structures. They, like the more encompassing arrangements of international regimes, are a means of achieving governance. Rosenau's own analysis of the United Nations posits the UN as the beneficiary of turbulence and as a change agent.[25] Other means include cartel arrangements among firms, networks among NGOs and members of a global social movement, coalitions of states alone or of several different types of actors. Each means also provides a context for political action that along with the nature of the governance issue itself, will shape the other instruments actors may use to exercise relational power or their ability to affect outcomes based on structural power.

A further aspect of the "how" of governance is leadership. International relations scholars, especially those concerned with structural power, have often neglected this aspect of politics: the roles of powerful, charismatic, visionary, or skillful individuals in shaping outcomes of efforts to govern (and the willingness of others to follow). Although endowed with the material resources of potential power and the "strength" of position, major powers have often neglected or been unable to lead for lack of domestic support, international followers, or skillful and visionary individuals. In speaking of the U.S. hegemonic role in establishing post–World War II international organizations and regimes, one must account not only for American predominance economically and militarily, but also for its leadership. Current, renewed optimism about its position as the sole remaining superpower seldom considers the absence of vision, skill, and leadership as well as the breakdown in congressional support for meeting U.S. financial obligations to multilateral institutions.[26]

One of the notable features of multilateral diplomacy is the opportunities afforded to small states and middle powers (and their skillful diplomats) as well as to coalitions of states to exercise leadership. Examples abound: Singapore's ambassador Tommie Koh and the UN Conference on the Law of the Sea; Malta's Ambassador Arvid Pardo and the UN resolution setting forth the principle of the "common heritage of mankind"; Belgium's Paul Henri Spaak and the European Common Market; Middle powers Australia and Canada and the GATT Uruguay Round bargains on agricultural trade; Canada's prime minister Lester Pearson and UN peacekeeping.

The postinternational, multicentric world is also one in which a UN secretary-general, or UNEP executive director, or Human Rights Watch, the World Wildlife Fund, the Union of Concerned Scientists, or a coalition of indigenous peoples may exercise leadership. This is not new, but the volume of examples appears to have increased and, hence, the difference to be more noticeable from the old pattern of major power, i.e., state, leadership.

Secondly, ideas and words matter (as do the agent or messenger). Knowledge counts, but there is still much we do not understand. Modernity has been distinguished by faith in technology and corresponding confidence in what we might call policy "engineering." Americans in particular have displayed great confidence in human ability to solve any problem with sufficient time, cash, and ingenuity.

Recent literature has given us a far greater understanding of the role ideas play in shaping politics, policy (foreign and domestic), and governance. The literature on NGOs is replete with illustrations of their role as agents for "principled ideas and values."[27] Yet, clearly, there is also much that is not fully understood about the choices of decision makers.

Given the changing mix of state and nonstate influence, it is difficult to posit how the crisis of governmental authority that lies at the heart of Rosenau's micro-macro parameter will play out in different domains of global governance. Furthermore, institutions—whether systems of rule, organizational structures, or patterns of practice—tend to change slowly. Currently the UN and many other IGOs face demands for reform, some representational, some organizational, some performance-oriented. The continuing dominance of IGOs by member states complicates efforts on the part of those advocating change, just as entrenched authorities do in other arenas. IGO reform, however, is but one further aspect of the issue of who gets what at the heart of the global politics of governance: the values and effectiveness of outcomes.

All Is Not Just, Fair, Wise, or Effective

Historically, many international organization scholars have operated with a mindset that "Multilateralism is good" and more of it is better.[28] The point is not necessarily to advocate less, however, in the mode of domestic conservatives calling for less government and regulation, but rather to reexamine the bases for our judgments of what is fair, wise, and effective, at what costs, and to whom. There has been far too little critical analysis of international policy and governance outcomes in terms of their impact on issues and problems themselves. As Baldwin cautions, however, there is "no such thing as a perfect influence attempt," only degrees of success and failure, best analyzed in the context of the difficulty of what is being attempted.[29] In this vein, Brian Urquhart once described the UN as "the world's emergency room"— the dumping ground for the most difficult problems that states could not solve on their own, but waited until situations reached the crisis point to seek help.[30]

The pieces of global governance are marked by competing ideas and value systems no less than politics in any domain. Among bankers and finance ministry officials of G-7 countries at least, the International Monetary Fund and World Bank are esteemed for the effectiveness of their conditionality and structural adjustment programs. Critics, however, note the high social and economic costs people in many countries have paid to meet these conditions and the net flow of monetary resources from South to North in their efforts to maintain debt repayment schedules.

In current UN reform proposals, we see the values of more equity in representation on the Security Council; more organizational efficiency, coordination, and rationality among the many organs dealing with economic development and social issues; smaller bureaucracies at the top or center and more funding for programs themselves; more attention to maintaining standards of staff productivity and less to representation of a distribution of the membership. Although rationality would eliminate the UN Conference on Trade and Development (UNCTAD), many developing states oppose this step because of UNCTAD's value as a forum for promoting their interests. The politics of UN reform is a contest over which sets of values and which groups of member states will prevail at what cost and to whom.

One could scrutinize any international regime or other governance mode with respect to prevailing values and effectiveness. Ultimately, in the politics of global governance, effectiveness depends upon the compliance of states as well as industries, regions, and people whose capacities to comply (and for whom the cost of compliance) vary widely.[31]

Finally, there are the inevitable unintended consequences—positive and negative—of policy choices. The limits of knowledge, of technology, of human and policy engineering, of resources, of leadership or of commitment, as well as the realities of changes "on the ground" make governance a matter of art and the politics of an imperfect "science."

RESEARCH CHALLENGES

In probing the parameters of postinternational change and the dynamics of the global politics of governance, who gets what, when, how, and at what cost are questions we must ask about the pieces of global governance. And, in so doing, we must consider the following:

- States that say no
- Regimes that do not develop (or persist)
- Citizens that think parochially
- Corporations that exploit, degrade, pollute, and denude
- NGOs that cannot agree to work with each other
- Movements that do not move
- Leaders who do not lead
- Governance attempts that fail as well as those that succeed

We must also ask what are the consequences of parametric change and turbulence for who gets what in the politics of global governance. What are the intended and unintended changes in who benefits and who loses, who grows richer and who becomes more impoverished, who is empowered and who is effectively "disenfranchised," or whose and which values determine what is fair, just, and effective?

The postinternational paradigm, then, provides a framework within which to organize the following three research and theory-building tasks:

1. Developing systematically structured, comparable case studies on the nature of post–Cold War governance arrangements, the mix of state and nonstate actors and authorities, the politics and processes of interaction among these different actors for different types of issues and domains.[32] These would form the empirical basis for comparative governance studies and policy-process tracing, enabling us to predict better where or when governance is likely to emerge or be absent and, hence, to develop better theories on the global politics of governance. They would also make clear whether the macro parameter is, in fact, now bifurcated between state and multicentric worlds or a continuum of different mixes in different domains. The design could incorporate cross-time comparisons as well as cross-issue and domain. This would enable us to test the hypotheses about the effects of turbulence and parametric change on the politics of governance.

2. If the crisis of authority structures afflicts more than governments per se, what types of governance arrangements will more likely be regarded as legitimate and effective, eliciting greater degrees of compliance? And, what is the nature and extent of the loyalty and identity attached to these governance domains?

3. Are more competent, skillful individuals aware of the pieces of "complex governance?" What evidence can we find of their greater capacity to know when and how to participate in the global politics of governance? What will happen if that is frustrated by lack of adequate means to express opposition or participate in shaping outcomes?

ORDER, DISORDER, COMPLEXITY, AND CHANGE:
CYCLES, LINES, AND CIRCLES

There is a human longing for order, simplicity, and stability, though some of us thrive on a certain amount of disorder, complexity, and change. So, it is not surprising that a number of individuals, groups, and even states worldwide should share a quest for order in what is clearly a disorderly and turbulent world. Some might prefer a world of neatly separated black boxes or billard balls, however much they may collide with each other. Others may be quite comfortable with a world that seems almost "neomedieval" in its multiple and overlapping authorities, absent any clear lines of territorial or spiritual space. Modernist, Western minds grope to see where the lines and stages of development may lead next or, alternatively, where the ending of one cycle may come and the beginning of another be discerned. Those of more Eastern (or holistic or indigenous) mind, like the "neomedievalists" think in terms of complex, concentric circles and coexisting contradictions that do not necessarily resolve in Hegelian syntheses.

Much of what has emerged to date in the way of global governance has been a product of Western conceptions of government and governance. This is one reason why the Asia-Pacific developments are so intriguing: many Asians are not readily accepting what they regard as foreign modes of interaction and organization (or, in the case of human rights, foreign principles and norms). What happens in this emerging community will have to reflect compromises or new combinations of these traditions.

For scholars, the challenge is to break out of the jail of single-level analysis; to explore the roles of many actors, not just states; to trace the networks that link some of those actors and through which ideas and knowledge circulate, movements coalesce, and actions take shape; then to study the structures and processes—formal and informal—through which politics plays out, power is exercised, choices are agreed upon and implemented (or only partially so), the values and ideas that guide those choices, the costs they incur, the identity of winners and losers, and the consequences—intended and unintended—for forests, species, lakes, human well-being, and global security.

Finally, our task is to put governance at the center of our study of global politics. As Rosenau argued with regard to the comparative study of foreign policies almost thirty years ago, so today, governance is neither fad, fantasy, nor a separate field. The global politics of governance is central to the field we likely, as habit-driven actors, will continue calling inter*national* relations even as we adopt a postinternational paradigm.

NOTES

1. It is with some trepidation that I write this essay, knowing that Jim Rosenau continues to think and write prolificly about global governance. Nonetheless, it is with affection and gratitude for many years of friendship and colleagueship that I have "penned" these thoughts. In doing so, I have been reminded of one early piece of advice Jim gave me, namely, the value I would ultimately derive from having taught many different courses from American government to my own specialty of international organizations. For

some of Rosenau's own thoughts on global governance, see "Governance, Order, and Change in World Politics," in James N. Rosenau and Ernst-Otto Czempiel, eds., *Governance without Government: Order and Change in World Politics* (Cambridge: Cambridge University Press, 1992), pp. 1–29; "Governance in the Twenty-first Century," *Global Governance* 1, 1 (winter 1995): 1–15; "Multilateral Governance and the Nation-State System: A Post–Cold War Assessment," (paper for the first meeting of a study group of the Inter-American Dialogue, Washington, D.C., April 24–25, 1995); and *Along the Domestic-Foreign Frontier: Exploring Governance in a Turbulent World* (Cambridge: Cambridge University Press, 1997).

2. On the subject of global civil society, see chapter 5 in this volume by Ronnie Lipschutz.

3. This formulation is a variation of Rosenau's in his introductory essay for the volume, *Governance without Government*. See "Governance, Order, and Change in World Politics," pp. 4–5.

4. See Thomas M. Franck, *Fairness in International Law and Institutions* (New York: Oxford University Press, 1995), particularly the discussion in chapter 1.

5. Lawrence S. Finkelstein, "What Is Global Governance," *Global Governance* 1, 3 (September–December 1995): 367–72.

6. For an intriguing discussion of markets as "governors" and the structural power of markets, see Susan Strange, *States and Markets* (London: Pinter, 1988) and *Retreat of the State: The Diffusion of Power in the World Economy* (Cambridge: Cambridge University Press, 1996).

7. Inis L. Claude Jr., *Swords into Plowshares: The Problems and Progress of International Organization*, 3rd rev. ed. (New York: Random House, 1974), chaps. 2–4.

8. John Gerard Ruggie, ed., *Multilateralism Matters: The Theory and Praxis of an Institutional Form* (New York: Columbia University Press, 1993).

9. Mark W. Zacher, "The Decaying Pillars of the Westphalian Temple: Implications for International Order and Governance," in Rosenau and Czempiel, *Governance without Government*, p. 60.

10. There is a growing literature both in international relations and international law on the social construction of reality. See, for example, Friedrich V. Kratochwil, *Rules, Norms, and Decisions: On the Conditions of Practical and Legal Reasoning in International Relations and Domestic Affairs* (Cambridge: Cambridge University Press, 1989); Audie Klotz, *Norms in International Relations* (Ithaca, N.Y.: Cornell University Press, 1995); Martha Finnemore, *National Interests and International Society* (Ithaca, N.Y.: Cornell University Press, 1996); Thomas M. Francke, *The Power of Legimacy among Nations* (New York: Oxford University Press, 1990); and John Searle, *The Construction of Social Reality* (New York: Basic Books, 1995).

11. See, for example, Thomas G. Weiss and Leon Gordenker, eds., *NGOS, The UN, and Global Governance* (Boulder, Colo.: Lynne Rienner, 1996) and Thomas Risse-Kappen, ed., *Bringing Transnational Relations Back In: Non-State Actors, Domestic Structures, and International Institutions* (Cambridge: Cambridge University Press, 1995).

12. For a particularly insightful discussion of the continuing role of customary practice, see chapter 4 of Anthony D'Amato, *International Law Anthology* (Cincinnati, Ohio: Anderson Publishing, 1994), pp. 51–119. On the subject of informal agreements, see Charles Lipson, "Why are Some International Agreements Informal?" *International Organization* 45, 3 (1991): 495–538.

13. See for example, Amitav Acharya, "Ideas, Identity, and Institution-Building: Making Sense of the 'Asia Pacific Way,' " *The Pacific Review* 10, 3 (1997): 319–46, vol. 10, no. 3.

14. For discussions of second-track diplomacy in Asia Pacific, see among others, Stuart Harris, "Policy Networks and Economic Cooperation: Policy Coordination in the Asia-Pacific Region," *The Pacific Review* 7, 4 (1994): 381–94; Paul M. Evans, "The Dialogue Process on Asia Pacific Security Issues: Inventory and Analysis," in Evans ed., *Studying Asia Pacific Security* (Toronto: Joint Centre for Asia Pacific Studies, 1994); Desmond Ball, "A New Era in Confidence Building: The Second-track Process in the Asia/Pacific Region," *Security Dialogue* 25, 2 (1994): 157–76; Lawrence T. Woods, *Asia-Pacific Diplomacy: Nongovernmental Organizations and International Relations* (Vancouver: UBC Press, 1993); and Diane Stone, "Networks, Second Track Diplomacy, and Regional Cooperation: The Role of Southeast Asian Think Tanks," (paper prepared for the 38th Annual Meeting of the International Studies Association, Toronto, 22–26 March 1997).

15. See Margaret P. Karns, "Ad Hoc Multilateral Diplomacy: The United States, The Contact Group, and Namibia," *International Organization* 41, 1 (winter 1987): 93–123.

16. I am indebted to Barry Hughes for suggesting this term.

17. Richard E. Benedick, *Ozone Diplomacy: New Directions in Safeguarding the Planet* (Cambridge: Harvard University Press), 1991.

18. The Commission on Global Governance, *Our Global Neighborhood* (New York: Oxford University Press, 1995).

19. For a discussion of this, see Robert Latham, "Politics in a Floating World: Toward a Critique of Global Governance," in *Approaches to Global Governance Theory* edited by Martin Hewson and Timothy Sinclair (Albany: State University of New York Press, 1998).

20. See among others, Strange, *Retreat of the State*, chaps. 6–12 for an interesting series of case studies; Craig N. Murphy, *International Organization and Industrial Change: Global Governance since 1850* (New York: Oxford University Press, 1994); Oran R. Young, *International Governance: Protecting the Environment in a Stateless Society* (Ithaca, N.Y.: Cornell University Press, 1994); and Mark W. Zacher with Brent A. Sutton, *Governing Global Networks: International Regimes for Transportation and Communications* (Cambridge: Cambridge University Press, 1996).

21. See Peter M. Haas, "Introduction: Epistemic Communities and International Policy Coordination," *International Organization* 46, 1 (winter 1992): 1–36 and other essays in this special issue.

22. On the subject of spaces, see John Gerard Ruggie, "Territoriality and Beyond: Problematizing Modernity in International Relations," *International Organization* 47, 1 (winter 1993) and Yale H. Ferguson and Richard W. Mansbach,

"Political Space and Westphalian States in a World of 'Polities': Beyond Inside/Outside," *Global Governance* 2, 2 (May–August 1996): 261–87.

23. The literature on identity is a growing one. See, for example, R. B. J. Walker, "Sovereignty, Identity, Community," in *Contending Sovereignties,* edited by Walker and Saul Mendlovitz (Boulder, Colo.: Lynne Rienner, 1990), pp. 159–85; Ole Waever, Barry Buzan, M. Kelstrup, and P. Lemaitre, *Identity, Migration and the New Security Agenda in Europe* (London: Pinter, 1993); Peter J. Katzenstein, ed., *The Culture of National Security: Norms and Identity in World Politics* (New York: Columbia University Press, 1996); Yale H. Ferguson and Richard W. Mansbach, *Polities: Authorities, Identities and Change* (Columbia: University of South Carolina Press, 1996); and Benedict Anderson, *Imagined Communities: Reflections on the Origin and Spread of Nationalism,* rev. ed. (New York: Verso, 1991).

24. David A. Baldwin, *Paradoxes of Power* (London: Basil Blackwell Publishers, 1989).

25. James N. Rosenau, *The United Nations in a Turbulent World* (Boulder, Colo.: Lynne Rienner, 1992).

26. See Margaret P. Karns and Karen A. Mingst, "The Past as Prologue to the Future: The United States and the United Nations," in *The United Nations System in World Politics: The Policies of Member States,* edited by Chadwick R. Alger, Gene M. Lyons, and John Trent (Tokyo: UN University Press, 1995).

27. Risse-Kappen, *Bringing Transnational Relations Back In,* p. 309. On the subject of ideas and foreign policy more generally, see Judith Goldstein and Robert O. Keohane, eds., *Ideas and Foreign Policy: Beliefs, Institutions, and Political Change* (Ithaca, N.Y.: Cornell University Press, 1993).

28. Inis L. Claude Jr. *States and the Global System* (New York: St. Martin's Press, 1988).

29. David A. Baldwin, *Economic Statecraft* (Princeton, N.J.: Princeton University Press, 1985).

30. Brian Urquhart was a longtime member of the UN Secretariat, Under Secretary-General for Political and Security Affairs in the 1980s, and often known as the "father of peacekeeping." The remark was made in a speech to the National Model United Nations Conference.

31. On the issues of effectiveness, compliance, and states' capacity, see Peter M. Haas, Robert O. Keohane, and Marc A. Levy, *Institutions for the Earth: Sources of Effective International Environmental Protection* (Cambridge: MIT Press, 1992); Abram Chayes and Antonia Chayes, *The New Sovereignty: Compliance with International Regulatory Agreements* (Cambridge: Harvard University Press, 1996); and Harold K. Jacobson and Edith Brown Weiss, "Strengthening Compliance with International Environmental Accords: Preliminary Observations from a Collaborative Project," *Global Governance* 1, 2 (May–August 1995): 119–48.

32. Two scholars who have undertaken extended, systematic studies of governance arrangements are Oran Young and Mark Zacher. Young's work focuses on international environmental governance, including polar regimes; Zacher's addresses international economic regimes, including infrastructure industries such as shipping and telecommunications.

CHAPTER 4

Justified Jailbreaks and Paradigmatic Recidivism

V. Spike Peterson

> Reality, it seems, is not what it used to be in International Relations.
> —Jim George, *Discourses of Global Politics*

> [T]heorizing must begin anew, and present premises and understandings of history's dynamics must be treated as conceptual jails from which an escape can be engineered only by allowing for the possibility that a breakpoint in human affairs is imminent, if not upon us, as the twentieth century comes to an end.
> —James Rosenau, *Turbulence in World Politics*

We confront a world of complementary, conflictual, and contradictory systems of differential power: what Jim Rosenau has aptly characterized as "turbulence." There is no simple or "essential" relationship among an ever expanding global capitalism, centralization and decentralization of political orders, the hierarchies of gender, class, and race/ethnic oppression, and the threatened biosphere upon which all else ultimately depends. These interlocking systems of power develop differentially (they are not reducible to each other) yet inextricably (they are mutually constituted through historical process). In this turbulent context, international relations (IR) theory is contested terrain. As an exploration of that terrain, this chapter locates Rosenau's work in relation to gender-sensitive and feminist international relations theory.

Preparation of this chapter was facilitated by a grant for Research and Writing from the John D. and Catherine T. MacArthur Foundation.

CONSTITUTING JAILS . . .

Abandoning existing assumptions is no easy matter. . . . [S]tudents of world politics, like politicians, are prisoners of their paradigms, unwilling or unable to escape the premise of state predominance and constantly tempted to cling to familiar assumptions about hierarchy, authority, and sovereignty.[1]

Chapter 2 of *Turbulence in World Politics* is titled "Justifying Jailbreaks" and, in Rosenau's words, "offers a justification for an unremitting effort to break out of the conceptual jails in which the study of world politics is deemed to be incarcerated."[2] Having delineated the limitations of conventional theories, in the same volume Rosenau presents a "new paradigm"[3] to address the anomalies and turbulence of contemporary life. He argues that it is the simultaneous interaction of changes in the main parameters of world politics (micro, macro, and mixed) that locates us in the most "thoroughgoing transformation since comparable shifts culminated in the Treaty of Westphalia in 1648."[4] To develop a paradigm able to accommodate the scale and complexity of this transformation, Rosenau attempts to rethink foundational categories, conventional assumptions, and theoretical frameworks. The sweep of this rethinking is elaborated in *Turbulence* and its specific contrast to realism is explored in *Thinking Theory Thoroughly*.[5]

From my perspective, the singularly most attractive and significant feature of Rosenau's work is his creative transgression of conventional boundaries. Especially in the past decade, Rosenau has been uniquely innovative as an IR theorist, producing a variety of works that chart new paths and celebrate new voices.[6] Given space restrictions, I cannot address this work in its entirety. Rather, I focus here on the role of dichotomies as a subtext both in Rosenau's critique of realism and in his construction of postinternational politics. On the one hand, Rosenau's subversion of givens—especially, either-or dichotomies—is one of the things I admire in his work and find most innovative, illuminating, and promising when assessing his recent contributions to IR theory. On the other hand, I am critical of how particular binaries—and their ontological and epistemological commitments—remain the basis for Rosenau's theory, which suggests that his rethinking is not in fact thorough enough. My argument, in brief, is that Rosenau breaks out of a jail cell, but not out of the paradigmatic prison of positivist and masculinist binaries.

The dichotomies that dominate conventional IR theory are a function of the discipline's self-definition (domestic politics versus international anarchy, war versus peace, us versus them) and its commitment to positivist understanding. The latter entails categorical separations—dichotomies—of fact (objectivity) versus value (subjectivity), theory versus practice, and subject (knower) versus object (that which is known). Linked to these foundational binaries and played out with varying degrees of visibility and force in IR theorizing are a number of other now familiar dichotomies: agent-structure, politics-economics, reason-affect, direct-indirect violence, public-private, masculine-feminine.

But in what sense are these dichotomies a conceptual prison? Critiques of positivism and its binary framing have occupied philosophers of science and social theorists throughout this century. The complexity of argumentation and diversity of positions defy brief summary; I refer readers to the appropriate literature[7] and confine my remarks here to the role and significance of dichotomies in contemporary epistemological debates.

In spite of important distinctions among critical and postmodern theorists, they agree on rejecting positivist dichotomies in favor of relational thinking. As I argue at length in "Transgressing Boundaries,"[8] rather than oppositional (either-or) and hierarchical dualisms (privileging the first term over the second), "objects" and the boundaries identifying them must be understood in relation, as interactively constituted in historical context. This insistence on situating claims by reference to contingent, historical conditions reflects (in part) the "linguistic turn," understood as a shift from thinking of language as a neutral or transparent medium (simply "representing" reality) to language and world as mutually constituted, as interactive and *relational*. In Eloise Buker's words

> While acknowledging that words do point to things, a semiotic theory of language emphasizes how words *constitute* phenomena as certain types of things. Semiotics explains that meanings reside not in speakers, but in the language of a group of speakers. Thus, it locates meaning in a language system which is stabilized by a community.[9]

Hence, to communicate intelligibly, we "submit" ourselves to systems of cultural meaning; we are constrained by the rules and grammar of language systems. At the same time, speakers "even as they are constrained by the language system, can over time change it and so exercise power over language."[10] The important point here is that, once in place (stabilized in hegemonic discourse) oppositional dichotomies act as a filtering device that "imposes" ways of thinking that shape how we "know" reality, including how we act in ways that effectively "produce" that reality—at the expense of alternative realities rendered visible/real through alternative linguistic filters. The point is less to question, for example, whether weapons and nation-states "really exist" but to ask how and why our discursive practices constitute these objects in particular contingent ways (precluding alternative constructions) and *what the effects of this particular constituting are*. It is to deny what Jim George calls the "spectator" theory of knowledge, where external "facts" impose themselves on subjects/observers, independent of the subject's meaning system, in favor of "theory *as* practice," where subjects and objects are related (mutually constituted) through stabilized linguistic/cultural meaning systems.

> Whatever else this alternative approach achieves, it problematizes the dominant modernist commitment to a world of given subjects and objects and all other dichotomized givens. In so doing, it reformulates basic *questions* of modernist understanding in emphasizing not the sovereign subject (e.g., author/independent state) or the object (e.g., independent world/text) but instead the historical, cultural, and linguistic practices in which subjects and objects (and theory and practice, facts and values) are constructed.[11]

In regard to dichotomies, suffice it to underscore two points: (1) that either-or thinking misconceives the relational dynamic of all concepts, understanding, and action, and (2) that binary constructions "promote patterns of thought and action that are static (unable to acknowledge or address change), stunted (unable to envision alternatives), and dangerously oversimplified (unable to accommodate the complexities of social reality)."[12]

(JAIL)BREAKING AWAY . . .

From a perspective critical of binary thought, Rosenau's postinternational politics is to be applauded for its many examples of post-dichotomous thinking. This is perhaps most striking in his discussion of micro-macro, where he rejects the conventional [read positivist] juxtaposition of "versus" in favor of "and," which focuses on the *interaction* of terms rather than their ostensible "conflict."[13] In short, Rosenau insists on favoring neither one nor the other in isolation but both and how they mutually affect each other. He specifically challenges the prevailing IR dichotomy that favors system explanation while it denies agency and changing attributes to individuals.[14] Not only does he alert us to the development of new skills and orientations among all of the world's people (the micro parameter), he argues that these are currently "preeminent" sources of turbulence. That is, the causal power of micro-level phenomena is accorded a *central* place in his model;[15] indeed he suggests that it may "constitute the single most important source of the turbulence that marks our time."[16]

Rosenau's commitment to relational thinking is also spelled out in his characterization of authority and how to more adequately understand "power". Without denying the significance of possessions (of sovereignty, resources, military might), Rosenau insists that developments in the multicentric world challenge conventional accounts of power, forcing us to more complicated understandings. As a guideline for jail-breaking, he instructs us

> to recognize that what makes actors effective . . . derives not from the sovereignty they possess or the legal privileges thereby accorded them, but rather lies in relational phenomena.[17]

Also consistent with a critique of either-or framing, Rosenau posits a continuum of control: brute force constitutes one extreme and persuasion (via scientific proof and reason) the other.[18] Rather than the poles, we need to focus on the more complex interactions between these extremes. Similarly, responses to control extend along a continuum, this time ranging from utter compliance to complete defiance, with the more relevant cases of bargaining, conditional agreement, and apathy falling between the extremes.

One can sight other examples of Rosenau's commitment to nonoppositional constructions: he coins the term "habdaptive actors" for those whose responses fall between the extremes of rote habit and calculated rationality;[19] he characterizes action sequences as "cascades" to emphasize their asymmetrical and multidirectional "flow";[20] and he rejects the dichotomy of "domestic" versus "international" politics. His boundary transgressions extend to: analyzing sovereignty as a restraint on actions and effectiveness; according agency and power to "all those who have authority to initiate and sustain actions" with transnational repercussions; arguing that subnational and supranational actors may be as relevant to world politics as states; denying the conventional notion of systemic levels; demoting the role of force in global politics; and proposing that "most important outcomes are produced by so many diverse whole systems and subsystems as to result in their effective control by none."[21]

In short, for those who are critical of the positivist and realist commitments that dominate IR scholarship, Rosenau's boundary transgressions are a welcome intervention. And not only did *Turbulence* present an elaborate alternative to realist orthodoxy, it was written by a highly respected senior theorist. Unlike dissident voices from the margin, one could hope that Rosenau's challenges would be engaged by those occupying the discipline's center. For those on the margins, Rosenau's profound challenge to realist adequacy in the face of contemporary reality marked new possibilities and a less constrained environment for alternative theories of IR.

CLARIFYING FEMINISMS . . .

I turn now to consider how Rosenau's work, and in particular, the role of dichotomies in his work, both opens up and also constrains spaces for feminist interventions in IR theory. My purpose here is twofold: to render visible some of the features of masculinism[22] at work in mainstream and in Rosenau's theorizing, and to illuminate feminist contributions to social and IR theorizing. In the process, I hope to suggest how gender is central to both contemporary global transformations and the development of IR theory capable of addressing those transformations. With other feminists, I am arguing that gender hierarchy is a constitutive, not coincidental, element of the interstate system and the global capitalist economy. On this view, gender relations *must* be examined to adequately apprehend how the world actually works, how "reality" is—every day and over centuries—constructed, reproduced, and transformed.[23]

Feminist scholarship is interdisciplinary, critical, and far from homogeneous. In early work, feminists sought to "correct" the gender-bias of knowledge claims by "adding women" to models and conceptual frameworks characterized as androcentric (assuming male experience as the norm). Adding women to conventional accounts is an important corrective: it documents women's agency in historical processes, exposes masculinist bias and error, and reframes our "picture" of social relations.[24]

By emphasizing individuals, the micro parameter, and the importance of nonstate actors, Rosenau's postinternational politics opens a space for "adding women." Rosenau does not, however, explore this opening. Had he done so, the gender of his micro actors (individuals, officials, leaders, private actors) would have been revealed as masculine, in the sense that his micro parameter presupposes only public-sphere actions and their political effects. That is, Rosenau fails to recognize and hence reproduces androcentric bias in his construction of micro agents.

Also typical of IR theorizing, Rosenau fails to attend to gender as an analytical category and systematic feature of social relations. In Terrell Carver's words, "gender is not a synonym for woman"[25] but a reference to the socially constructed (historical, contingent) dichotomy of masculine-feminine that shapes not only personal identities but also cognitive categories, language, stereotypical assumptions, social practices, and institutions (see note 22). The important point here is that, while the gender dichotomy is ostensibly derived from biological difference, cultural constructions of masculinities and femininities have little to do with biological phenomena. Indeed, feminists are critical of how putatively "biological" phenomena are deployed in social relations to naturalize, therefore depoliticize, gendered language, practices, and institutions that converge in reproducing masculinism as "ideology" and male dominance as practice.

At no point, however, does Rosenau address gender as an analytic category nor the power of gendered concepts, assumptions, frameworks, and worldviews. For example, it is the presumption of masculine agency in the definition of "citizen" that conceals how women (and feminized "Others") are effectively excluded from public sphere power. It is an androcentric understanding of "work" and "development" that ignores—even as it takes for granted—women's productive and reproductive labor in the "private sphere." And it is commitment to masculinist philosophy that privileges instrumental reason at the expense of more nuanced and complex theories of knowledge.

It is now a staple of feminist scholarship that conventional models of human nature, categories of social theory, and paradigms of knowledge construction are androcentric, taking male (especially elite, "Western" male) experience as the norm.[26] In particular, feminists argue that the binary logic of Western logocentric philosophy and the hierarchical dichotomies it generates are conceptually and empirically gendered.[27] This gendering is visible if we consider how the privileged first term of conventional dichotomies is associated with masculine qualities and the denigrated second term with feminine qualities: subject-object, autonomy-dependence, rational-irrational, order-anarchy, mind-body, culture-nature, public-private, freedom-necessity, hard-soft.

Whereas critical and postmodern theorists decry the reign of dichotomies in Western theory/practice, feminists go further and argue that these dichotomies are "rooted in" or dependent on the ostensibly "foundational" dichotomy of male/masculine-female/feminine. Stated simply, the gender dichotomy gains its "givenness" by (mistaken) association with biological ("natural") sex difference, and dichotomies more generally acquire the status of "givens" insofar as they readily "map onto" the gender dichotomy. As a consequence, feminists argue that attempts to move beyond dichotomizing *cannot succeed* unless they challenge the underlying dichotomy of masculine-feminine that renders dualizing filters so "natural."

Gender is thus not only a variable that must be added to conventional accounts, but an analytic category with profound consequences for how we "see," understand, and "know" the world. Hence, while "adding women" (as an empirical category) is a crucial step, the systemically transformative force of feminist interventions lies in its critique of gendered language/meaning systems (gender as an analytic category) and their pervasive, diffuse effects. In short, rethinking theory thoroughly requires taking gender seriously, as both an empirical and analytical category. Failure to do so leaves gendered assumptions in place and generates theories that are inadequate because they neglect central and pervasive features of social life.

Although men as a group are privileged vis-à-vis gender hierarchy, we *all* act as its agents insofar as we internalize, reinforce, and reproduce the dichotomy of masculine over feminine—through personal identifications, linguistic habits, social practices, and institutional dynamics. Ideologically, and especially in relation to the study of IR, the importance of masculinism is that it naturalizes not only the subordination of women and the invisibility of women's ways of being and knowing, but it also naturalizes (depoliticizes) the "othering" objectification—and corollary domination—of that which is associated with femininity: nature, females, and nondominant males.[28] And objectification matters, perhaps especially in international relations. Perceptions of "the enemy," military engagements, economic exploitation, and ecological destruction (as well as processes of a less conflictual nature) that dominate the attention of IR theorists cannot be analyzed, anticipated, or transformed if we continue to neglect how objectification is promoted and naturalized in social relations.

In the discussion that follows, I bring a critical feminist perspective to bear on the topics of power politics, states, and global capitalism. I hope to suggest how various systems of power and their constitutive dichotomies interact, and how gender-sensitive analyses constitute more adequate theorizations of turbulence.[29]

Feminist Analyses of Power/Politics

It is now a commonplace among feminists that power needs to be redefined if the hierarchical effects of gender are to be rendered systematically visible.[30] For the most part, conventional accounts identify power, in its direct expression, with coercion or violence and, in less direct expression, with the capacity to control or influence the behavior of others. Political scientists, of course, discipline their examination of power by focusing on its manifestations in the public sphere and rely on the dichotomy of public-private to distinguish their object of inquiry from personal, sex/affective, familial, household relations. In IR, by contrast, it is the dichotomy of domestic-international that disciplines our examination of power. Denying that politics in the classical sense can obtain under conditions of anarchy, IR theorists focus on "power politics" as the high-stakes game that nations play.

For those critical of dichotomized modes of thought, the categorical separation of public and private spheres, domestic and international "levels," and direct and indirect violence is incoherent—and for many, dangerously so. While Rosenau pushes us to abandon certain dichotomies, he retains several of singular importance to the reproduction of masculinism and its related social hierarchies. In particular, while he doubts the utility of separating domestic-international or micro-macro, he fails to question the assumption of power/politics as exclusively public-sphere activity. Even his relational authority does not address power relations associated with the private sphere, intimacy, families, and households. By neglecting the private sphere, Rosenau cannot account for prominent—even constitutive—features of all three parameters at the core of turbulence theory (e.g., how individuals, collectivities, authority, power, and social structures are gendered constructions).

Drawing on extensive, multifaceted interrogations of the public-private divide, feminists argue that when power is understood through a conventional dichotomizing lens, significant expressions of power—and specifically, the systemic relations of gender domination—are overlooked. A focus on public-sphere activities has precluded understanding how power in intimate relations and the family/household is linked, for example, to competition, violence, group identifications, and ideological allegiances. Power relations in the private sphere include not only domestic violence but the naturalization of inequalities promoted by conventional family forms (heterosexual, male-as-breadwinner, etc.) that reproduce dichotomized (and ethnicized/racialized) gender identities and gendered divisions of power, labor, and authority.

Consider, as Susan Okin does,[31] how structures of hierarchy and subordination (injustice) in the family affect understanding and expectations of justice in social relations more generally—including those at the interstate level. Or notice how patriarchal families/households are typically the *basis* of authority and power relations in fundamentalist movements, the "religious right," social revolutions, and nationalist claims.[32] In relation to women's agency—as private- and public-sphere actors—Rosenau's multicentric world of sovereignty-free actors looks suspiciously like male-bonding practices familiar from conventional states, which to a significant extent are at the expense of women's interests qua women (while they may be in the interest of women as members of particular groups). In particular, the authority crisis prompting Rosenau's new paradigm might more adequately be analyzed as a crisis—indeed multiple crises—of masculinism.[33]

In IR, preoccupation with the power politics of interstate conflict has precluded the study of that power in relation to structures of indirect violence, which transcend political and territorial boundaries.[34] Rosenau has broken away from conventions here. He argues that previous sources of power in the state-centric world have now been fragmented; alternative expressions of power in the decentralized multicentric world necessarily complicate traditional assumptions regarding military capacity and elite wealth as definitive. Rosenau forces us to recognize greater complexity in expressions of power and authority, but fails to extend that complexity beyond a conventional understanding of "power" that presupposes, and thereby reproduces, the dichotomy of public and private. His paradigmatic recidivism leaves the power of and against women invisible.

In political theory, the binary of public-private is inextricable from the dichotomy of politics-economics, which continues to burden IR theorizing. I do not doubt that Rosenau understands politics and economics to be related, but economic power is a very muted thread in his depiction of postinternational *politics*. This neglect has multiple gendered consequences. Of particular relevance here is IR theory's failure to recognize and address the indirect violence wrought by systems of economic inequality, in which gender is a major factor. IR's narrow definition of security forestalls questions of "Whose security?" and "At what expense to alternative forms of social organization?"[35] Addressed in greater detail below, economic relations in the context of turbulence are powerfully gendered. For example, how restructuring affects individuals, families, and states, how dramatic increases in informal sector activities shape political-economic dynamics, and how privatization shapes crises of the welfare state—none of these can be analyzed adequately without attention to gendered divisions of labor and power.

In sum, feminists argue that neither power/politics nor turbulence can be adequately theorized until direct and indirect violence (like public-private, politics-economics, domestic politics-interstate

anarchy) are understood in terms of *relations*—being mutually constituted—not either-or dichotomies. If we remain incarcerated in the
public-private binary, we cannot theorize power relations that perme-
ate all social relations and shape contemporary turbulence. By turning
to feminist analyses of the state as a masculinist project, we can begin
to see the gendering of violence, in/security, and power.

Feminist Analyses of State Making

As many have noted, IR theories of the state are underdeveloped and
markedly ahistorical. While Thucydides is often heralded as IR's founding father and our first realist, the context in which he wrote—early
(rather than modern) state-making—is rarely investigated for insights
on contemporary states and the historical intersection of objectivist
metaphysics, the centralization of political authority, and realist political theory.[36] While political theorists acknowledge the canonical importance of Athenian texts, IR theorists—including Rosenau—tend to
ignore how these texts established (often dichotomized) constructions
of authority, identity, politics, security, and public-private spheres that
continue to discipline the theory/practice of world politics.

What particularly drops out of sight in an ahistorical picture of
states is the institutionalization of domination relations associated with
early state making. It is here that the "human story" took a decisive
turn, marked by the effective centralization of political authority and
accumulation processes, military consolidation, a hierarchical division
of labor by gender, age, and "class," the reconfiguration of individual
and collective identities appropriate to that division of labor, and ideological legitimation of these transformations. Subsequent *normalization*—that is, depoliticization—of these arrangements effectively
obscures how these particular power arrangements were *made* in historical process. The point here, which I believe Rosenau would endorse, is that coercive power alone tells us little about state making, as
sociocultural, economic, and ideological dimensions are crucial to the
success and especially the reproduction of centralized power. Unfortunately, although Rosenau urges us to move beyond state-centrism to
recognize the contemporary importance of sovereignty-free actors, he
does not interrogate conventional characterizations of the state, nor
press us to seek more critical and historical understanding of states.

Feminists analyze the state from diverse perspectives.[37] In anthropological and historical studies, feminists theorize the institutionalization and ideological normalization of the patriarchal heterosexual family/
household, dichotomized gender identities and gendered divisions of

labor, power, and authority, masculinist language systems, and the separation of public and private spheres. As the basic socioeconomic unit defined by the state, the patriarchal family/household marks citizenship claims and facilitates resource extraction, conscription, regulation of property (including women), and centralized (infrastructural) control more generally. But it also marks the site where intimate and reproductive sexual relations are expressed, physical and emotional needs are met, and culturally appropriate personal and collective identities are formed. It is where we learn to be who we are and to believe in what we are taught. This early learning and believing profoundly shapes the individuals that constitute Rosenau's micro parameter, but processes of identification and socialization are not areas addressed in his postinternational politics. This neglect of identification processes has particular relevance in IR—especially, turbulent IR—where limited comprehension of emotional investments, identification processes, and ideological allegiances seriously compromises our understanding of, for example, nationalisms and fundamentalisms, genocidal massacres, new social movements, or possibilities for transnational and global solidarities.

As Rosenau reminds us, micro-level effects are necessarily linked to macro phenomena. The state's ideological promotion of gendered identities in the household extends into the labor market, situating women in low-wage, low-profile "servicing" jobs. Moreover, states often promote a "family wage" model that elevates men's earnings, treats women's work as supplemental, and denies the extent of female-headed households (estimated at 30 percent worldwide).[38] In the context of global restructuring (discussed below), privatization and liberalization, which tend to weaken public programs and their delivery of social benefits, are feminist issues because poverty is a feminist issue. And these are citizenship (political identity) issues because in contemporary states the well-being of individuals is linked to citizenship claims that mark who is inside (and outside) of the state's responsibility for protecting rights and providing welfare.

In regard to security issues, state militarism produces and is produced by gendered identities and divisions of violence manifested both internally and externally. While men are socialized (in the family as well as in the military) to be aggressive, competitive, protectors of the nation, and even life takers, women are typically socialized to be passive, supportive, those in need of protection, and life givers. Moreover, the costs of militarism are not just direct violence but (gendered and global) structural violence entailed by loss of welfare provision (to military spending), distorted labor markets and economic maldevelopment (to suit military priorities), environmental degradation (from military actions), and increased traffic in women and sexually transmitted disease (as a corollary of military bases and impoverished local populations). These aspects of today's world cannot be adequately addressed by state theories that ignore gender.

In short, the state is a bearer of masculinist values—even when it is ostensibly "helping" women through welfare dependency and military protection. State theories like Rosenau's that fail to question the public-private divide and focus only on the public sphere render invisible far too much of how reality—including nation-states, wars, structural violence, and global capitalism—is *made* in everyday practice, in everyday lives, homes, and families.

Feminist Analyses of Global Capitalism

By privileging politics at the expense of economic analyses, Rosenau fails to offer adequate illumination of today's global capital dynamics and divisions of labor. Offering an alternative to realism, world-system theorists analyze the global economy as a single system best understood in terms of a global division of labor. Less familiar are feminist accounts that theorize the household[39] within the world system[40] and deploy "housewifization" as a metaphor for nonwaged labor—subsistence provision and social reproduction—essential to capitalist accumulation.[41] That is, feminists reject the conventional dichotomies of formal-informal economies and paid-unpaid work and insist on bringing productive and reproductive labor into *relation* to better analyze today's economic relations. For these theorists, understanding the global division of labor—and its transformations—requires taking seriously the gendered division of labor constituted within patriarchal households. The exploitation entailed in the latter is obscured by ideologies of (hetero)sexual difference that naturalize both women's systemic subordination and the dichotomy of labor-for-wages (paid, public-sphere production) versus labors-of-love (unpaid, private-sphere reproduction). Moreover, the naturalization of gender hierarchy and exploitation within the household is then extended to hierarchies—of class, race, and nation—and the exploitative dynamics everywhere imposed by capitalist relations.

Hence, feminists theorize linkages between the household and the modern state as "two of the universal institutionalized products of historical capitalism."[42] Whereas Rosenau and traditional accounts tend to ignore family/household relations as noneconomic (lacking waged, "productive" labor) and apolitical (lacking formal and coercive powers associated with the state), theories of the household and "house-wifization" illuminate crucial relations: states structure the family/household to meet their reproductive and productive needs and do so in the context of a global economy that shapes those needs. Similarly, gender relations lived and learned within the household tend to support the state's legitimation project and capitalism's accumulation dynamic. Households are central to capitalism as the site of invisible, "primitive accumulation"[43] and socially necessary labor. As noted earlier, they are also sites of identity formation and cultural socialization that are key to the reproduction of domination ideologies. But the ensemble of linkages is not static. In particular, the household is a focal point not only of collaboration and reproduction but also resistance and transformation. Hence, gender dynamics have upward, downward, and lateral effects on topics of IR concern. While Rosenau's cascading metaphor may be apt in regard to these effects, he does not employ it to analyze gendered divisions of identification or labor.

In short, families/households have always been definitive sites of power. While patriarchs, states, and capitalists have dominated in controlling the greater part of that power, women (and subordinated others more generally) have not only colluded in but also resisted and reconfigured relations of domination.[44] Rosenau's attention to cross-cutting and asymmetrical "flows" of power is an important step in expanding how we think about power. When constrained, however, within the conventional dichotomies of production-reproduction, paid-unpaid labor, formal-informal sector activities, and public-private power, its analytical utility is undercut and we remain within a conventional framework—a prison!—that is not adequate for comprehending turbulence in either gender or global terms.

CONCLUSION

For the greater part of its history, the terrain of IR theory has been dominated by positivist commitments. Dichotomies have filtered our thinking, structured and limited the questions asked, and organized how answers were sought. In spite of disciplinary debates and the innovations of theorists like James Rosenau, there has been little "progress" beyond these constraining dichotomies and their unfortunate, even oppressive, effects. It is in this sense that the occasional jailbreak fails to rethink theory thoroughly enough and leads instead to paradigmatic recidivism.

In spite of its dominance, positivist-realism has been profoundly challenged, as much by "world events" as by intellectual developments. Surely the dichotomy of politics-economics has been laid to rest by the force of global capital relations that so profoundly alters (but does not eliminate) state-centric power. And binary oppositions of us-them, internal-external, micro-macro, state-nonstate, and domestic-international have just as surely been subverted by increasingly visible processes of interdependence and deterritorialization. At the same time, IR is gradually coming to terms with theoretical developments that challenge positivist premises and insist on a paradigmatic escape from dichotomizing theory/practice.

I have argued here that a paradigmatic break requires not simply the deconstruction of dichotomies—a project Rosenau ably and admirably begins—but the interrogation of masculine-feminine as the "foundational" dichotomy that normalizes positivism's and masculinism's binary mode. Jailbreaks require daring, courageous, and creative leaders. Jim Rosenau is all of these. His rethinking of realism broke boldly away from entrenched "givens" and opened new spaces for alternative theorizing as exemplified in this chapter! For this and more, I greatly admire Rosenau and deeply appreciate his work. My constructive criticisms here are meant to honor, not diminish, his pivotal contributions. Escaping from paradigmatic prisons, however, is clearly a more demanding (and even troubling) project, but one we postpone at great risk. As Rosenau fully appreciated, we live in "new times," in conditions of turbulence, or what others call postmodernity, and our theorizing *must* address the quality and scale of these changes. For this task, positivism's dichotomies are not only inadequate, they are actively misleading. We must abandon them, and to do so, we must rethink more thoroughly the power of gender.

NOTES

1. James N. Rosenau, *Turbulence in World Politics: A Theory of Change and Continuity* (Princeton, N.J.: Princeton University Press, 1990), p. 244.

2. Ibid., p. 22.

3. Ibid., p. 241.

4. Ibid., p. 10.

5. James N. Rosenau and Mary Durfee, *Thinking Theory Thoroughly* (Boulder, Colo.: Westview Press, 1995).

6. For example, James N. Rosenau, *Global Voices* (Boulder, Colo.: Westview Press, 1993).

7. George's *Discourses of Global Politics* is an accessible yet sophisticated and comprehensive treatment of the philosophical arguments as they pertain to IR. See also: special issues of *International Studies Quarterly* 33 (September 1989) and 34 (September 1990); V. Spike Peterson, "Transgressing Boundaries:

Theories of Knowledge, Gender, and International Relations," *Millennium* 21 (Summer 1992): 183–206; Claire Turenne Sjolander and Wayne S. Cox, eds., *Beyond Positivism: Critical Reflections on International Relations* (Boulder, Colo.: Westview Press, 1996); Steve Smith, Ken Booth, and Marysia Zalewski, eds., *International Theory: Positivism and Beyond* (Cambridge: Cambridge University Press, 1996); Mark Neufeld, *The Restructuring of International Relations Theory* (Cambridge: Cambridge University Press, 1995).

8. Peterson, "Transgressing Boundaries."

9. Eloise Buker, "Sex, Sign and Symbol: Politics and Feminist Semiotics," *Women and Politics* 16 (winter 1996): 34.

10. Ibid., p. 37.

11. George, *Discourses of Global Politics*, p. 192.

12. V. Spike Peterson and Anne Sisson Runyan, *Global Gender Issues*, 2d. ed. (Boulder, Colo.: Lynne Rienner Press, 1999), p. 39.

13. Rosenau, *Turbulence in World Politics*, p. 142.

14. Ibid., p. 25.

15. Ibid., p. 242.

16. Ibid., p. 103.

17. Ibid., p. 40.

18. Ibid., p. 185.

19. Ibid., p. 228.

20. Ibid., p. 293.

21. Ibid., p. 42.

22. For purposes of this essay, masculinism and gender hierarchy refer to systems of power that privilege that which is associated with (hegemonic) masculinity over that which is associated with femininity. As subsequently clarified in the text, gender refers not only to the empirical categories of male/men and female/women but also to conceptual categories, symbol systems, discourses, activities and institutions. Hence, the "privileging" of that which is associated with masculinity includes not only the appropriation of women's productive and reproductive labor, regulation of women's bodies/sexuality, and men's dominance in society's important institutions, but also the dominance of masculinism in symbol systems and discursive practices. Masculinism may refer to the system (masculine privileging) or to the ideology (naturalization) of gender hierarchy. Although I do not elaborate here, masculinities are not homogenous; in this essay I am referring to dominant or hegemonic constructions of masculinity. For further discussion, see R. W. Connell, *Masculinities: Knowledge, Power, and Social Change* (Berkeley: University of California Press, 1995).

23. Here I echo Sandra Whitworth's (*Feminism and International Relations* [London: Macmillan, 1994], p. x) demand that IR theorists move beyond pseudo-inclusion, where anthologies include a feminist chapter, "but most of the work that appears throughout the rest of those anthologies seems unfamiliar with, and unaffected by feminist scholarship." The literature in feminist-IR has expanded rapidly: a selected bibliography on "gender and IR" compiled by Kenneth Boultin (*Gender and International Relations: A Selected Historical*

Bibliography [Toronto: York Center for International and Strategic Studies, Occasional Paper No. 23]) totals 145 pages; Jacqui True ("Feminism," in Scott Burchill et al., *Theories of International Relations* [London: Macmillan, 1996]) provides an excellent current review of feminist innovations and literature. Books that broadly address IR themes from feminist perspectives include Cynthia Enloe, *Bananas, Beaches and Bases: Making Feminist Sense of International Politics* (Berkeley: University of California Press, 1990); Cynthia Enloe, *The Morning After: Sexual Politics at the End of the Cold War* (Berkeley: University of California Press, 1993); Ann J. Tickner, *Gender in International Relations: Feminist Perspectives on Achieving Global Security* (New York: Columbia University Press, 1992); V. Spike Peterson, ed., *Gendered States: Feminist (Re)Visions of International Relations Theory*, (Boulder, Colo.: Lynne Rienner Press, 1992); Peterson and Runyan, *Global Gender Issues*; Christine Sylvester, *Feminist Theory and International Relations in a Postmodern Era* (Cambridge: Cambridge University Press, 1994); Peter Beckman and Francine D'Amico, eds., *Women, Gender, and World Politics* (Westport, Conn.: Bergin and Garvey, 1994); Jan Jindy Pettman, *Worlding Women: A Feminist International Politics* (London: Routledge, 1996); Marysia Zalewski and Jane Parpart, eds., *The 'Man' Question in International Relations* (Boulder, Colo.: Westview Press, 1998); Jill Steans, *Gender and International Relations* (Cambridge: Polity Press, 1998); Gillian Youngs, *International Relations in a Global Age* (Cambridge: Polity Press, 1999).

24. For example, Gerda Lerner, *The Creation of Patriarchy* (New York: Oxford University Press, 1986); Arlene Saxonhouse, *Women in the History of Political Thought: Ancient Greece to Machiavelli* (New York: Praeger, 1985).

25. Terrell Carver, *Gender is Not a Synonym for Woman* (Boulder, Colo.: Lynne Rienner Press, 1996).

26. For example, Sandra Harding, *The Science Question in Feminism* (Ithaca, N.Y.: Ithaca University Press, 1986); Sandra Harding, ed., *Feminism and Methodology* (Bloomington: Indiana University Press, 1987); Susan Heckman, *Gender and Knowledge: Elements of Postmodern Feminism* (Oxford: Polity Press, 1990).

27. I cannot review the extensive argumentation here. It may be cast in anthropological, linguistic, philosophical psychoanalytical or historical-empirical terms. For an example relevant to IR theorists, I argue that the gender of binarism is an effect of the interaction of early state formation, accumulation dynamics, writing systems, instrumental reason, and patriarchal relations. See V. Spike Peterson, "The Gender of Rhetoric, Reason, and Realism," in Francis Beer and Robert Hariman, eds., *Post-Realism: The Rhetorical Turn in International Relations* (East Lansing: Michigan State University Press, 1996); V. Spike Peterson, "Whose Crisis? Early and Postmodern Masculinism," in Stephen Gill and James H. Mittelman, eds., *Innovation and Transformation in International Relations Theory* (Cambridge: Cambridge University Press, 1997).

28. The scholarship in support of these claims is extensive. Masculinism justifies gender hierarchy by reference to ostensibly "natural" sex differences that effectively essentialize (dehistoricize) "woman" in narrow terms of sexuality and reproduction. The history and social construction of sex/gender difference (for example, Pat Caplan, ed., *The Cultural Construction of Sexuality*

[London: Tavistock, 1987]; Michel Foucault, *The History of Sexuality*, trans. R. Hurley [New York: Vintage, 1980] is thus obscured and the naturalization of sex difference and gender hierarchy is then extended to justify other hierarchies of "difference." For example, racism associates people of color with undesirable (feminine) qualities: lack of reason, excessive sexuality, dependence, closeness to nature. Denied the status of reasoning agents and free subjects, subordinated peoples (or nature) become "objects." As objects, their exploitation is "naturalized" in the double sense that the subordinated group is "naturally" an object and that "man" (as agent and subject) "naturally" exploits objects.

29. I am not claiming, however, that it is only feminists who make some of the critiques to follow, nor that all feminists would agree with the arguments as I articulate them. Moreover, my very general remarks should be understood simply as a sketchy introduction to very complex arguments; they do not do justice to the nuance and sophistication of the research underpinning them.

30. Kathleen Jones and Anna Jonasdottir, *The Political Interests of Gender: Developing Theory and Research with a Feminist Face* (London: Sage, 1988).

31. Susan Moller Okin, *Justice, Gender, and the Family* (New York: Basic Books, 1989).

32. Nira Yuval-Davis and Floya Anthias, *Woman-Nation-State* (London: Macmillan, 1989); Nira Yuval-Davis, ed., *Unholy Orders: Women against Fundamentalism* (London: Virago, 1992); Mary Ann Tetreault, ed., *Women and Revolution in Africa, Asia and the New World* (Columbia: University of South Carolina Press, 1996); V. Spike Peterson, "The Politics of Identity and Gendered Nationalism," in Laura Neack, Patrick Haney, and Jeane Hey, eds., *Foreign Policy Analysis: Continuity and Change in Its Second Generation* (Englewood Cliffs, N.J.: Prentice Hall, 1995).

33. Peterson, "Whose Crisis," pp. 185–201.

34. J. Ann Tickner, *Gender in International Relations*; Jan Jindy Pettman, *Worlding Women*.

35. J. Ann Tickner, *Gender in International Relations*; V. Spike Peterson, "Security and Sovereign States: What Is at Stake in Taking Feminism Seriously?" in V. Spike Peterson, ed., *Gendered States*.

36. But see Peterson, "The Gender of Rhetoric"; G. E. R. Lloyd, *Magic, Reason, and Experience: Studies in the Origins and Development of Greek Sciences* (Cambridge: Cambridge University, 1979). The appropriation of Thucydides in support of neorealism *has* been challenged in a number of recent works. See, for example, Hayward R. Alker, "The Dialectical Logic of Thucydides' Melian Dialogue," *American Political Science Review* 82 (September, 1988): 805–20; Daniel Garst, "Thucydides and Neorealism," *International Studies Quarterly* 17 (March, 1989), but the relevance of Athenian state making for contemporary IR theory remains underdeveloped.

37. See, for example, Anne Showstack Sassoon, ed., *Women and the State: The Shifting Boundaries of Public and Private* (London: Macmillan, 1987); Linda Gordon, ed., *Women, the State, and Welfare* (Madison: University of Wisconsin

Press, 1990); Jane Parpart and Kathleen Staudt, eds., *Women and the State in Africa* (Boulder, Colo.: Lynne Rienner Press, 1990); Sophie Watson, ed., *Playing the State: Australian Feminist Interventions* (London: Verso, 1988); Deniz Kandiyoti, *Women, Islam, and the State* (Philadelphia: Temple University Press, 1991); V. Spike Peterson, *Gendered States*; Diane Sainsbury, ed., *Gendering Welfare States* (London: Sage, 1994); Wendy Brown, *States of Injury: Power and Freedom in Late Modernity* (Princeton, N.J.: Princeton University Press, 1995).

38. United Nations, *The World's Women: 1970–1990 Trends and Statistics* (New York: United Nations, 1991), p. 18.

39. In this chapter, household refers broadly to multiple dimensions of social reproduction, including sex/affective familial relations and non-waged/informal sector activities. It thus may include activities outside of the family, narrowly defined, or the "house," spatially understood. My treatment of the household draws especially on the work of Joan Smith and Maria Mies, but differs from each. For a lengthier discussion, see V. Spike Peterson, "The Politics of Identification in the Context of Globalization," *Women's Studies International Forum* 19 (January–April, 1996): 5–15.

40. Joan Smith and Immanuel Wallerstein, eds., *Creating and Transforming Households: The Constraints of the World-Economy* (Cambridge: Cambridge University Press, 1992); Kathryn Ward, *Women Workers and Global Restructuring* (Ithaca, N.Y.: Ithaca University Press, 1990); Joan Smith, "The Creation of the World as We Know It," in Valentine Moghadam, ed., *Identity Politics and Women* (Boulder, Colo.: Westview Press, 1993).

41. Maria Mies, *Patriarchy and Accumulation on a World Scale: Women and the International Division of Labour* (London: Zed Books, 1986); Maria Mies, Veronika Bennholdt-Thomsen, and Claudia von Werlhof, *Women: The Last Colony* (London: Zed Books, 1988).

42. Joan Smith, "The Creation of the World," p. 36.

43. Mies, *Patriarchy and Accumulation*.

44. Isabella Bakker, ed., *The Strategic Silence: Gender and Economic Policy* (London: Zed Books, 1994).

PART 2

The Role of Citizens in a Postinternational World

Individuals are the most important actors in a postinternational world. Rosenau truly believes it is the enhanced skill levels of individuals that have brought about profound changes in the international arena and cannot be discounted, as so much of international relations theory has often done.

The chapters in this part elaborate on the role of individuals, with each author employing his or her own special view of that evolving role. Ronnie Lipschutz begins this part with his examination of global civil society, its evolution, successes, limitations, and most importantly, its relevance for a postinternational world.

Nick Onuf brings perspective to the topic, offering a postmodern critique of the individual as evidenced in the writings of Hume, and the extent to which Rosenau's views are informed by others. While Onuf is more critical of Rosenau's views from an historical, theoretically developed point of view, he does applaud their relevance for a modern world.

Finally, Ole Holsti, Rosenau's longtime friend and coauthor, brings his research on public opinion as the measured expression of individuals to bear on a postinternational worldview. He is particularly illuminating in identifying what is unique about the individual from a postinternational perspective as opposed to the realist and liberal paradigms.

CHAPTER FIVE

Politics among People:
Global Civil Society Reconsidered

Ronnie D. Lipschutz

Where in discussions about the future of international relations are the
people? Few writers besides James Rosenau have tried to fit people
into the "postinternational" world politics of the next century.[1] Instead, most analysts peering into the future have tried to describe the
big picture: The world will be richer. It will be happier. It will be
crowded. It will be poorer. It will be violent. Religions will clash across
continental fault lines. Anarchy will reign throughout much of the
world. Democracy will triumph. Borders will vanish and peace will
come. Perhaps. Perhaps not.[2]

The difficulty with such global generalizations, encapsulating in
trite phrases the actions and fates of 10 billion people, is that they do
not tell us very much about what those people are up to now, or what

This chapter is drawn from *After Authority: War, Peace and Global Politics in the
21st Century* (Albany: State University of New York Press, 2000), as well as
from Ronnie D. Lipschutz, "Reconstructing World Politics: The Emergence of
Global Civil Society," pp. 101–33, in Rick Fawn and Jeremy Larkins, eds.,
International Society after the Cold War—Anarchy and Order Reconsidered (Lon-
don/New York: Macmillan/St. Martin's, 1996); Ronnie D. Lipschutz, "From
Place to Planet: Local Knowledge and Global Environmental Governance,"
Global Governance 3, 1 (January–April 1997): 83–102. Many of the arguments
presented here grow out of those made in Ronnie D. Lipschutz, with Judith
Mayer, *Global Civil Society and Global Environmental Governance—The Politics of
Nature from Place to Planet* (Albany: State University of New York Press, 1996).

they could be up to in that future. Yet, what people do *will* matter, whether they do it alone or in groups, peacefully or violently, or with an eye to the present or to the future. Indeed, it is more probable that future politics will originate less in the actions of the "great women and men" of state, than in patterns of everyday politics, of politics among people. These patterns will have to do with fairly mundane matters, with everyday questions of governance.[3] Such patterns and questions are already evident in a number of transnational political arenas, including environmental restoration and protection, human rights, gender, indigenous peoples, labor and culture, as well as in economic ones, such as trade, investment, property rights, and product standards. These are part of what I call "global civil society." It is here that we must look in order to see the emerging outlines of twenty-first-century postinternational politics.

The skeptical reader might ask, "What is the evidence for this global civil society? Moreover, if such a thing exists, what does it presage?" Would it mean the disappearance of the state system and a truly "postsovereign, postinternational" world politics? Are not "sovereignty-free" transnational networks and actors so dependent on the structures created and supported by "sovereignty-bound" states that they cannot exist without them? And, is a global civil society plausible in the face of the communitarian and ethnic forces tearing apart so many countries? Moreover, if it does exist, isn't global civil society simply a conservative product of a globalizing bourgeois capitalist class and therefore merely another move to consolidate the dominance of the rich over the poor? Or, is it possible that global civil society might be the site of an incipient counterhegemonic bloc, engaged in a "war of position," that could offer an emancipatory path to a democratic world politics? The answers to these questions are, for the most part, "yes," as we shall see.[4]

Making such an argument does not, however, imply some sort of teleological "triumph" of reason over emotion or irrationality. Not all of the networks and actors comprising global civil society are necessarily supportive of global governance. Some act through these networks in order to resist the state, others engage in attacks on states as treacherous collaborators with emerging institutions of global governance. Similarly, global economic actors—primarily corporations and other institutions of capital—also constitute an aspect of "global civil society" in their efforts to regulate politics at the transnational level and, in some instances, to intervene in domestic settings through sponsorship of functional projects at the local level. Finally, the ultimate form of these mutually constitutive "entities" is, as yet, underdetermined; a collapse back into a more traditional international state system cannot be ruled out. Nonetheless, the growth of various mechanisms of transnational governance, strongly driven by processes linked to economic globalization, suggest otherwise.

In this chapter, I offer a reconsideration of the concept of global civil society in light of questions and objections raised about it since the publication of my *Millennium* paper in 1992.[5] I argue here that, although the concept of global civil society has been underdefined, for a variety of reasons it remains useful. Drawing on the work of Michael Mann,[6] Steven Gill and others, I offer a more concrete conceptualization, illustrating parallels between the historical emergence of the modern national state and domestic civil society, and a developing system of global governance and global civil society. These matters, and the phenomena they interrogate, are clearly relevant to Rosenau's postinternational politics and his "two worlds of world politics," the sovereignty-bound composed of nation-states and their offspring and the sovereignty-free, driven by information and communication and populated by enhanced elites, powerful people, and various nongovernmental actors. Whether, however, the emergence of global civil society is a sign of "triumphant subgroupism" or a broad social response to the seemingly chaotic nature of market-based civilization, remains to be seen.[8]

WHAT IS GLOBAL CIVIL SOCIETY?

The two most familiar notions of civil society draw on Locke, on the one hand, and Marx and Hegel, on the other.[9] Locke contrasted political or civil society with the paternal authority of the state of nature. For Hegel and Marx, civil society, or *burgerliche Gesellschaft*, referred to the state of human development reached by advanced peoples, where the economic and social order moved according to its own principles, independent of the ethical demands of law and political association. Unlike Locke, however, Hegel and Marx thought civil society to be self–seeking and lacking in the moral cohesion of primitive societies.

These two conceptions—the political and the bourgeois—are commonly used to inform the normative stances of both proponents and critics of the beliefs and practices of civil society. Thus, to neo-Marxists, civil society is said to constitute something like a "fetish" propagated by a self-interested bourgeoisie, while, to Lockean liberals, it is the highest manifestation of democratic politics and morally superior to the state. Yet, "really existing states" are a hodgepodge of institutional forms, matching neither the black boxes of Cold War realism nor the eternally vigilant and balanced watchman state of the idealizers of market democracies. Civic associations, understood in the broadest sense, fulfill multiple roles and, although the balance between altruism and selfishness can vary greatly, some of both can be found in all of them. Indeed, many associations that fall into this category go beyond collective self-interest to active pursuit of the collective political good.[10] Furthermore, although civil society might be a liberal bourgeois fetish, it cannot be denied that most of the world's richer and more powerful states are both liberal and bourgeois. For better or worse, ideology informs practice, and vice versa.

What is, perhaps, more important for our purposes is that political civil society and the state are neither independent nor autonomous of each other; Rosenau's sovereignty-bound and sovereignty-free worlds are, to a large degree, mutually constitutive. A state, whether liberal or not, relies on some version of civil society for its legitimacy; conversely, a civil society cannot thrive without the legitimacy bestowed on it by the state, whether or not it is democratic. One example of this relationship can be found in Indonesia, where until recently an authoritarian state coexisted with a dynamic civil society of as many as eleven thousand nongovernmental organizations (NGOs), by some counts.[11] Many of these groups occupy a kind of uncertain middle ground, supporting the state in some instances, opposing it in others. Similarly, at times, the state finds it necessary to rely on these groups for certain functional needs as well as support.[12]

One example of the complexities of global civil society is the Climate Action Network (CAN),[13] a global alliance of regional coalitions made up of national and local environmental organizations and individuals. The members of CAN are engaged in a continuous and reciprocal exchange of knowledge and practice, some of it universal, some of it contingent and contextual.[14] Members and organizations participate in local educational activities, regional and national lobbying, and international negotiations, such as those dealing with the UN Framework Convention on Climate Change. They act as technical and political advisors to governments and their agencies in some settings, and as adversaries of governments in others. They become involved in management at the local, regional, national, and global levels, both as Network and as individuals and groups in specific locales. And, CAN is only one such network of global civil society; there a many more, some of them subnational, some among a few countries, others with global reach.[15]

WHY GLOBAL CIVIL SOCIETY NOW?

But why should global civil society be developing now? Is it actually something new?[16] My explanation for the emergence of global civil society at this time rests on certain notions about global political economy since 1945. One of the consequences of the "information revolution," rooted in the discovery and application of new knowledge through a Fordist version of scientific research on a large scale during and after World War II, was a vast expansion in the supply of higher education throughout the world.[17] To be sure, the enormous growth in sources and availability of information and the increase in modes of transnational communication were both empowering, as Rosenau has argued, but for most of the 1950s and well into the 1960s, these powerful people were absorbed rather easily by state and economy. What changed? In many countries, the expansion of higher education led to a large increase in the supply of college graduates, which came to exceed the demand for them. Beyond a certain point, moreover, state control of the economic and political systems made expansion of employment opportunities problematic (a problem evident today across Europe). In the United States, however, growing numbers of educated cadres struck out on their own, establishing the plethora of consultancies, think tanks and other such institutions so familiar to us today, disseminating knowledge and practice throughout the society and the world.

The growth in numbers of powerful people has been globally significant, but to explain the significance of this phenomenon we need to look not only at material factors or institutions, but also to the progenitors of ideas. Michael Mann has drawn on the writings of Antonio Gramsci to explain the emergence of national states in Europe and North America during the 1700s and 1800s, and the economic, political, and social revolutions and changes that took place throughout the "long" nineteenth century.[18] Put briefly, Mann sees the rise of what Gramsci called "organic intellectuals" as central to the transition from royal to popular sovereignty and the creation of the modern state. These organic intellectuals filled a discursive role in a gradual process of social change, by developing and articulating the ideas and practices that animated the political and social upheavals of those times. Mann observes that, while material interests and needs were always central to popular mobilization, emotional and ideational incentives were as important, if not more so.

More than this, these ideas and arguments were framed in terms of "progress," promising a better future through political, economic, and social reorganization. The ideologies of nationalism, liberalism, socialism, and other -isms that reified the strong state were created by these organic intellectuals. Without the communication and putting into practice of their arguments, the nineteenth century might have been a much quieter time. As it was, the centralized nation-states that dominated world politics for the past century were, for better or worse, legitimated by the ideas of these intellectuals, if not constructed by them. As Mann has put it

> Capitalism and discursive literacy media were the dual faces of a civil society diffusing throughout eighteenth-century European civilization. They were not reducible to each other, although they were entwined. . . . Nor were they more than partly caged by dominant classes, churches, military elites, and states, although they were invariably encouraged and structured by them. Thus, they were partly transnational and interstitial to other power organizations. . . . Civil societies were always entwined with states—and they became more so during the long nineteenth century.[19]

Below, I will describe how such organic intellectuals have, in recent years, become central to the emergence of global civil society. First, however, it is necessary to explore in greater detail the further consequences of the globalization of capitalism and communication.

FROM NATIONAL TO GLOBAL GOVERNANCE?

In recent years, research into transnational social movements, nongovernmental organizations, global networks and coalitions, and global governance structures has become a popular and profitable endeavor. Virtually all of the resulting works take note of extensive patterns of transnational interaction that suggest a fundamental change in world politics. Although there are those who insist that little has changed,[20] there are reasons to believe that more is happening than meets the eye. What is most conspicuous about this change are seemingly contradictory tendencies evident in world politics, what Rosenau has tagged with the somewhat ungainly term "fragmegration."[21]

On the one hand, we are offered the notion of a single world, integrated via the global economy, in which the sovereign state appears to be losing much of its authority and control over domestic and foreign affairs.[22] This trend seems to point toward a single world market in which economics dominates politics. Contrary to the expectations of neofunctionalists and others, however, such global economic integration does not seem to generate a parallel process in the political realm. Instead, we see the rise of what, pace Huntington, we might call *geocultural politics*, through which countries fracture into conflict- and war-ridden fragments, with a sovereignty exercised over diminishing pieces of territory.

How can these two seemingly opposing phenomena be explained? In part, this phenomenon is a consequence of the growing mobility of capital, but it can also be understood as a reaction against the political decomposition of states that capital requires in order to be secure in its mobility. This is not new. In the late nineteenth and early twentieth century, the first steps toward globalization were brought to a halt by national governments and elites who saw threats to their autonomy and prerogatives; the same pattern followed in the 1930s.[23] Today, nation-states are caught in a similar contradiction.

On the one hand, states are decentralizing, deregulating, and liberalizing in order to provide more attractive economic environments for financial capital.[24] On the other hand, as they do so, the safety net provided by the welfare state is being dismantled. That safety net, it should be noted, includes not only assurance of health and safety, environmental protection, public education, and so on, but also standard sets of rules that "level the economic playing field" and ensure the sanctity of contracts. The latter two are especially important to capital. As deregulated capitalism works its way on national economies, however, the playing field develops pits, holes, and undulations, and the distribution of wealth across countries, groups, and classes becomes more uneven (uneven development is one reason capitalism is so dynamic). This, as might be expected, can pose political problems both domestically and internationally.[25] But individual countries cannot move to reregulate because there are powerful interests who benefit from domestic deregulation. Furthermore, to reimpose political control over the economy might also be to give up a competitive advantage over other countries and their firms.

Under globalization, the greatest profits are to be found in the high-tech and information industries, in transnational finance and investment, and in flexible and niche production and accumulation. This means looking beyond national borders for ways in which to deploy capital, technology, and design in order to maximize returns on investment and gain access to foreign markets. One obstacle to economic growth is the transaction costs associated with 190 sets of national regulations. From the perspective of investors, it is preferable to deal with single sets of rules that apply to *all* countries, as is supposed to be the case within the European Union or among the members of international regimes.[26] Globalization of production and capital has thus been accompanied by liberalization and, at the rhetorical level, at least, a commitment to the deregulation of markets. But therein lies a central paradox of our times: a market system cannot exist without rules; indeed, markets *require* rules in order to function in an orderly fashion.[27] So, where are the rules?

It is often argued that there is no global government, and that regulatory harmonization is not only difficult to achieve (as seen in the recent failure of the Earth Summit +5 meeting) but also unfair (especially as regards environmental and labor law).[28] The fact is, however, that global rules are quite common and additional ones are being promulgated constantly. While "deregulation" is the mantra repeated endlessly in virtually all national capitals and by all international capitalists, it is domestic deregulation that they desire, not the wholesale elimination of all rules.[29] Selective deregulation at home may create a lower-cost environment in which to produce, but deregulation everywhere creates uncertainty and economic instability. Hence, transnational regulation and global welfarism—the successors to Bretton Woods—are becoming increasingly important in keeping the system together and working.

The General Agreement on Trade and Tariffs, and its successor, the World Trade Organization, provide examples of regulatory harmonization for the benefit of capital and country. The Montreal Protocol on Substances that Deplete the Ozone Layer is a regulatory system designed to harmonize rules governing ozone-damaging substances. The Comprehensive Nuclear Test Ban Treaty is intended to regulate the production and use of atomic bombs by its signatories. The human rights regime is meant to set a standard for the fair and just treatment of citizens by their states as well as their fellow citizens. International meetings such as the Conference on Population and Development in Cairo aim at the promulgation of a globally shared set of norms and rules governing family planning.

Indeed, the raft of regimes and international institutions associated with the United Nations system constitutes something of an incipient global welfare system (even though there are many holes in this "safety net"). As such, it serves two critical functions. First, it provides global norms and rules that are meant to apply everywhere (even though these standards are sometimes less rigorous than the citizens of particular countries would like, and enforcement remains problematic). Second, it allows national governments to tell their citizens that they have no control over the content of global regulatory systems, and that domestic politics must not be permitted to intrude into the functioning of these rules. There is political intervention into the market system here, but it takes place out of reach of domestic interest groups, lobbyists and logrolling. The absence of accountability on the part of these global institutions is not so easily shrugged off and serious questions are being raised about this matter.[30] Nevertheless, we have here the beginnings of global governance (and taxation) although there remains the question of representation, which I take up later in this chapter.

FROM NATIONAL TO LOCALISM AND GLOBALISM

This explains only one part of the puzzle of fragmegration. What about fragmentation? In my view, fragmentation does not presage a return to a more traditional international relations among five hundred or more states.[31] Nor does it necessarily point toward any of the other scenarios sketched out by Rosenau or others. It is better understood, instead, as an integral part of the postinternational dialectic. The state remains the primary actor in *international relations*, but the *jurisdictional authority* of states is being spread throughout an emergent, multilevel and, for the moment, very diffuse system of globalizing governance. Within this system, "local" management, knowledge, and rule are as important to coordination within and among local, national, and global political "hierarchies," regions, and countries as the international management manifested in traditional regimes, both political and economic. The two apparently contradictory tendencies actually involve the transfer of *authority* downward to the regional and local levels as well as upward to the global level. All of this is taking place, moreover, through the actions of national governments.

What might the resulting political arrangements look like? Some have suggested that such social innovation constitutes a "new mediaevalism"; others have proposed as organizing principles "heteronomy" or "heterarchy."[32] In discussing the first of these three concepts, Ole Wæver argues that

> For some four centuries, political space was organized through the principle of territorially defined units with exclusive rights inside, and a special kind of relations on the outside: International relations, foreign policy, without any superior authority. There is no longer one level that is clearly *the* most important to refer to but, rather, a set of overlapping authorities.[33]

What is critical in Wæver's point is not space, but *authority*—in the sense of the ability to get things done because of one's legitimacy, as opposed to one's ability to apply force or coercion. Such distributed authority arrangements are most clearly seen in the environmental arena.

In the postinternational "heteronomy," authority will be distributed among many centers of political action, often on the basis of specific issues rather than delineated territories, and as a result of the control and dissemination of knowledge and practice. In a way, this will generate a form of global functionalism (really, functional differentiation) rather than world federalism, inasmuch as different authorities will deal with specific applied problems—toxic wastes, marshland protection—rather than a broad range of generalized ones. Moreover, because these problems are embedded within a global economic system, such local functionalism will, inevitably, reach beyond localities into and through that global system.[34] Note that this concept is not the same as the functionalism of Mitrany or neofunctionalism of Haas.[35] Whereas those theories envisioned political *integration* as the outcome of international functional coordination, it appears that contemporary functionalism will operate at multiple levels.

In the present instance, this form of functionalism can be understood as a consequence of rapid *innovation*, of the generation of new scientific-technical and social knowledge(s) required to address different types of contemporary issues and problems.[36] This differs in a number of ways from Rosenau's "skills revolution," which focuses more on the individual acquisition of new capabilities and the power that supposedly flows from them. Inasmuch as there is too much scientific and social knowledge for any one actor, whether individual or collective, to assimilate, it becomes necessary to establish knowledge-based alliances and coalitions whose organizational logic is only partly based on space or, for that matter, hierarchy. "Local" knowledge is spatially situated while "organizational" knowledge—how to put knowledge together and use it—is spaceless (but possibly time dependent). Combined together, the two become instrumental to rapid technical and social innovation at a scale, and in a manner, that leads to broad social change and reorganization.[37]

Acquisition of functional knowledge and practices leads, in turn, to new forms and venues of authority,[38] in that only those with access to such capabilities can act successfully. Successful action, based on knowledge and practice, generates legitimacy and authority. Completing the circle, those organizations with such legitimacy and authority are then sought out for their management expertise when other circumstances appear, similar to those that first led to the group's launch. Some of this expertise is scientific, in the traditional sense, some of it is contextual and contingent, in the sense of being "indigenous knowledge."[39]

To a significant degree, therefore, the governance function will be located at that level of social organization at which the appropriate combination of "local" and "global" knowledges come together.[40] This level is more likely to be regional or local—in the lab, the research group, the neighborhood, the watershed—than in some undifferentiated global realm. Or, as Richard Gordon has put it,

Regions and networks . . . constitute interdependent poles within the new spatial mosaic of global innovation. Globalization in this context involves not the leavening impact of universal processes but, on the contrary, the calculated synthesis of cultural diversity in the form of differentiated regional innovation logics and capabilities. . . . *The effectiveness of local resources and the ability to achieve genuine forms of cooperation with global networks must be developed from within the region itself.*[41]

The notion of functionalist regionalization helps to illuminate the puzzle of fragmegration: lines must be drawn somewhere, whether by reference to Nature, power, authority or knowledge. From a constructivist perspective, such lines may be as "fictional" as those that currently separate one country, or one county, from another. Still, they are unlikely to be wholly disconnected from the material world, inasmuch as they will have to map onto already existing patterns and structures of social and economic activity.

MUST THE FUTURE REPEAT THE PAST?

The framework offered above does suggest a postinternational future that might, just possibly, be less dismal than that of the realists and catastrophists, and it also indicates how and why global civil society comes into play. Earlier in this chapter, I suggested that the sovereignty-bound and sovereignty-free worlds are mutually constitutive, a reflection of a dialectic of simultaneous fragmentation and integration. The globalizing of civil society is an integral part of this process, emerging to supplement institutions of global governance while also providing functional authority and rules at the local and regional levels. But this begs one question: If *global* civil society is a really existing formation, where, then, is the "state" that gives rise to it and, in turn, it relies on?

Two possibilities offer themselves. On the one hand, it might be that individual states themselves "authorize" the civil societies within their borders to extend themselves transnationally, in some cases fulfilling functions that states cannot or will not while, in other instances, extending state power across borders via proxies.[42] This seems plausible, inasmuch as there is not much yet visible evidence of a civil society within, for example, the People's Republic of China. On the other hand, it is also possible that the institutions of an incipient system of global governance provide the legitimacy and cover for the transnationalization of civil society. Such transnationalization in turn

giddens

helps to support and validate various international institutions, even as it also changes them. Certainly, the role of the United Nations system in opening up international politics to a broad range of nongovernmental groups is suggestive of this. There is no reason to think that both explanations might not be correct: states as well as international institutions might both play a role in fostering global civil society.

But there is also a critical role here for enhanced elites and powerful people, working individually and together. Recall that, according to Michael Mann, the organic intellectuals of centuries past played a central role in the emergence of the modern nation-state. Today's organic intellectuals are to be found thinking and acting, I would argue, within global civil society. They constitute a cadre of transnational intellectuals—not necessarily because they travel, but through transnational "discursive literacy"—who fill a role in the development of systems of global governance parallel to those described by Mann. These organic intellectuals are also filling what is, so far, a rudimentary representational role in this process. Indeed, just as modern democracies came into being in a symbiotic relationship with their domestic civil societies, so is this emergent system of global governance coming into being in concert with a "global civil society."

There is a strong intersubjective element at work here: analysis informs action and vice versa. Today's organic intellectuals engage in the examination of transnational phenomena and articulate their significance (as in the chapters in this volume), eschew determinism, and offer alternative conceptualizations of how things might be done. They also transfer both knowledge and practice via national and transnational coalitions, alliances, and communications, and create the organizations and institutions that propagate these notions and carry them to various levels of government and governance. In this way, the architecture of postinternational politics is emerging in the interstices of the current world system, just as the state system and capitalism grew out of feudalism 300 to 400 years ago.[43]

Note, however, that this development is neither teleological nor necessarily progressive. The emergence of global governance and a transnational welfare system could serve the interests of a narrow stratum of political and economic elites and prove profoundly conservative and reactionary.[44] The result might be a repetition of the previous catastrophes described by Polanyi, as the pain of globalization bites deeply and states and entrenched domestic interests strike out in reaction. There are disquieting trends to which one can point: the globalization of surveillance through information technologies, struggles to construct new, albeit bankrupt, states, the transnationalization of militias and other reactionary groups, and demands by capital to minimize social and environmental costs.

Still, the future is not (yet) etched in stone. We could also be witness to the democratization of societies and states through mechanisms of global governance, and the emancipation of peoples and cultures as states lose their historical roles as defensive containers and become distinctive political and cultural communities within a postinternational world society.[45] This will require our active involvement at all levels of politics and government, an involvement that goes beyond parties, elections, and indirect representation to a commitment to a local politics. Whether this politics involves health, human rights, housing, education, environment, transportation, energy, or another social issue, it must be consciously practiced within the framework of a democratic global system and an active global civil society, at all levels.

NOTES

1. James N. Rosenau, *Turbulence in World Politics* (Princeton, N.J.: Princeton University Press, 1990).

2. Samuel P. Huntington, *The Clash of Civilizations and the Remaking of World Order* (New York: Simon & Schuster, 1996); Benjamin R. Barber, *Jihad vs. McWorld* (New York: Times Books, 1995); Francis Fukuyama, *The End of History and the Last Man* (New York: Free Press, 1992); Kenichi Ohmae, *The End of the Nation State—The Rise of Regional Economies* (New York: Free Press, 1995); Robert D. Kaplan, "The Coming Anarchy," *Atlantic Monthly*, February 1994, pp. 44–76 and *The Ends of the Earth: A Journey at the Dawn of the Twenty-first century* (New York: Random House, 1996); Julian L. Simon, *The Ultimate Resource 2*, rev. ed. (Princeton, N.J.: Princeton University Press, 1992).

3. For a discussion of governance, see Lipschutz, "From Place to Planet," and the references therein.

4. For a general overview of perspectives on civil society, see Michael Walzer, ed., *Toward a Global Civil Society* (Providence, R.I.: Berghahn Books, 1995); and Jean L. Cohen and Andrew Arato, *Civil Society and Political Theory* (Cambridge: MIT Press, 1992).

5. "Reconstructing World Politics: The Emergence of Global Civil Society," *Millennium* 21, 3 (winter 1992): 389–420. For a critique, see, e.g, André C. Drainville, "The Fetishism of Global Civil Society: Global Governance, Transnational Urbanism, and Sustainable Capitalism in the World Economy," (Paper presented at the annual convention of the American Political Science Association, San Francisco, Calif., August 29–September 1, 1996).

6. Michael Mann, *The Sources of Social Power—The Rise of Classes and Nation-States, 1760–1914*, vol. 2 (Cambridge: Cambridge University Press, 1993).

7. Stephen Gill, "The Global Panopticon? The Neoliberal State, Economic Life and Democratic Surveillance," *Alternatives* 2, 1 (1995): 1–49. See also:

Yoshikazu Sakamoto, ed., *Global Transformation—Challenges to the State System* (Tokyo: UN University Press, 1994).

8. The *locus classicus* for discussions about market society is Karl Polanyi, *The Great Transformation* (1944; reprint, Boston: Beacon Press, 1957).

9. This section draws on Lipschutz, "Reconstructing World Politics."

10. Lipschutz, *Global Civil Society*, chaps. 4–6.

11. Jeri Laber, "Smoldering Indonesia," *New York Review of Books* 44, 1 (January 9, 1997): 43.

12. See Lipschutz, *Global Civil Society*, chaps. 4–5.

13. For information about the Climate Action Network, see http://www.igc.org/climate/Eco.html.

14. Lipschutz, *Global Civil Society*, chap. 3.

15. Among the many recent works on the subject, see: Paul Wapner, *Environmental Activism and World Civic Politics* (Albany: State University of New York Press, 1996); Thomas Princen and Matthias Finger, eds., *Environmental NGOs in World Politics* (London: Routledge, 1994); Jessica T. Mathews, "Powershift," *Foreign Affairs* 76, 1 (January–February 1997): 50–66; Lipschutz, *Global Civil Society* and the citations therein.

16. Craig Murphy, *International Organization and Industrial Change: Global Governance since 1850* (New York: Oxford University Press, 1994).

17. This argument is made in greater detail in Ronnie D. Lipschutz, "The Great Transformation Revisited," *Brown Journal of International Affairs* 4, 1 (winter/spring 1997): 299–318; Lipschutz, *After Authority*, ch. 2.

18. Mann, *Sources of Social Power*.

19. Mann, *Sources of Social Power*, p. 42.

20. John J. Mearsheimer, "The False Promise of International Institutions," *International Security* 19, 3 (winter 1994): 5–49.

21. Rosenau has taken the contrary tendencies into account by theorizing "sovereignty-bound" and "sovereignty-free" actors. This, I think, does not capture the entire dynamic, in that some of the actors in the latter category would dearly love to move into the former.

22. The literature on this point is vast and growing, but see, for example, Ohmae, *The End of the Nation State*; and Pam Woodall, "The World Economy: Who's in the driving seat?" *The Economist*, October 7, 1995, special insert.

23. See Polanyi, *The Great Transformation*.

24. For an argument that such deregulation has *not* taken place, see Steven K. Vogel, *Freer Markets, More Rules—Regulatory Reform in Advanced Industrial Countries* (Ithaca, N.Y.: Cornell University Press, 1996).

25. Andrew Pollack, "Thriving, South Koreans Strike to Keep it That Way," *New York Times*, January 17, 1997 (national edition), p. A1; "Protests Erupt across Haiti as Leaders Push Austerity," *New York Times*, January 17, 1997 (national edition), p. A3. For a more general assessment, see Ethan B. Kapstein, "Workers and the World Economy," *Foreign Affairs* 75, 3 (May–June 1996): 16–37.

26. David Vogel, *Trading Up—Consumer and Environmental Regulation in a Global Economy* (Cambridge: Harvard University Press, 1995).

27. See Walter Russell Mead, "Trains, Planes, and Automobiles—The End of the Postmodern Moment," *World Policy Journal* 12, 4 (winter 1995/96): 13–32; Jacques Attali, "The Crash of Western Civilization—The Limits of Market and Democracy," *Foreign Policy* 107 (summer 1997): 54–63.

28. Jagdish Bhagwati, "Trade and the Environment: The False Conflict?" in Durwood Zaelke, Paul Orbuch, and Robert F. Houseman, eds., *Trade and the Environment—Law, Economics, and Policy* (Washington, D.C.: Island Press, 1993), pp. 159–90.

29. See, for example, Edward M. Graham, *Global Corporations and National Governments* (Washington, D.C.: Institute for International Economics, 1996).

30. See Gill, "The Global Panopticon?"

31. Bob Davis, "Global Paradox: Growth of Trade Binds Nations, but it Also Can Spur Separatism," *Wall Street Journal*, June 20, 1994 (western ed.), p. A1.

32. The best-known discussion of the "new mediaevalism" is to be found in Hedley Bull, *The Anarchical Society—A Study of Order in World Politics* (New York: Columbia University Press, 1977), pp. 254–55, 264–76, 285–86, 291–94. The notion of "heteronomy" is found, among other places, in John G. Ruggie, "Continuity and Transformation in the World Polity: Toward a Neorealist Synthesis," *World Politics* 35, 2 (January 1983), p. 274, n. 30. A heterarchy is a system of functionally differentiated and overlapping sovereign and semisovereign authorities, while a society is composed of individual entities embedded in webs of institutional relationships. The term "heterarchy" comes from C. Bartlett and S. Ghoshal, "Managing Innovation in the Transnational Corporation," pp. 215–55, in C. Y. Doz and G. Hedlund, eds., *Managing the Global Firm* (London: Routledge, 1990), quoted in Richard Gordon, "Globalization, New Production Systems and the Spatial Division of Labor," pp. 161–207, in Wolfgang Litek and Tony Charles, eds., *The Division of Labor: Emerging Forms of World Organization in International Perspective* (Berlin: Walter de Gruyter, 1995), p. 181.

33. Ole Wæver, "Securitization and Desecuritization," pp. 46–86 n. 59, in Ronnie D. Lipschutz, ed., *On Security* (New York: Columbia University Press, 1995).

34. One example of this is the growing environmental justice movement, which is becoming globalized and addresses not only the local disposition of toxic wastes but its export and disposal in other places around the world; see, e.g., Jennifer Clapp, "The Toxic Waste Trade with Less-Industrialised Countries: Economic Linkages and Political Alliances, *Third World Quarterly* 15, 3 (1994).

35. David Mitrany, *A Working Peace System* (Chicago: Quadrangle Books, 1966); Ernst B. Haas, *Beyond the Nation-State* (Stanford: Stanford University Press, 1964).

36. The following paragraphs are based on Gordon, "Globalization." He argues for the existence of three "logics" of world-economic organization: internationalization; multi/transnationalization; and globalization. The last is

"heterarchical" and nonmarket and, as he puts it, involves "valorization of local-ized techno-economic capabilities and socio-institutional frameworks . . . [with] mutual reciprocity between regional innovation systems and global networks" ("Concurrent Processes of World-Economic Integration: A Preliminary Typology," handout in colloquium, November 30, 1994, UC-Santa Cruz).

37. Judith Mayer has pointed out that even organizational knowledge is, to a large degree, also contextual, inasmuch as successful organization aimed at solving a localized functional problem must be based on a solid under-standing of local social relations. Personal communication, January 26, 1995.

38. See Rosenau, *Turbulence in World Politics*, chap. 14.

39. See Lipschutz, *Global Civil Society*, chaps. 4–6.

40. Lipschutz, *Global Civil Society and Global Environmental Governance*, chap. 2.

41. Richard Gordon, "Globalization," pp. 196, 199; emphasis added.

42. This was the point made by Robert Gilpin in *U.S. Power and the Multinational Corporation* (New York: Basic, 1975).

43. Mann, *Sources of Social Power*, chap. 2.

44. Gill, "The Global Panopticon?"

45. Rather as Judith Butler has argued in terms of a proliferation of so-cially constructed genders; see *Gender Trouble—Feminism and the Subversion of Identity* (New York: Routledge, 1990), p. 112. See also Lipschutz, *After Author-ity*, ch. 8.

CHAPTER 6

Writing Large:
Habit, Skill, and Grandiose Theory

Nicholas Onuf

[M]ost students in the international field have not treated their
subject as local politics writ large.
—James N. Rosenau, *The Scientific Study of Foreign Policy*

Most students in the international field see *Turbulence in World Politics*
as a dramatic shift in James Rosenau's thinking about world politics,
brought on by dramatic changes in the world of politics.[1] Rosenau
thinks about politics in dramatic terms.[2] He has even written a publicly performed play. Despite decades of work in which he has developed and tested his ideas in the manner of normal science, Rosenau
has proven himself better attuned to the dramas of the last few years
than any other major figure in the field.

It does not do, however, to conclude that Rosenau has abandoned
a magnificent body of work, or repudiated its conceptual underpinnings, in favor of a new "turbulence paradigm." Even if Rosenau speaks
in terms that suggest such a paradigm shift, we ought not to be fooled
by his dramatic inclinations.[3] Just before *Turbulence* appeared, Rosenau
claimed to be an unrepentant behavioralist.[4] So he remains.

What then in Rosenau's thinking has changed so dramatically? I
suggest that changes in the world forced him to formulate, for the first
time systematically, the behavioral theory underlying all of his work.
How can someone who counts thinking theoretically among his "long-
standing habits" *not* have done so long ago?[5] After all, Rosenau's early
essay on "calculated control" presents a tightly organized conceptual
framework, elements of which occupy an important position in *Turbulence*. Yet by Rosenau's own reckoning, this essay presents no theory:

"it does not explain why international affairs unfold as they do."[6] Even with respect to foreign policy, Rosenau claimed to offer nothing more than a "pre-theory."[7] His modesty stems from the conventional positivist assumption that normal science conducted within the terms of an increasingly refined conceptual framework would eventuate in a general theory whose propositions had already passed the test of scientific scrutiny. When the world began to change far more dramatically than existing frameworks seemed to be able to account for, Rosenau was jarred from his theoretical slumber.

Rosenau declared his new stance on theory in a long, highly visible review essay, which he published several years before *Turbulence* appeared. "The need for theorizing—good and bad—is especially acute in world politics today. Change is so pervasive in both the internal and external lives of communities and nation-states that old formulations no longer feel comfortable."[8] Under review was "the best of 'bad theory'." Rosenau called for a better alternative—"grandiose theory"—meeting grandiose requirements.[9]

The term "grandiose" is itself rather grandiose. "Grand" might have been a better choice, both for the ambition "to roam across vast theoretical vistas" and for the demands placed on those daring to do so.[10] Four of the criteria for good grandiose theory "come straight from the philosophy of science."[11] Nevertheless, they do not require "operationalized hypotheses or systematic data," at least initially.[12] Such a requirement would effectively prevent theorizing on an appropriately grand scale.

Another three criteria constitute "the substantive core" of Rosenau's "theoretical predispositions."[13] Rosenau's substantive criteria insure that a properly grandiose theory reaches across "macro and micro levels of aggregation."[14] While these criteria would seem to favor neither level over the other, the complexity of micro-macro interactions forces the grandiose theorist to start somewhere. Ever the behavioralist, Rosenau's clear preference is the microlevel.

HABIT

Constituting the micro level are "habit-driven actors"—"both officials and citizens who strive for goals and respond to challenges in habitual ways."[15] Habits differ, as do their "bases," but everyone has a "habit function."[16] So-called rational actors are "habituated" to making self-consciously rational choices.[17] Indeed, no actor can be dismissed as a mindless victim of habit. According to Rosenau, *the readiness to learn is part of an actor's habit pool.*[18]

Rosenau makes habit an abiding feature of human behavior. Perhaps not consciously, he follows an august predecessor in doing so: David Hume, whose analysis of causality helped awaken Immanuel Kant from his self-described dogmatic slumber. Hume argued that we experience the "constant conjunction" of objects, events, or properties in nature, leading us to infer a "necessary connexion," or causal relation, between them.[19] Yet we can never demonstrate that such conjunctions are necessary, because we have no way of knowing if they will continue to take place in the future. Only by experiencing them can we know for sure, and this is so no matter how often we have experienced them in the past. In Hume's words, "there can be no *demonstrative* arguments to prove, *that those instances, of which we have had no experience, resemble those, of which we have had experience.*"[20]

Lacking arguments, why are we so confident that constant conjunctions will continue as they have? Hume's answer is habit (a term he used interchangeably with custom). "All inferences from experience . . . are effects of custom, not of reasoning."[21] We come to expect what we are accustomed to experiencing. Indeed the principle *"that like objects, plac'd in like circumstances, will always produce like effects"* is a product of experience. Having "establish'd itself by a sufficient custom, it bestows an evidence and firmness on any opinion, to which it can be apply'd."[22]

Hume's inference that habit causes us to infer causal relations from the evidence of constant conjunctions is, by his own account, unproven and unprovable. Nevertheless, Hume bestowed considerable firmness on his opinion by calling habit a "principle"—one that "determines" our causal conclusions.[23] Even more striking is Hume's claim that "habit is nothing but one of the principles of nature, and derives all its force from that origin."[24] This principle seems no more justified than the principle that nature is uniform, which Hume dispatched as an argument for causality.[25] Nevertheless, Hume seems to have believed that nature is uniform. Our ability to recognize and act on this condition sets us apart from animals. Like us, they are guided by the habit of drawing inferences from experience, as well as by instinct. Unlike us, they do not make arguments about the state of nature, or about anything else.[26]

The principle that nature is uniform is not just an argument, but an article of faith for positivist science. It encourages us to formulate scientific laws or, in Hume's terms, "general rules," and theories, or arguments, purporting to explain the existence and operation of these general rules.[27] Science depends on generalization. More precisely, science makes the process of generalization a collective undertaking guided by general rules.

Hume thought that generalizing from our experiences is the first and foremost of our habitual activities. The difficulty comes when we seek to generalize in the face of ambiguous or contradictory evidence. As Hume noted, "when any cause fails of producing its usual effect, philosophers [clearly including himself] ascribe not this to any irregularity in nature; but suppose, that some secret causes, in the particular structure of parts, have prevented the operation."[28] In such instances, we ought to assign probabilities, not to nature, but to our assessments of its causal relations.[29]

In generalizing, we are prone to mistakes. Following "certain and infallible rules," scientists make fewer mistakes than the rest of us perhaps, but they do make them because of their "uncertain and fallible faculties."[30] Haste causes mistakes, as does narrow-mindedness.[31] A particular failing that the rules of good science seek to prevent is the formulation of a general rule before the evidence warrants. Hume's term for a rashly formulated general rule is prejudice.[32]

To generalize with Hume: everyone generalizes all of time. It is a universal habit, but not one that is uniformly practiced. We can learn to generalize better by being self-conscious about the process, by learning from our mistakes and by formulating rules in aid of generalization. Rosenau's position is identical.

Consider four of Rosenau's nine rules for "creative theorizing" about "international phenomena."[33]

1. To think theoretically one must be able to assume that human affairs are founded on an underlying order.

2. To think theoretically one must be predisposed to ask about every event, every situation, or every observed phenomenon, "Of what is it an instance?"

3. To think theoretically one must be tolerant of ambiguity, concerned about probabilities, and distrustful of absolutes.

4. To think theoretically one must be consistently ready to be proven wrong.[34]

Rule 1 simply and unequivocally reaffirms the principle of the uniformity of nature in the most inclusive sense. Rule 2 makes generalization a maximally self-conscious activity. As any of Rosenau's students will attest, he attaches great importance to the question, Of what is this event, object, property or relation an instance? "Of all the habits that one must develop to think theoretically, perhaps none is more central than the inclination to ask this question at every opportunity."[35]

Rule 3 seeks to combat prejudice and its concomitants. Rule 4 reaffirms Hume's claim that we can never prove anything anyway.

Implicit in the Hume-Rosenau position on habit as a human universal that can be cultivated to good effect is the division of humanity into two groups. There are those who generalize rashly, without sufficient attention to evidence. There are those who generalize circumspectly but effectively in solving nature's "secrets" or "puzzles."[36] Just this division made Hume an emblematic figure in the Enlightenment of the eighteenth century.

Philosophers and other enlightened individuals of the time saw themselves free from the thrall of tradition—of superstitious beliefs, mindless habit and blinding prejudice. Superstition willfully misreads nature, mindless habit refuses change for the better, prejudice resists correction. Worst of all from Hume's point of view is the widespread belief in miracles. By definition, a "miracle is a violation of the laws of nature."[37] Believing an event to be a miracle denies the possibility of a natural explanation for the event. Miracles appeal to the gullible masses, who "receive greedily, without examination, whatever soothes superstition and promotes wonder."[38]

As far as I know, Rosenau has never attacked traditional, popular beliefs the way Hume did. Nevertheless, the behavioral theory that he systematically formulated in *Turbulence* exhibits a strongly Humean tendency to differentiate between an enlightened few with exemplary habits, and the mass of ordinary people who are unable to rise above their bad habits. Even if habit is the source of all learning and progress, habits that drag humanity down constitute the great problem to be vanquished, the puzzle to be solved, at every level of human aggregation.

HABDAPTION

In *Turbulence*, Rosenau reaffirmed the importance of habit in understanding human behavior. There is, however, a subtle change in the way he formulated this proposition. All people are simultaneously rational about some situations of choice and habit-driven about other such situations. When rational, they learn from experience and adapt to changing circumstances; when habit-driven, they respond to situations unreflectively and repeat the same patterns of behavior even when circumstances have changed.

> Empirically, in short, the vast preponderance of officials and citizens are both rational and habitual, both intellectual and emotional, and our understanding of turbulence in world politics is thus more likely to be advanced if we employ a perspective that posits individuals as

falling between two ideal types. What is needed is a model organized around a central premise in which the form and direction of micro action is conceived to spring from a combination of habits that perpetuate continuity and orientations that allow for thoughtful estimates and are open to change. It is the shifting balance between rote behavior and adaptive learning that forms the conditions of postinternational politics. To reflect this model, it seems worthwhile to coin a new term that expresses the synthesis of habitual and adaptive responses. Henceforth, where appropriate, we shall refer to individuals as *habdaptive actors* and to their location on the continuum between rote behavior and adaptive learning as their *habdaptive function*.[39]

Rosenau seems to have revised his earlier view that people, as creatures of habit, are habitual learners. In this new formulation, some people are adaptive learners, while others learn habits and then stop learning. The former have "developed analytic skills," "complex cognitive maps," "active and refined cathectic capacities," "questioning compliance orientations," and "performance criteria" for their "legitimacy sentiments." Conversely, the latter have "rudimentary analytic skills," "simplistic cognitive maps," "dormant and crude cathectic capacities," "unthinking compliance orientations," and "traditional criteria" for their "legitimacy sentiments."[40]

Rosenau's Enlightenment opposition of tradition and enlightenment is analytically rudimentary, crudely cathectic (indeed, highly prejudiced in its cathectic thrust), and, two and a half centuries after Hume, thoroughly traditional. Nevertheless, its utility for Rosenau is undeniable. The simple proposition that everyone is habit-driven is no foundation for theory. Taken together, the propositions that everyone combines habitual and adaptive behavior but in different proportions, and that these proportions can shift individually and in aggregate, constitute a model. With this model in place, Rosenau had positioned himself to formulate a theory of behavior applied to the circumstances of world politics.

As stated in *Turbulence*, the theory itself has a simple grandeur.

[T]he possibility of change on the part of the habdaptive actor . . . underlies a prime argument of this book: that turbulence has engulfed world politics partly, even largely, because citizens and officials have moved away from the habit end of the learning continuum and toward the adaptive end. The movement may be no more than minimal—on the order of one JND—for any individual, but the aggregative consequences of the movement are not minimal at all. On the contrary, the breakdown of habits is a major reason for the transformation of the state-centric system . . .[41]

Rosenau's habitual reluctance to declare himself theoretically is still in evidence—why not call this "prime argument" the "grandiose theory" that it is? On the other hand, Rosenau's habitual preference for probabilistic formulation is to be commended. The introduction of a "just noticeable difference" (JND) as a "measurement unit" is regrettable, and not just because it is methodologically misleading.[42] Claiming that the aggregate effects of just noticeable changes "are not minimal at all" is unwarranted. Why cannot the many individual changes in habdaptive actors offset each other, with the result of little or no noticeable change at the level of the aggregate?

Turning first to the methodological difficulties with JND as a measurement unit, we might ask, just noticeable to whom? When differences are just noticeable to observers (this was clearly Rosenau's frame of reference when he introduced the concept of JND early in the book), different observers may not agree on what they have observed, errors in observation are most likely, and changes in observers' instrumental capacities can dramatically change the field of noticeable differences. Furthermore, the fact that some observer just notices a change in an individual's behavior has no demonstrable relation to the degree of individual change needed for Rosenau's theory to work. Individual changes that are too subtle or minute for any observer to notice may nevertheless aggregate to major change. Conversely, the observer may notice all sorts of changes in all degrees and not know which ones are responsible for the aggregate pattern of change.

If individuals whose behavior has changed are the ones who do the noticing, then Rosenau's theory has acquired a significant additional term. Reference to JND is not just a methodological aside that interrupts the statement of the theory. Instead it is an important if cryptically formulated proposition linking individual changes to aggregate change. When individuals begin to notice changes in themselves, then these changes (the changes noticed and the additional change represented by the act of noticing) add up to major change. In order to maintain the theory's simple grandeur, we should construe this additional term as a necessary one: major movement depends on people noticing that they—themselves and all those whom they can observe closely—have begun to change.

I am not at all sure that Rosenau intended to make self-awareness an integral feature of his theory, even if his conception of rational, adaptive behavior includes just this property. From a positivist point of view, measuring self-awareness is highly problematic, and offering JND as a measurement unit is not even close to a solution. More to the point, making individual self-awareness a necessary condition for major change would not seem to comport with Rosenau's theoretical disposition to emphasize the unintended consequences of small changes. If people begin to notice changes in their behavior and act on what they have noticed, then these second-order changes are hardly unintended, whether and to what degree, from any observer's point of view, they are noticeable.

CHANGE

Rosenau set his theory up as an alternative to the standard liberal theory of unintended consequences, which of course is Adam Smith's invisible hand and the entire edifice of modern microeconomics.[43] This theory asserts that small, noticeable changes in behavior yield aggregate conditions that have the effect of encouraging small changes by others in a compensatory direction. If many individuals begin to demand more of some good, other individuals produce more of this good until supply and demand have returned to balance. Major movement is dampened, precisely because everyone notices small differences and responds accordingly.

Rosenau would likely say (indeed, may have said somewhere) that the liberal theory of unintended consequences is a good theory. He would also say that it is unduly grandiose. It fails to account for a major class of unintended consequences—those that have amplifying rather than dampening effects. By implication, the standard liberal theory makes habit its centerpiece. People have learned the habit of calculating marginal utilities, and that is all they ever need to do.

Rosenau's habdaptive actors engage in other kinds of behavior, no less calculating, but far more likely to produce macro-level change. To make space for a theory that features an elastic habdaptive function, Rosenau had to explain why any rational person would abandon old habits when they are so obviously useful. Change itself—"changing circumstances"—is the key.[44] There are two sorts of changes in circumstances that prompt a change in an actor's habdaptive function: "(1) when external stimuli are persistently and startlingly new; (2) when new skills and orientations develop within the actor."[45] External stimuli that are likely to prompt a significant, readily noticed shift toward learning include war, revolution, or a rapid change in the material conditions affecting daily life. "Internally induced habit change is illustrated by the effects of the microelectronic revolution on people's analytic capabilities."[46] Both sorts of change are much in evidence in today's world.

The kind of behavior that changing circumstances prompt people to learn differs from the habit-driven behavior that markets rely on and economists concern themselves with. Implicitly Rosenau has reaffirmed the liberal division of political and economic domains. For Rosenau, "politics is conceived of as activities in which one actor . . . seeks to modify or preserve the behavior patterns of functionally distant others."[47] This is what Rosenau has always called "calculated control." Not just calculated, but self-consciously oriented to the achievement of specific consequences, control thus conceived would seem to be the antithesis of habit-driven behavior yielding an orderly set of unintended consequences.

Yet even here habit enters the picture. Enduring relations of control are authoritative, authority being "that set of premises and habits on which macro leaders are entitled to rely to obtain automatic compliance from their followers."[48] After reviewing the reasons that "people accord legitimacy to acts of authorities," Rosenau concluded that compliance is mostly "a matter of habit; repeated instances of compliance become deeply ingrained."[49] Hume held the same view: "men, once accustomed to obedience, never think of departing from that path, in which they and their ancestors have constantly trod, and to which they are confined by so many urgent and visible motives."[50]

According to Rosenau, a shift along the continuum from habit to adaptive learning undermines authority. "It is in the deterioration of habit that authority crises originate: the more the membership moves away from automatic acceptance and toward outright rejection, the more is an authority relationship subjected to strain."[51] When challenged, authority is far more likely to be dislocated than destroyed. When compliance orientations shift from unthinking to questioning, the "locus of control" tends to shorten.[52] In particular, states become "[m]ore decentralized, less coherent and effective"; their "[a]uthority more diffuse, hierarchy weakened; and their "[c]itizens more defiant, loyalties more tenuous." In a compensating movement, subgroups become "[m]ore numerous, centralized, coherent, and effective"; their "[a]uthority more concentrated, hierarchy strengthened; their "[m]embers more compliant, committed, and loyal."[53]

In our time, states are losing ground to subgroups, many (but not all) of which are "located within states and at least technically subject to their authority."[54] Size matters. States reap economies of scale due to their large size but depend on the uniform habits of a passive citizenry to be able to operate on the scale they do. Active learners find small groups and organizations more responsive to their concerns. For them, local politics pay off with at least some chance of achieving intended consequences at the local level.

Republican theory has always concerned itself with the size problem in politics. Hume thought the best solution was a pyramid of representative bodies—a solution Madison seconded in *Federalist* No. 10, as did Rosenau in *Turbulence*, if only in passing.[55] Yet contemporary republicans doubt that voting for representatives sufficiently activates habit-dominated citizens or satisfies active, adaptive citizens with consequences worthy of their intentions. Having studied the problem of mobilizing citizens between elections, Rosenau would seem to have had the same misgivings.[56]

Contemporary republicans have turned their attention to social movements that challenge as well as mediate the state's authority. So has Rosenau. As *Turbulence* makes clear, Rosenau is a republican thinker who has come to believe that local politics writ large can only go so far in saving the state from the perils of scale. Now more than ever, local politics have global consequences.

The largest such consequence is, for most citizens, hardly intended, indeed hard to imagine. The world itself is bifurcating. A "multicentric world" of "sovereignty-free actors" has begun to take its place along side the "state-centric world" with which we have long been familiar.[57] Whether one world will prevail over the other, bifurcation continue, or a cyclical pattern set in is a matter of speculation.[58] The theory predicts a range of outcomes depending on the extent to which citizens experience a change in their habdaptive functions.

Rosenau observed that one's preferences are likely to affect one's assessment of the possibilities. His preference is bifurcation.

> It has the potential for a creative reconciliation of all the great antitheses of politics—the conflicts between order and freedom, between the will of majorities and the autonomy of minorities, between individual needs and collective welfare, between technological innovation and cultural integrity, between growth and stability, and between change and continuity.[59]

Thus concludes *Turbulence*, its theory offered not just to explain turbulence in today's world, but to reassure us, and perhaps even to help bring bifurcation to fruition as an intended consequence of one scholar's adaptive learning.

SKILL

Rosenau's behavioral theory of politics explains stable, predictable relations of authority by reference to mindless habit. It explains our own era of turbulence by reference to a general change from habit-driven behavior at the micro-level to adaptive behavior. Great change at the micro level is, as far as Rosenau is concerned, a recent phenomenon that is easy enough to substantiate. Not only is turbulence a conspicuous feature of our times but, thanks to television, the evidence is constantly before our eyes, stimulating us to think politically as never before. Far more important is the spectacular increase in analytic skills engendered by the microelectronic revolution. This is, indeed, a "skill revolution."[60]

Rosenau's behavioral theory starts with change in actors' habdaptive functions and ends with a bifurcating world. One might object that he significantly weakened his theory, or at least the claim that it stands grandly on its own terms, by finding the cause of behavioral change in worldwide changes in material conditions. Presumably these changes are the result of (somebody's) adaptive learning at an earlier interval. Thus stated, the theory suffers from infinite regress, and the charge that its point of departure—recent behavioral change— is glaringly arbitrary.

Rosenau's implicit answer to this charge is that the skill revolution is just that—a revolution that has no precedence. As a step-level shift toward adaptive learning for a very large number of people, its consequences are world shaking. Rosenau has considered the obvious criticism that the effects of the skill revolution are anything but equal. Some people have privileged access to the means for improving their analytic skills, others have much less access. The point, however, is aggregate change. As Rosenau and Mary Durfee put it, "the gap between the two ends of the skill continuum may be no narrower than in the past." Nevertheless, "the advancement in the competencies of those at every point on the continuum is sufficient to contribute to a major transformation in the conduct of world affairs."[61]

At first glance, this claim is empirical and, as such, contestable. Indeed, the gap between the two ends of the skill continuum may be far wider now than in the recent past. Possibly the gap is growing so dramatically that the world's bifurcation is an unintended consequence, but not the sort of bifurcation that Rosenau has had in mind. After bifurcation, one world would consist of materially privileged, analytically skillful people. The other is a nether world, made up of all those who have been left behind analytically and materially, despised or pitied for their bad habits and retrograde attitudes by those who have abandoned them.[62]

The issue is not simply empirical. Implicitly, Rosenau's theory makes habit the rule and adaptive learning an exception. Habit reigns because we are all good at repetitive behavior, which is, often enough, socially efficient. Adaptive learning is exceptional because it is hard work for individuals and costly to society. Rosenau seems to believe that the material changes underlying the skill revolution somehow annul time-tested propositions that are embedded in the structure of his theory. Without offering a compelling amendment to the theory—a set of propositions to the effect that microelectronics have altered our capacity to learn and rid us of the tendency to revert to habit—Rosenau's empirical claims fail to convince for theoretical reasons. If he is right, then his theory cannot be very good.

NORMATIVITY

Rosenau's behavioral theory of politics is undeniably grandiose. I believe, however, that something is missing—something Hume might have supplied—that would make it a better theory without undue cost to its simple grandeur. Adding self-consciousness is neither warranted on Humean grounds (although there may be Kantian grounds for doing so) nor, as I observed above, is it methodologically tractable for anyone with positivist commitments. Instead, Rosenau's theory would benefit from the addition of a normative element. I am not suggesting that Rosenau make his theory any more normative than he already has (i.e., make it "value theory"; *Turbulence* is "value-explicit").[63] An early proponent of the distinction between facts and values, Hume nevertheless made a great deal of the fact that values systemically affect human conduct.[64]

Rosenau did include "normative prescriptions" in a laundry list of factors contributing to every actor's habit pool.[65] He also speculated that turbulence fostered the emergence of new "global norms."[66] To illustrate this trend, he offered an especially Humean instance—increasingly actors at every level insist on scientific criteria in evaluating truth claims. Nevertheless, Rosenau failed to consider where norms come from, and why they might matter more (given their origin) than other factors making up anybody's habit pool. Instead, norms belong to a residual category of macro-phenomena—call it culture—that somehow bears on every actor's habdaptive function.

Hume, by contrast, used the proposition that people are creatures of habit to explain both how norms happen to be everywhere and, if only implication, why norms matter when people have habits to guide them. Armed with a Humean understanding of normativity, we can then rewrite the terms of Rosenau's habdaptive function to avoid the gratuitous, though Humean, opposition between the benighted holders of tradition and the enlightened seekers of truth. The key to this move is recognition that behavior is always, necessarily social. Individuals have habits but share customs. The latter are habits writ large.

To acquire a habit, people must engage in repetitive behavior. If two people simultaneously engage in behavior that is mutually beneficial, or one imitates another, and they and others repeat the behavior in question to further benefit, all begin to generalize from the experience and then to count on its repetition—by everyone, for everyone's benefit. In Hume's compelling analysis, the process of generalizing from observed regularities of conduct (a process exactly analogous to that of inferring cause from regularities in nature) assures us that "the sense of interest has become common to all our fellows, and gives us a confidence of the future regularity of their conduct."[67]

The product of our collective generalizing is a rule or convention "which arises gradually, and acquires force by a slow progression, and by our repeated experience of the inconveniences of transgressing it."[68] According to Hume, conventions account for language, property, and everything else that makes society possible. Even *"natural"* justice is *"invented"*: "it derives its origins from human conventions."[69] The "force" that conventions acquire is normative; expectation gives rise to obligation. "They are contriv'd to remedy like inconveniences, and acquire their moral sanction in the same manner, from remedying those inconveniences."[70]

Normativity seems natural because we—people in general—think that we should behave as we customarily have behaved. We habitually come to this generalization from the particulars of our daily lives, and not from the requirements of any particular moral system.[71] People slip from fact to value, and back again, with amazing facility and splendid insouciance. We do so, in my opinion, because we know how to use language to have people (ourselves included) act as we think they should. Hume's brilliant analysis of promising as a performative use of language suggests instead that the relevant cognitive skills precede language and its invented rules, even if our linguistic abilities strengthen those skills.[72]

For Rosenau's purposes, it does not matter why people are so adept at traversing the fact-value divide—why we are so quick to draw normative conclusions from observed regularities and so sure of ourselves when we do so. He need only accept that, as social beings, we make rules just as readily as we form habits. Furthermore, we make rules on the expectation that we, and others, will follow them. Ruled as we are by habit and instinct, we are even more ruled by our rules.

Following rules is, often enough, a matter of habit. It works well for us. We also know when it works better for us to disregard a rule. Or to evade a rule. Or to claim that it is not a rule or at least not applicable to us. Or to change a rule or claim that others' evasions or endeavors have already changed it. Or to follow the rule to the letter but not in spirit, or follow it in spirit but not to the letter.

Pierre Bourdieu has called this ensemble of activities "*habitus*": "the durably installed generative principle of regulated improvisations."[73] Bourdieu claimed it a mistake to speak of rules—"a euphemized form of legalism"—where *habitus* is in evidence.[74] Bourdieu was mistaken—mislead, actually, by a too formal conception of rule as "an institutionalized call to order" that people are bound to follow.[75] People deal with rules all the time. However formal these rules are and whatever the institutional support for them, we do so with consummate skill and a high degree of self-awareness. We are quite aware, for example, that disregarding an informal, local, and provisional rule is likely to weaken the rule, or that making a rule more formal and general will contribute to the likelihood of its being followed. Intending such consequences is an integral feature of our collective normative competence.

No doubt people vary in their normative skills. Nevertheless, all of us who are able to get along as social beings possess this skill abundantly. To paraphrase Rosenau and Durfee, the gap between the two ends of the normative skill continuum is far narrower than it is for the continuum of analytic skills. Nor would it matter if the gap in normative skills changes, for it is unlikely to change enough to have any revolutionary consequences.

It does matter who has the institutional position to make rules formal and their violation costly, just as it matters what the people in this position want for themselves and others. It matters that particular sets of rules are difficult to learn and costly to teach. For example, rules for obtaining and using analytic skills, like the rules of good science, are notoriously demanding, even if some of these rules are needlessly arcane, practically irrelevant or routinely disregarded by those who know them. It matters that informal rules colonize formally ruled environments, making it doubly difficult for outsiders to know how to conduct themselves.

These are political matters, all of them affecting whether and to what degree the rules accompanying the microelectronic revolution are likely to narrow the gap in analytic skills around the world or, as an unintended consequence, to exacerbate it. I doubt that the gap will narrow, because the normative competence that we all possess so abundantly seems, perversely enough, to foster asymmetrical distributions of privilege and control. That we are all so good with rules means that some people always rule over others. This is less a complication for Rosenau's theory than a setback for his normative preferences. In practical terms, it suggests that, with modest alteration, his theory can help to account for turbulence wherever it occurs *and* the way people respond to it, not just individually, but socially.

NOTES

1. James N. Rosenau, *Turbulence in World Politics: A Theory of Change and Continuity* (Princeton, N.J.: Princeton University Press, 1990). After this essay was completed, Rosenau published *Along the Domestic-Foreign Frontier: Exploring Governance in a Turbulent World* (Cambridge: Cambridge University Press, 1997). Even if I had seen this large, rich book beforehand, I believe that I would still have written the essay much as it now appears.

2. James N. Rosenau, *The Dramas of Political Systems: An Introduction to the Problems of Governance* (North Scituate, Mass.: Duxbury Press 1972); Rosenau, ed., *Global Voices: Dialogues in International Relations* (Boulder, Colo.: Westview Press, 1993).

3. James N. Rosenau and Mary Durfee, *Thinking Theory Thoroughly: Coherent Approaches to an Incoherent World* (Boulder: Westview Press, 1995), pp. 31–35.

4. James N. Rosenau, "The Scholar as an Adaptive System," in Joseph Kruzel and Rosenau, eds., *Journeys through World Politics: Autobiographical Reflections of Thirty-four Academic Travelers* (Lexington, Mass.: Lexington Books, 1989), p. 64.

5. *Ibid.*, p. 59. Also see James N. Rosenau, "Thinking Theory Thoroughly," in K. P. Misra and Richard Smith Beal, eds., *International Relations Theory: Western and Non-Western Perspectives* (New Delhi: Vikas, 1979), reprinted in Rosenau, *Scientific Study*, pp. 19–31.

6. James N. Rosenau, *Calculated Control as a Unifying Concept in the Study of International Politics and Foreign Policy*, Research Monograph No. 15, Center of International Studies, Princeton University, reprinted in Rosenau, *The Scientific Study of Foreign Policy*, rev. and enlarged ed. (London: Frances Pinter, 1980), p. 281.

7. James N. Rosenau, "Pre-Theories and Theories of Foreign Policy," in R. Barry Farrell, ed., *Approaches to Comparative and International Politics* (Evanston, Ill.: Northwestern University Press), reprinted in Rosenau, *Scientific Study*, pp. 115–69.

8. James N. Rosenau, "Before Cooperation: Hegemons, Regimes, and Habit-Driven Actors in World Politics," *International Organization* 40 (1986): 849–50.

9. Ibid., p. 851.

10. Cf. Quentin Skinner, ed., *The Return of Grand Theory in the Social Sciences* (Cambridge: Cambridge University Press, 1985).

11. Rosenau, "Before Cooperation," p. 855.

12. Ibid., p. 853.

13. Ibid., p. 855.

14. Ibid., p. 861.

15. Ibid.

16. Ibid.

17. Ibid., p. 862.

18. Ibid., p. 864, his emphasis.

19. David Hume, *A Treatise of Human Nature*, (1739–1740), 2d ed. rev. by P. H. Nidditch (Oxford: Clarendon Press, 1978), p. 87.

20. Ibid., p. 89, his emphasis.

21. Ibid., p. 87

22. Ibid., p. 105, his emphasis.

23. David Hume, *An Enquiry concerning Human Understanding* (1748), ed. by Antony Flew (La Salle, Ill.: Open Court, 1988), p. 86.

24. Hume, *Treatise*, p. 179.

25. *Ibid.*, p. 89.

26. Hume, *Treatise*, pp. 176–79; *Enquiry*, pp. 139–42.

27. Hume, *Treatise*, p. 141.

28. Hume, *Enquiry*, p. 99.

29. Hume, *Treatise*, pp. 130–72; *Enquiry*, pp. 98–100.

30. Hume, *Treatise*, p. 181.

31. Hume, *Enquiry*, p. 142.

32. Hume, *Treatise*, p. 146.

33. Rosenau, "Thinking Theory Thoroughly," pp. 20–31. They are reproduced in Rosenau and Durfee, *Thinking Theory Thoroughly*, pp. 178–90.

34. Ibid., pp. 23, 25, 27, 30. On Rosenau's list these are rules 3, 4, 6, and 9.

35. Ibid., p. 25.

36. "Secrets" is Hume's term: "nature has kept us at a great distance from all her secrets." *Enquiry*, p. 77. "Puzzles" is Rosenau's. Another rule for thinking theoretically requires that we be "genuinely puzzled." "Thinking Theory Thoroughly," p. 29.

37. David Hume, "Of Miracles," in Hume, *Essays: Moral, Political and Literary, (1741–1742)* (Oxford: Oxford University Press, 1963), p. 524.

38. Ibid., p. 539.

39. Rosenau, *Turbulence*, p. 228, his emphasis; two footnotes deleted.

40. Ibid., table 9.1, p. 211.

41. Ibid., p. 228.

42. See ibid., pp. 32–33, for JND as a measurement unit.

43. Cf. ibid., p. 51

44. Ibid., p. 233.

45. Ibid., p. 234.

46. Ibid., p. 235.

47. Ibid., p. 184.

48. Ibid., p. 186.

49. Ibid., p. 187.

50. David Hume, "Of the Origin of Government," in *Essays*, p. 37; also see *Treatise*, p. 566.

51. Rosenau, *Turbulence*, p. 190.

52. Ibid., table 9.1, p. 211.

53. Ibid., table 6.1, p. 119.

54. Ibid., p. 133.

55. David Hume, "Idea of a Perfect Commonwealth," in *Essays*, p. 502; Douglass Adair, " 'That Politics May Be Reduced to a Science': David Hume, James Madison, and the Tenth *Federalist*," *Huntington Library Quarterly* 20 (1957): 343–60; Rosenau, *Turbulence*, p. 241.

56. James N. Rosenau, *Citizenship between Elections: An Inquiry into the Mobilizable American* (New York: The Free Press, 1974).

57. Rosenau, *Turbulence*, pp. 249–53.

58. Ibid., p. 445.

59. Ibid., p. 461.

60. Rosenau and Durfee, *Thinking Theory Thoroughly*, pp. 35–37. Rosenau seems not to have used this phrase in *Turbulence*.

61. Ibid., pp. 36–37. Also see Rosenau, *Turbulence*, pp. 364–67.

62. See Robert B. Reich, *The Work of Nations: Preparing Ourselves for 21st Century Capitalism* (New York: Alfred A. Knopf, 1991), for a popular assessment along these lines.

63. Rosenau, "Thinking Theory Thoroughly," p. 22; *Turbulence*, p. 33. Rosenau finally turned to normative matters in *Along the Domestic-International Frontier*, pp. 174–88, but even there has not made them integral to his grandiose theory.

64. According to Hume, "morality consists not in any relations, that are the object of science; but if examin'd, will prove with equal certainty, that it consists not in any *matter of fact*." *Treatise*, p. 468, his emphasis. See, however, Arnold Brecht's skeptical assessment of Hume's contribution to the fact-value distinction. *Political Theory: The Foundations of Twentieth-Century Political Thought* (Princeton, N.J.: Princeton University Press, 1959), pp. 539–41.

65. Rosenau, *Turbulence*, p. 229. The 1986 version of this list referred to "cultural norms." "Before Cooperation," p. 861.

66. Rosenau, *Turbulence*, p. 425.

67. Hume, *Treatise*, p. 490.

68. Ibid.

69. Ibid., p. 543, Hume's emphasis.

70. Ibid., p. 543.

71. Cf. Hans Kelsen's "basic norm." *Principles of International Law*, 2d ed. rev. by Robert W. Tucker (New York: Holt, Rinehart and Winston, 1967), pp. 556–65.

72. Hume, *Treatise*, pp. 516–25.

73. Pierre Bourdieu, *Outline of a Theory of Practice*, trans. by Richard Price (Cambridge: Cambridge University Press, 1977), p. 78. Bourdieu chose the term *"habitus"* "to set aside the common conception of habit as a mechanical assembly or preformed programme, as Hegel does when in the *Phenomenology of Mind* he speaks of 'habit as dexterity'." Ibid., p. 218, n. 47.

74. Ibid., p. 17.

75. Ibid.

CHAPTER 7

Pondering the Postinternational Perspective on the Public: A Prescient or Peripheral Paradigm?

Ole R. Holsti

In one of the first efforts to explore systematically the role of public opinion in the formulation of foreign policy, James Rosenau painted a rather dismal portrait of the public, or at least of the vast majority— 75 to 90 percent according to his reckoning—who constitute the "mass public." Using one of the many colorful metaphors that have marked his voluminous writing, Rosenau's description emphasized both the distance between the average citizen and the policy arena and the public's lack of interest in moving to a more proximate venue.

> The notion of a stationary pyramid is perhaps a poor way of introducing behavioral differences among the three strata of the public. A more appropriate analogy is that of a gigantic theater, with a tense drama unfolding on the stage. The mass public, occupying the many seats in the balcony, is so far removed from the scene of action that its members can hardly grasp the plot, much less hear all of the lines or distinguish between the actors. Thus they may sit in stony silence or applaud impetuously, if not so vigorously as to shake the foundation of the theater. Usually, however, they get thoroughly bored and leave, declining the invitation to occupy the empty seats in the orchestra.[1]

Rosenau not only described the ordinary citizen's profound lack of interest in public affairs, but he also expressed deep doubts that, if aroused to express its views and preferences, the public could play a constructive role in the conduct of foreign relations.

117

On the rare occasions when it does awaken from its slumber, the mass public, being no more informed than previously, is impulsive, unstable, unreasoning, unpredictable, capable of suddenly shifting direction or of going in several contradictory directions at the same time.[2]

Some three decades later, in a wide-ranging treatise that transcends established theories of world politics, Rosenau has moved the ordinary citizen from the peanut gallery to center stage. No longer is the average citizen an uninformed, passive, and uninterested observer of events that he can only dimly perceive—much less understand or influence—from a great distance. Owing to what Rosenau terms the closely linked "skills revolution" and "micro-electronic revolution," the ordinary citizen has been transformed into an important actor on the world stage, a fact that neither governments nor analysts of world politics can afford to neglect. "Turbulence," the central concept in his model, "derives from the changes that are transforming the analytic skills, affective capabilities, and legitimacy sentiments of individuals in all parts of the world."[3]

The remarkable metamorphosis of the ordinary individual's relevance to world politics can be traced in large part to a microelectronic revolution whose communications products—ranging from radio, television, and audio tapes, to personal computers, video tapes, and fax machines—have made available to average citizens the means for becoming informed about public affairs and for undertaking meaningful political action, thereby transforming the nature of politics on a global scale. "The very facets of the microelectronic revolution that have strengthened the competence of the state have also enlarged the competence of citizens to articulate their interests, press their demands, redirect their support, and otherwise participate in public affairs."[4] More specifically, "the analytic skills of citizens everywhere are being refined, so that their understanding of world politics is more elaborate and complex," with enormous consequences for the traditional central actors of world politics—sovereign states—as well as for the international system itself.[5]

The "postinternational" conception of world politics articulated in *Turbulence* clearly represents a challenge of more than marginal proportions to the "realist" and "liberal" theories that have dominated the debate. The realist, liberal, and postinternational models of world politics differ in a number of important respects. Because the role of the individual—as a member of the general public rather than as an opinion leader or top-ranking policymaker—in the three models is among the most striking of these differences, this essay will undertake an examination of public opinion with several goals:

1. To explicate the conception of public opinion articulated by proponents of realism, liberalism, and postinternationalism. The effort will be to identify some of the more important differences within each school of thought, but there is not sufficient space to permit fine-grained analyses to explore fully some of the more subtle ones.

2. To review some of the evidence about public opinion that may be relevant to the three models.

3. To propose some elements of a research agenda, with special attention to the postinternational model, that might provide further insight on the merits of the competing conceptions of public opinion.

The discussion will begin with realism, the most venerable of the models and the one that has usually set the terms of the debate, not only among theorists of world politics, but also among practitioners and reformers.

REALIST PERSPECTIVES ON PUBLIC OPINION

Classical realism and the more recent variant, structural or neorealism, share a number of important ideas, including an emphasis on several key features of world politics: the anarchical nature of the international system, states as the primary actors, the central role of power relations, and security and survival as the primary goals of states. However, they differ somewhat on the role of public opinion. Neorealist theories focus on the structure of capabilities within the international system and, at least in some versions, explicitly bypass internal political variables as a source of explanation. Public opinion accounts for a sufficiently small amount of the variance that it can largely be disregarded, or at least consigned to the attention of "reductionists"—that is, foreign-policy analysts.

Almost without exception, proponents of the more venerable classical school of realism espouse a very jaundiced view of the public. Realism has generally been grounded in a pessimistic theory of human nature, either a theological version (for example, St. Augustine or Reinhold Niebuhr) or a secular one (for example, Machiavelli, Hobbes, and Hans Morgenthau). Man is by nature self-regarding and is largely motivated by such passions as greed and fear, qualities that are not lost when men are aggregated into political units such as nation-states.

Realist skeptics include the founding fathers who formulated and debated the U.S. Constitution. For example, the authors of the *Federalist Papers* argued that the appointed Senate rather than the directly elected House of Representatives is best suited to play a key role in the conduct of foreign affairs. Their arguments constitute a concise statement of the realist case for shielding the nation's foreign and security policy from the assumed vagaries of the public and the institution, the House of Representatives, which most directly represented it.[6]

Several decades later, Alexis de Tocqueville, a sympathetic French analyst of American society and politics, questioned whether democracies could satisfy the requirements for the effective conduct of diplomatic affairs. After admitting that it is "very difficult to ascertain, at present, what degree of sagacity the American democracy will display in the conduct of . . . foreign policy," he nevertheless expressed his own judgment in terms applicable not only to the United States but to all democracies: "As for myself, I do not hesitate to say that it is especially in the conduct of their foreign relations that democracies appear to be decidedly inferior to other governments." He went on to identify the "propensity that induces democracies to obey impulse rather than prudence, and to abandon a mature design for the gratification of a momentary passion" as the essential barrier to effective foreign policy-making. In contrast to the aristocracy—"a firm and enlightened body"—the "mass of the people may be led astray by ignorance and passion."[7]

These putative qualities of the general public—ignorance and passion—lie at the heart of virtually all realist critiques of public opinion, including that of Hans Morgenthau, dean of the post–World War II realists: "The rational requirements of good foreign policy cannot from the outset count upon the support of a public opinion whose preferences are emotional rather than rational."[8] Similar realist arguments about the dangers and deficiencies of public opinion have been espoused by journalist Walter Lippmann, diplomat-historians E. H. Carr and George F. Kennan, diplomatic historian Thomas A. Bailey, and political scientist Gabriel Almond.[9]

Because he has had such an enormous impact on analyses of public opinion, Walter Lippmann's views merit a brief summary. In two book-length analyses of politics from a social-psychological perspective, he challenged the core premises of classical democratic theory that the public, if given the facts, could and would make reasonable decisions. In reality, according to Lippmann, the average citizen cannot make a constructive contribution to public affairs because, "He lives in a world which he cannot see, does not understand, and is unable to direct."[10] The common man is too fully involved in the requirements of earning a living and in otherwise attending to his most immediate needs to have the time or inclination to satisfy the heroic but unrealistic assumptions about the informed and engaged citizen celebrated in classical democratic theory.

According to Lippmann, the chasm between theory and reality is especially wide in the realm of foreign affairs, which are typically far removed from the direct experiences of the general public. Because the "pictures in the head" of the average citizen are unlikely to have much correspondence to the real world of international affairs, even were the public inclined to take an active part in foreign affairs, it could scarcely make an informed and constructive contribution. In fact, these "pictures" are likely to be little more than stereotypes that, in turn, color the manner in which reality is perceived. Thus, average citizens are not unlike those portrayed in Plato's allegory of the cave; instead of observing reality directly, they can see only indirect and inadequate representations of it. His remedy also resembled Plato's: the salvation of the democratic polity requires greater reliance upon the experts.

Realists may sometimes concede that the quality of domestic policy might be enhanced by public deliberations but the benefits of public participation do not extend to foreign affairs. Effective diplomacy must often be based on sensitive intelligence or other confidential information that cannot be shared with the public; it usually requires secrecy, flexibility, speed of action, and other qualities that would be seriously jeopardized were the public to have a significant impact; and public passions would often make it impossible to conduct sensitive negotiations with either friends or adversaries.

Because realists are skeptical of institutional arrangements for promoting international cooperation in an anarchical system, to say nothing of philosophers' blueprints for regulating international relations or ensuring peace, they typically rely upon balance-of-power strategies for defending national interests. Palmerston's widely quoted aphorism that Britain has no permanent friends or enemies, only permanent interests, summarizes a cardinal rule of realist statecraft. But the flexibility required to pursue balance-of-power politics may

Table 7.1
Public Opinion in Three Models of World Politics

	Realist	Liberal	Postinternational
Conception of international system	State-centered and anarchic	State-dominated but international institutions can mitigate effects of anarchy	Bifurcation into state-centric and multi-centric worlds
Conception of nation-state	Largely impermeable	Permeable	Fragmented
Dominant level of analysis	System [third image]	States and system [second and third images]	Individuals, states, and system [first, second, and third images]
Crucial issues	Security	Security and prosperity	Security conceived as interdependence issues such as environmental pollution, currency crises, the drug trade, AIDS, etc.
Nature of public opinion:			
• Interest in foreign affairs	Generally very low	Sporadic, depending on the issue	Moderate but increasing
• Willingness to be engaged in foreign affairs	Generally very low, but can be unpredictable	Sporadic, depending on the issue	Moderate but increasing
• Cognitive/analytic skills relevant to foreign affairs	Very low; mostly "non-attitudes"	Low, but sufficient for sensible "public judgment"; "cognitive misers"	Variable; ability for complex and multivariate thinking is increasing
• Stability of public opinion	Very low; emotion driven	Generally stable; habit driven	Variable; learning-driven

(continued on next page)

Table 7.1 *(continued)*
Public Opinion in Three Models of World Politics

	Realist	*Liberal*	*Postinternational*
• Sources of change in public opinion	Emotion; lack of coherent world view	Reasonable responses to events	Events; growth of analytic skills
• Manipulability of public opinion	High; microelectronic technology increases elite ability to manipulate public	Variable; role of media is crucial	Decreasing; microelectronic technology increases public information and skills
• Loyalties	Focused on nation-state	Nation-state; also other groups	Multiple; those to nation-state are declining in the face of "subgroupism"
• Criteria of legitimacy	Traditional; patriotism	Variable	Utilitarian; performance-based
Impact of public opinion:			
• Nature of engagement in foreign policy	Emotional; thus rarely rational	Rational—"low information rationality"	Increasingly engaged due to the "skill revolution"
• Impact of foreign policy	Often irrelevant	Often relevant	Often relevant; initiating as well as reacting
• Effects on quality of foreign policy	If engaged, often a barrier to effective foreign policies	If engaged, often a barrier against ill-advised policies	Variable, but increasing analytic skills enhance chance of favorable impact

run contrary to public sentiments. Because the public is likely to be interested in "nationality, justice, or traditional friendships and enmities," selling the proposition that yesterday's friend is today's enemy, and vice versa, may not be easy.[11] Realists have typically viewed both friends and enemies from an instrumental perspective; they are means to the common end of defending vital national interests. In contrast, according to realist critics, the public is more likely to view relations with other countries as ends in themselves. Thus, realists usually describe public opinion as a barrier to any thoughtful and coherent foreign policy, hindering efforts to promote national interests that may transcend the moods and passions of the moment.

Indeed, one of the worst realist nightmares is that leaders, who have a sound appreciation of vital national interests—that is, what is both desirable and possible—will be prevented from taking necessary actions by a public that is neither capable of understanding those interests nor willing to pay the price for protecting or promoting them. That nightmare scenario is exceeded only by one other, in which the public, emotionally aroused by some horrifying injustice, forces leaders to undertake actions that are unlikely to rectify the injustice, while also entailing high costs, perhaps even catastrophic ones. Several examples illustrate this point. Hans Morgenthau frequently cited French and British plans to send assistance to Finland, the victim of unprovoked Soviet aggression in 1939, as a paradigmatic example of the folly to which an emotional public can push governments; only Sweden's refusal to permit the aid to cross its territory prevented France and Britain, already at war with Nazi Germany, from adding the Soviet Union to its list of enemies.[12] The controversy about American policy toward China following the bloody crackdown on dissidents in Beijing featured warnings by such prominent realists as Henry Kissinger on the dangers of permitting public sentiments about human rights to stand in the way of prudent efforts to pursue American interests in the Far East.[13] An essay by George Kennan about the damaging role that the public allegedly played in the decision to use American troops to deliver humanitarian aid to Somalia is a more recent indictment of leaders—President Bush in this case—who should know better than to allow an emotional public to force them into undertakings that do not engage any vital national interests.[14]

Table 7.1 provides a brief summary of the realist perspective, as well as the liberal and postinternational ones, on public opinion.

LIBERAL PERSPECTIVES ON PUBLIC OPINION

A long liberal tradition, dating back at least to Jeremy Bentham, places public opinion at the center of legitimate and effective public policy. Bentham described public opinion, or "The Public-Opinion Tribunal," as "the sole remedy" for many problems of government. His "Plan for an Universal and Perpetual Peace" also proposed removing the veil of secrecy from the conduct of foreign affairs: "That secresy [sic] in the operation of the foreign department ought not to be endured in England, being equally repugnant to the interests of liberty and those of peace."[15] James Mill effectively summarized the liberal case for public opinion as a repository of wisdom: "every man, possessed of reason, is accustomed to weigh evidence, to be guided and determined by its preponderance. . . . [T]here is a moral certainty, though some few may be misguided, that the greatest number will judge aright."[16]

Rousseau and Kant developed similar themes with respect to public opinion and war. Monarchs may engage in wars for reasons that have nothing to do with the interests of their subjects. In contrast, the foreign policies of republics are more peaceful, at least in part because the public can play a constructive role in constraining policymakers; accountability to the public can restrain any war-making proclivities of leaders. Kant based his argument on the constraints that republics and nonrepublics face when they contemplate engaging in war. The former are likely to be more peaceful because the public, which bears most of the costs, will be cautious about engaging in war: "If (as must inevitably be the case, given this form of constitution) the consent of the citizenry is required in order to determine whether or not there will be war, it is natural that they consider all its calamities before committing themselves to so risky a game." The situation is quite different under nonrepublican constitutions, according to Kant, because, "The easiest thing in the world is to declare war. Here the ruler is not a fellow citizen, but the nation's owner, and war does not affect his tables, his hunt, his places of pleasure, his court festivals, and so on."[17]

Among nineteenth-century statesmen, William Gladstone most explicitly adhered to the liberal vision "which favors the pacific, not the bloody settlement of disputes, which aims at permanent and not temporary adjustments; above all, which recognizes as a tribunal of paramount authority, the general judgement of civilized mankind."[18] The essence of the liberal thesis is thus a distinction between the peaceful public and leaders who may, for a broad range of reasons, pursue policies that lead to war. British foreign minister Ernest Bevin reiterated the Kantian case for public opinion as a barrier to war when he told Parliament: "There has never been a war yet which, if the facts had been put calmly before ordinary folk, could not have been prevented. The common man is the greatest protection against war."[19]

World War I, which might be described as the first public-relations war, was an especially significant milestone in the realist-liberal debate on public opinion. President Wilson's hopes for a new postwar world order depended significantly on democratizing foreign affairs and diplomacy. In his war message of April 2, 1917, he declared that,

> A steadfast concert for peace can never be maintained except by partnership of democratic nations. No autocratic government could be trusted to keep faith within it or observe its covenants. It must be a league of honor, a partnership of opinion. . . . Only free people can hold their purpose and their honor steady to a common end and prefer the interests of mankind to any narrow interest of their own.[20]

"Open covenants openly arrived at," an important feature of Bentham's blueprint for perpetual peace, was the first of Wilson's Fourteen Points and among his most important procedural prescriptions for reforming an international order in which secret diplomacy allegedly had dragged nation after nation into the catastrophic war against the will and interests of its ordinary citizens. The last of the Fourteen Points, creation of a general international organization, had a similar goal of bringing diplomacy within the purview of world public opinion. During the war Wilson had stated:

> The counsels of plain men have become on all hands more simple and straightforward and more unified than the counsels of sophisticated men of affairs, who still retain the impression that they are playing a game of power and are playing for high stakes. This is why I have said that this is a people's war, not a statesman's. Statesmen must follow the clarified common thought or be broken.[21]

Liberal approaches to world politics, especially as articulated by President Wilson during and after World War I, came under merciless attack from realists during the period of more than a half century encompassing the prelude to World War II, that conflict itself, and the Cold War that followed soon after the defeat of Nazi Germany and Imperial Japan. But the end of the Cold War and the replacement of authoritarian regimes by democratic ones in many parts of the world have revived interest in liberal theories, notably in the thesis of "democratic zones of peace." The resuscitation of liberal theories has, in turn, contributed to a reconsideration of the realist "Almond-Lippmann consensus" on the dubious quality and damaging impact of public opinion. An even more dramatic reassessment of the public emerges from Rosenau's postinternational model of world politics, to which we now turn.

THE POSTINTERNATIONAL PERSPECTIVE
ON PUBLIC OPINION

The postinternational perspective has transformed members of the general public from passive and largely voiceless spectators to central actors in world politics. The metamorphosis is the result of significant changes in a multitude of individual traits, including modes of learning, analytic skills, cognitive maps, role scenarios, cathectic capabilities, compliance orientations, legitimacy sentiments, and political loyalties.[22] Thanks largely to the microelectronic revolution, ordinary people in even the least developed areas of the world now have access to a vast new array of information sources, some of which lie beyond the ability of authoritarian governments to control. Thus, unlike the situation that prevailed only a few decades ago, it has now become possible for most of the planet's five billion people to compare their lot, not only with immediate neighbors, but also with those living in the adjoining country, or even half a world away.

Although the postinternational perspective does not suggest that members of the general public are uniformly well informed about world affairs, it posits that they are acquiring sufficient information as well as the enhanced analytical skills necessary to make politically relevant judgments, even complex ones. For example, readily available information about the social, political, and economic gap between their own situations and those of others—and the resulting sense of relative deprivation—can be a powerful source of motivation for political action. At the same time, the revolution in communications technology has increased the ability of the general public to articulate its demands, mobilize for purposes of promoting its interests, and take action if governments are unwilling or incapable of satisfying them.

Among the most consequential changes for world politics are those arising from the general public's sentiments about political legitimacy and loyalties to the state. Citizens have traditionally regarded the state as legitimate if it was able to maintain peace within its borders and provide protection from external threats. Their willingness to do so was heightened by patriotic sentiments and loyalties to the symbols and institutions of the state, as well as habits of compliance to authorities.

In contrast, the postinternational depiction of the general public is vastly different. Rather than according legitimacy and loyalty out of sentiment and habit, the postinternational citizen is a more autonomous, savvy utilitarian with a well-developed sense of how the state should be performing to satisfy his demands. Depending on that performance, he is prepared either to bestow or to withhold his loyalties. Whereas the traditional citizen would respond favorably to the toast, "My country, right or wrong," today's citizen is more likely, according to the postinternational perspective, to ask his country, "What have you done for me lately?"

Because demands on states, even the wealthiest ones, are likely to expand faster than the resources to meet them, the replacement of traditional with performance criteria of legitimacy is widespread and has important political consequences. As the gap between citizen expectations and state performance widens, the focus of political loyalties is shifting to subgroups, including but not limited to those rooted in ethnicity, religion, tribe, language, class, or combinations of these attributes. Whether the subgroups exist wholly within states or transcend national boundaries, increasing loyalties to them serve to fragment the state.

Technological advances have often been perceived as having contributed to the growth of the state and the ability of ruling authorities to cajole, manipulate, or coerce compliance by the public. The postinternational perspective recognizes that modern communications technology can be put into the service of ruling authorities; it also emphasizes, however, that the microelectronic revolution has at the same time enhanced the ability of ordinary citizens to pose effective challenges to regimes and states and thereby to become important actors in the dramas of world politics.

WHAT DOES THE EVIDENCE TELL US ABOUT THE PUBLIC?

Proponents of realism, liberalism, and postinternationalism can point to some important evidence supporting their perspectives on the nature of the public and its impact on the conduct of foreign affairs. Because a thorough analysis of the evidence is far beyond the scope of a single chapter, this review will only touch upon a few of the more general points that can be cited by supporters of the three perspectives.

Some realists criticize the public for holding parochial, myopic, and chauvinistic attitudes; according to Alvin Johnson, "As in the bosom of the earth vestiges of all earlier life may still be found, so in the bosom of public opinion are to be found vestiges of the early dinosaurs of thought."[23] But the strongest card in the realist's hand is the consistent and compelling evidence that the general public remains very poorly informed about almost all aspects of public affairs and, most especially, of world politics. Whether measured by absolute standards or compared to citizens of other developed nations, the level of public information is especially low in the United States.[24] In the same vein, realists argue that the meager store of public information amounts to little more than random bits of knowledge that lack any structure or coherence. Consequently, mass opinions can shift in quite unpredictable, perhaps even random, patterns.

Much of the microelectronic revolution originated in the United States; the United States ranks at or near the top of countries in the per capita ownership of radios, television sets, VCRs, facsimile machines, and personal computers; and it has the highest percentage of students enrolled in postsecondary educational institutions. These facts notwithstanding, there are few indications that the availability of more information has given rise to increased interest or engagement of the American public in the political process. And when it does choose to become engaged, realists ask, how can such an informationally impoverished public possibly make a valuable contribution to the quality of foreign policy? Thus the conclusion that the profound doubts expressed by de Tocqueville, Lippmann, Kennan, and other realists have lost none of their relevance.

Liberals do not deny that most members of the general public have a very limited store of factual information about world affairs; the evidence on this point is, after all, quite overwhelming. Their responses tend to take several forms. First, they often question whether the kinds of factual questions that the public has such difficulty answering provide a sufficient basis for the dolorous conclusions of realists. Even if average citizens have great difficulty in naming world leaders, identifying parties to international disputes, or locating countries on a map of the world, they are nevertheless capable of expressing "public judgment" on such important questions as the nature of national interests, the degree to which they may be engaged in a given situation, and the appropriate responses when those interests are challenged.[25] This ability has been described as "low information rationality."[26]

Second, even though the members of the general public may be poorly informed about the factual aspects of international affairs, their attitudes are in fact structured in moderately coherent ways, even if they do not fit the intellectual's definition of coherence.[27] Indeed, low information and an ambiguous international environment may actually motivate rather than preclude having some type of attitude structure. "Cognitive misers" may use a limited number of beliefs to make sense of a wide range of facts and events.

Finally, reacting to the realist prescription that foreign policy is too important to be left to the vagaries of public whims—that only experts can cope effectively with a dangerous world—liberals point to the rather substantial evidence that aggregate opinions tend to reflect events and trends in the real world and that, when shifts in public attitudes do take place, they are neither random nor systematically out of touch with reality. Indeed, the public sometimes "gets it right" even before the experts. As two veteran pollsters put it, "The American people do not show themselves as fickle and prone to sudden shifts in points of view, but rather as reasonably sensible and shrewd observers of the global environment."[28]

Direct political actions rather than surveys provide the most persuasive support for the postinternational perspective on the public. Recent years have witnessed many and sometimes dramatically effective uprisings against ineffective, corrupt, and authoritarian governments. Demonstrations against stolen elections by outraged citizens of Belgrade, beginning at the end of 1996 and continuing for many weeks into 1997, forced the Milosevic government in Serbia to acknowledge opposition victories and restore the winning candidates to their city council offices. This is but one demonstration of how ordinary citizens can mobilize for action against authoritarian regimes; they have done so in countries as disparate as Russia, Poland, Albania, the Philippines, East Germany, South Africa, China, Burma, Romania, Iran, Hungary, Bulgaria, and Czechoslovakia. Not all of these movements have been successful and some, such as in China, ultimately have been crushed with tragic consequences for the protesters. But even the failed ones have left indelible images such as the photo of a single young Chinese man standing up to one of the tanks deployed to crush the Tienanmen Square protest movements. There is also evidence that the products of the microelectronic revolution have played an indispensable role in mobilizing the protest movements. For example, videotapes of the assassination of Benino Aquino by the Philippine army played a critical role in rallying the public against the corrupt Marcos regime.

Finally, evidence of "subgroupism" abounds, not only in war-torn post–Cold War states such as Bosnia and parts of the former Soviet Union, but also in long-established democratic states, including Canada and the United States.

CONCLUSION

The postinternational perspective clearly depicts the public and its role in ways that differ significantly from the realist and liberal renditions. Most importantly, it emphasizes that the average citizen is an active player rather than a passive and indifferent observer of world politics. Does it, however, provide us with a clearer set of lenses for analyzing and understanding political dynamics in a world that is, indeed, characterized by turbulence? After posing three questions this conclusion turns to some research tasks that might shed additional light on its validity.

First, has the microelectronic revolution really enhanced the political skills of the general public? These technologies have certainly revolutionized entertainment and helped to create and sustain our most widely known national "heroes"—the celebrities of sports, movies, television, and popular music that much of the public can identify and whose achievements, lives, and foibles are staples in the popular media. Is there compelling evidence that the microelectronic revolution has stimulated a comparable interest in politics or enhanced the quality of political discourse? Although casting a ballot on election day is one of the least demanding forms of political involvement, voter turnout in established democracies suggests that interest in politics has, at best, remained rather stable in some democracies since the end of World War II, while it has fallen rather steadily in others, including Japan and the United States. Indeed, although poll taxes and other efforts to prevent minority Americans from voting have been sharply curtailed during the past several decades, voter turnout in the 1996 election was the lowest since 1924.

Second, do features of the postinternational perspective actually represent fundamentally altered political dynamics that are transforming world politics, or are they more accurately depicted as stages in recurring cycles? For example, there appear to be some striking similarities between the 1920s and 1990s, at least in the impact of new communications technologies in the United States. The earlier period also witnessed major innovations, including the introduction of the radio and national networks, talking movies, and a vast increase in ownership of telephones and automobiles. All of these new technologies made it possible for the average citizen to learn more about the world and to have greater contact with citizens in distant parts of the country. Few students of the period have discerned a concomitant increase in interest and participation in politics—that would await the great depression of the 1930s—but almost all of them agree the impact on most forms of entertainment and popular culture was enormous.

Similarly, the widespread availability today of audiotapes, videotapes, VCRs, personal computers, facsimile machines, desktop publishing, cable television networks, e-mail, and the Internet has increased by many orders of magnitude the information available to the public throughout the world, but once again the use of this technology for entertainment appears to have outstripped by a vast margin its impact on politics; indeed, it may have done a great deal to blur the line between politics and entertainment.

Third, is the postinternational perspective on the public equally valid for all countries? The most impressive evidence of the public's enhanced political skills, participation, and impact is to be found in the countries of the former Soviet empire, as well as in a few others such as the Philippines and South Africa, in which ordinary citizens were able to topple corrupt and authoritarian regimes. Yet, after achieving a greater public voice, have many citizens in even these countries experienced reduced interest in public affairs?

These questions suggest the need to go beyond anecdotes by generating systematic evidence relevant to the postinternational depiction of the public. A research agenda might include but not be limited to some of these tasks.

1. Development of indicators of political skills and participation. Some standard methods for assessing political skills—for example, asking respondents factual questions about politics—are not likely to do more than confirm what we already know. Part of the task is therefore to develop indicators that will provide better evidence about the extent to which there has in fact been a "skills revolution." The same is true of political participation. Voting turnout, while not irrelevant, is at best a one-dimensional measure. It would be helpful to add others to measure and depict trends about participation in public affairs.

2. Development of indicators for "subgroupism," one of the key concepts of the postinternational perspective. Are publics generally shifting their legitimacy sentiments and loyalties from the state to subgroups, with the consequence that the former are being fragmented? If so, are the changes cyclical or do they represent a more or less permanent transformation of public sentiments?

3. Process tracing to measure the impact of the public. This is a most difficult aspect of research on the public. At times the impact can be obvious, as it was when Lech Walesa led the

Solidarity movement to power in Poland, or when the Russian public took to the streets to protest the coup against the Gorbachev regime in 1991. But the postinternational perspective also posits changes that arise from less dramatic actions whose impact may be more subtle but no less significant over the longer run.

4. Comparative research. It seems important to assess how localized or widespread the dynamics outlined by the postinternational perspective might be, indicating the need for cross-national research.

In summary, the postinternational paradigm presents an intriguing and sufficiently plausible depiction of the public to warrant additional development and investigation. Until we have more systematic evidence on the nature and role of the public, and the political dynamics to which they give rise, perhaps the most appropriate conclusion is that unique Scottish verdict: "Not proven."

NOTES

1. James N. Rosenau, *Public Opinion and Foreign Policy: An Operational Formulation* (New York: Random House, 1961), p. 34.

2. Rosenau, *Public Opinion and Foreign Policy*, p. 36.

3. James N. Rosenau, *Turbulence in World Politics: A Theory of Change and Continuity* (Princeton, N.J.: Princeton University Press, 1990), p. 25.

4. Rosenau, *Turbulence in World Politics*, p. 130.

5. Ibid., p. 205.

6. Alexander Hamilton, John Jay, and James Madison, *The Federalist* 1787–1788 (New York: Modern Library, 1937), nos. 62–64, 75.

7. Alexis de Tocqueville, *Democracy in America*, vol. 1 (New York: Vintage, 1958), pp. 243–45.

8. Hans J. Morgenthau, *Politics among Nations*, 5th ed. (New York: Knopf, 1978), p. 558.

9. Walter Lippmann, *Public Opinion* (New York: Macmillan, 1922); Lippmann, *The Phantom Public* (New York: Harcourt Brace, 1925); Lippmann, *Essays in the Public Philosophy* (Boston: Little Brown, 1955); Edward Hallett Carr, *The Twenty Years' Crisis, 1919–1939: An Introduction to the Study of International Relations* (London: Macmillan, 1941); George F. Kennan, *American Diplomacy, 1900–1950* (New York: Mentor Books, 1951); Thomas F. Bailey, *The Man in the Street: The Impact of Public Opinion on Foreign Policy* (New York: Macmillan, 1948); and Gabriel Almond, *The American People and Foreign Policy* (New York: Harcourt Brace, 1950).

10. Lippmann, *The Phantom Public*, p. 14.

11. Quincy Wright, *A Study of War* (Chicago: University of Chicago Press, 1942), p. 265.

12. Morgenthau, *Politics among Nations*, pp. 12–13.

13. Henry A. Kissinger, *Diplomacy* (New York: Simon and Schuster, 1994).

14. George F. Kennan, "Somalia, through a Glass Darkly," *New York Times*, September 30, 1993, p. A25.

15. Jeremy Bentham, *Works of Jeremy Bentham*, 11 vols. (New York: Russell and Russell, 1962), 8: 561, 2: 547.

16. James Mill, "On Liberty of the Press for Advocating Resistance to Government: Being Part of an Essay for the Encyclopedia Britannica," 6th ed. (1821; reprint, New York: Free Speech League, 1913): pp. 16, 18.

17. Immanuel Kant, *Perpetual Peace and Other Essays on Politics, History, and Morals*. Translated with an introduction by Ted Humphrey, (1796; reprint, Indianapolis, Ind.: Hackett Publishing, 1983), p. 113.

18. Quoted in Kissinger, *Diplomacy*, p. 164.

19. Ernest Bevin. Speech to the House of Commons, United Kingdom, November 1945. Quoted in John Bartlett, *Familiar Quotations*. 13th ed. (Boston: Little Brown, 1955), p. 926.

20. *New York Times*, April 3, 1917, p. 1.

21. Quoted in Carr, *Twenty Years' Crisis*, p. 44.

22. Rosenau, *Turbulence in World Politics*, p. 211.

23. Alvin Johnson, *On German Pacification*.

24. Michael A. Dimock and Samuel L. Popkin, "Who Knows?: Political Knowledge in a Comparative Perspective," (paper presented at the annual meeting of the Midwestern Political Science Association, Chicago, April 3, 1993).

25. Daniel Yankelovich, *Coming to Public Judgment: Making Democracy Work in a Complex World* (Syracuse, N.Y.: Syracuse University Press, 1991); Yankelovich and I. M. Destler, eds. *Beyond the Beltway: Engaging the Public in U.S. Foreign Policy* (New York: W.W. Norton, 1994); Alan F. Kay, "Discovering the Wisdom of the People," *World Business Academy Perspectives* 6 (1992): 19–28; and Kay, *Uncovering the Public View on Policy Issues: Evidence that Survey Research Can Address Intractable Problems in Governance* (Washington, D.C.: Americans Talk Issues Foundation, 1992).

26. Samuel L. Popkin, *The Reasoning Voter* (Chicago: University of Chicago Press, 1991).

27. Yankelovich, *Coming to Public Judgment*.

28. Lloyd Free and William Watts, "Internationalism Comes of Age . . . Again." *Public Opinion* 3 (April–May 1980): 50. That conclusion is supported by a number of other important studies, including: Bruce W. Jentleson, "The Pretty Prudent Public: Post-Vietnam American Opinion on the Use of Military Force," *International Studies Quarterly* 36 (1992): 49–73; Benjamin I. Page and Robert Y. Shapiro, *The Rational Public: Fifty Years of Trends in Americans' Policy Preferences* (Chicago: University of Chicago Press, 1992); and Eugene R. Wittkopf, *Faces of Internationalism: Public Opinion and American Foreign Policy* (Durham, N.C.: Duke University Press, 1990).

PART 3

Postinternationalism: A Paradigm for the Twenty-First Century?

Postinternationalism is far from a refined, testable paradigm and the authors in this part attempt to design ways to move Rosenau's writings toward a more analytically useful framework.

Mary Durfee begins the process by defining what a complex system is and what it is not. Drawing on other frames of reference, most notably, in the hard sciences, but also extending the analogy to the U.S. Constitution, Durfee pushes postinternationalism toward a more critical examination.

Joseph Lepgold follows in this form, placing postinternationalism in the liberal tradition and identifying areas where hypotheses may be found. Lepgold's arguments are particularly relevant to much of the discussion in the field today and locates the postinternational paradigm neatly within those debates.

Ralph DiMuccio and Eric Cooper offer a somewhat different view of the process by examining the relevance of postinternationalism to the field of international relations. They examine this question by performing a citation comparison with Kenneth Waltz's *Theory of International Politics*. While it may be early to make such a comparison, this parsimonious analysis is particularly true to many of the tenets of Rosenau's own perspective of scholarship, which is also carefully delineated in this piece as well.

Yale Ferguson concludes this part with a cry for innovation in the field of international relations and invites the discipline to move beyond its narrow focus on state's behavior. Ferguson argues that the degree to which postinternationalism will become a useful paradigm relies on the extent to which it is adopted both as a frame of reference in the study of international relations and perhaps even futher, as an organizational division within associations dedicated to understanding the world around us.

The final part of the book is "A Postinternationalist's Response." It is here that James Rosenau responds to his critics and explores his own perceptions of the utility of the postinternational paradigm and its prospects for the future.

CHAPTER 8

Constituting Complexity: Order and Turbulence in World Politics

Mary Durfee

When the framers of the U.S. Constitution set out to do their work, they had in mind a model of the physical world. This physical world was mechanistic and driven by laws that could yield understanding of both past and future states of the system. They thought of the movement of the heavens and built into the document the weights and counterweights, pulleys and gears of a clock. It was to be a "machine that would run of itself."[1] A machine that would run of itself would, of course, be a perpetual-motion machine. We know that kind of machine is not possible to build in the physical world. And yet, there is a peculiarity to the machine they wrote; it does go and it has done so in environments quite different from the one in which it was invented. Even the civil war that almost stopped the machine was over the source of its running, namely the balance between the centralization and decentralization of power.

The document works because it is always becoming something new. Perpetual motion is not possible, but perpetual organization might be. Perpetual motion means the machine will do the exact same thing over and over and over again; perpetual organization means it will do themes and variations endlessly—and may "live" at the very edges of its range of viability. In this sense, the Constitution encourages self-organization

I want to thank Don Durfee, Yale Ferguson, Matt Hoffmann, David Johnson, and Ole Holsti for reading earlier versions of this chapter. They improved the final result and caused none of its weaknesses.

137

by promoting local interactions in a decentralized system; it relies on individual agents employing their knowledge of the system to make the system work. There is no mention in it of parties or committees or interest groups, but they evolved nonetheless.

The "machine" the framers built was what science might now call a complex adaptive system. No clock this. Complex adaptive systems exist everywhere; they may be life itself. They arise at the edge of chaos between the certainty of death and the uncertainty of chaos. These systems originate when individual agents, following simple rules, produce an organization of systems that one could not predict simply from the original players and rules; system and agents coevolve. They are one type of dynamic system. Herbert Simon said these systems are "made up of a large number of parts that interact in a nonsimple way. In such systems, the whole is more than the sum of its parts, not in an ultimate, metaphysical sense, but in the important pragmatic sense that, given the properties of the parts and the laws of their interaction, it is not a trivial matter to infer the properties of the whole."[2]

Unlike the Framers who sought to set in motion a clock with orderly and predictable behavior, James N. Rosenau set out to understand the sources of instability in political systems in his *Turbulence in World Politics*. Like the Constitution, his framework is no clocklike machine. Although world politics may not be as patterned as the American constitutional system, the world(s) he described in *Turbulence* fit the characteristics of complex adaptive systems, and not just chaotic ones. Turbulent, chaotic systems, where systems reach no stable state between potential equilibria are just one type of dynamic system. Complex ones, where order appears for free and without command, represent another. So, while Rosenau emphasizes the destruction of patterns in *Turbulence,* the theory contains much that accounts for their reappearance.

This chapter attempts to separate the chaotic from the complex in Rosenau's theory. It is just a first, rough cut; but, in clarifying the two types of dynamic systems better, we will see even more clearly the utility of postinternational theory for understanding and explaining world politics. Critical assumptions in his theory, namely, the existence of the multicentric world and the changing capacities of individuals, are themselves orderly patterns. Thus, the theory, for all its emphasis on turbulence, depends on order. This order is not merely in the sense that turbulence implies some nonturbulent time. Rather, it has a theory-specific meaning. Complexity's "order out of chaos" is not equivalent to stability from instability; rather it represents the processes by which patterns emerge and refresh themselves.

Separating the complex and the chaotic in his postinternational theory does require reshaping the relationships between empirical concepts. In brief, this is the argument. Rosenau's notion of individuals being able to move between habit and adaptation on the "habdaptive function," is partially misspecified. This function is not disembodied from systems around the individual. While this change moderates to some degree the profoundly "micro" orientation of his theory, it still gives strong play to the importance of individuals in world politics. The second change recasts the relational parameter by allowing it to operate in two places: between the micro and macro parameters, as Rosenau describes, and also between the state- and multicentric worlds. In the first instance, micro actors may, through their learning, change themselves and shape the macro parameter. Turbulence theory, however, has no ready way to explore how interactions between the two worlds in the macro parameter may yield patterns in either or both worlds. Thus, there are times when it may be best to place the relational parameter between the two worlds rather than between the macro and micro parameters. Placed in this way, it becomes a kind of "space" in which new patterns of collective life form, change, and weaken.

COMPLEX SYSTEMS

Before setting off to constitute complexity from *Turbulence in World Politics*, let us consider the nature of complex adaptive systems. This exercise should help show why both chaotic and complex dynamics are present in postinternational theory. There may well be times in world politics where instability of a fundamental kind takes hold of a system; far more frequently, however, systems adapt over time to new inputs and develop new capacities to use information through enduring processes. Change that produces orderly patterns is the realm of complex, adaptive systems.

Six Characteristics of Complex Adaptive Systems

What is it that complex adaptive systems do and how do they do it? This question is currently puzzling biophysical scientists as well as social scientists and historians. I propose we use six propositions about these systems.[3] Propositions 1 and 6 answer the question what do they do, while 2 through 5 suggest how the systems come to perform their functions.

1. Complex adaptive systems distribute action over space and time. This means they are process dominant, rather than structure dominant.

2. The elements of the system contain the information of the system.

3. Local interaction rules (which are probabilistic) provide the central tie between individual and system; these provide the conjunction between internal rules of the individuals[4] and external constraints of the environment. Local interaction rules thus provide the bases for self-organization.

4. Micro choices based on the interplay of information and rules actually cause organization. In this situation new information is created by the interactions that is not contained in the interacting parts. In the process, both actor and system may change. The actor changes by updating imperfect knowledge of the consequences of action. The system changes when the updated knowledge retained by the elements of the system changes or reinforces the rules.

5. Complex adaptive systems have history (chaotic ones might be said to have a past).[5] Micro actors retain and use knowledge of history in making choices about action. Thus, past states of the system as well as the narrowing of "options" caused by the moving front of the system shape behavior; this use of knowledge can potentially produce adaptation.[6]

6. Complex systems provide resiliency against shifts to alternate-system states by allowing subsystems and individuals to operate at fluctuating, overlapping, and often wide ranges of variation.

Since these characteristics may seem unfamiliar, let's return to the example of the U.S. Constitution. This relatively familiar example, at least to U.S. readers, may aid in clarifying both the nature of complex adaptive systems and the ensuing discussion of postinternational politics. A look at any day in the United States (or any other country or organization) ought to cause wonder about the organization that does and does not appear. The Constitution balances between centralization and decentralization of power and between private and public action. Thus, it distributes action between coequal branches and between territorial units. It parses and distributes action through time through many checks and balances and other time-dependent processes (elections, the census). It also links individual choices and ambitions to these defined political spaces and times. As Madison put it in Federalist 51, "Ambition must be made to counteract ambition. The interest of the man must be connected with the constitutional rights of the place."[7] Thus micro actors are joined by relational rules to the macro structure and the entire system produces action neither might do in the absence of the other.

The rules that scatter interactions over time and space make action possible, but the parts of the system rarely operate at the same time on precisely the same problem. Therefore, considerable nonlinearity, even creativity, is possible. Thus, to use an environmental example, at any one time Congress might be passing a new environmental law, the president might be signing an international agreement on the environment, the EPA might be regulating via an existing congressional statute, the states might be passing their own variants of environmental law, and private organizations might be litigating a specific EPA decision through the courts in order to undo or advance a rule. All of these things can readily be explained, even qualitatively predicted, by the fairly simple rules of the Constitution. Yet, it is hard to say *exactly* how the system will look at any point in the future. Like a flock of birds that suddenly shifts direction, yet stays together, we can be fairly confident that the system will cohere by virtue of the rule-guided interactions between historically informed actors that operate the subsystems.

The many actors in the American system possess a range of information about the system, other actors, and themselves. As indicated in characteristic 5, they are likely to have historical information, although the extent of the information may vary dramatically between actors. Various actors also have an array of goals and scenarios as they act on current choices and anticipate the future. Thus, a regulated firm will be able to estimate what current EPA requirements and likely behavior will be, the pros and cons of trying to change the law, and how a court decision might affect them. This produces an interplay between expectations and anticipation, between continuities from the past and plans for change.

It requires micro-actor choice to make the potential organization manifest. The members of Congress (or of state legislatures) have to decide to change a law—and hope the executive will sign; the president has to launch his agencies to negotiate a new international agreement; EPA staffers have to write and apply regulations; the judges in courts have to decide a case. Once the choice is made, then both the choosers and others "nearby" who are influenced by the choice will update what they know about the system. Like the bird flock the actors in this system change direction not so much because there is a definite leader in the system, but because they "take cues" from the behaviors of others nearby. On the day of a court decision, especially if it is from the Supreme Court, the flock heads in one direction; if Congress and the president can agree on a new law, then the Court's decision may not matter. Those two outcomes are also, in theory, predictable from the rules we can all read for ourselves in the Constitution.

Very often some turbulence has to accompany a change in direction.[8] This happens often enough in politics: a pattern forms, deforms, and reforms as new actors or new conditions arrive. That firm working amidst environmental regulations is adjusting its behavior relative to other elements in the system at all times, and vice versa. Other inputs to the actors of the system come from the overlapping systems in which they participate. The firm probably stays alert to developments in technology, markets, and the regulations of other countries. It will be able to attend to these inputs only in varying degrees and this will be constrained by its own history, its own systems, its own people.

So why do we need these rambling, intersecting subsystems at all? Why is there so much organization in so many spots, all seemingly near the edge of collapse? This is where the sixth principle comes in. Ecologist C. S. Holling argues that complexity in biological systems increases their resiliency by helping both the individual components and the system resist a rapid change to a different system state. It also provides a setting for considerable evolutionary self-organization. He illustrates this claim with the example of temperature maintenance by mammals. "Five different mechanisms, from evaporative cooling to metabolic heat generation, control the temperature of endotherms. Each mechanism is not notably efficient by itself. Each operates over a somewhat different but overlapping range of conditions and with different efficiencies of response. It is this overlapping 'soft' redundancy that seems to characterize biological regulation of all kinds. It is not notably efficient or elegant in the engineering sense. But it is robust and continually sensitive to changes in internal body temperature."[9] This kind of "functional diversity" provides "great resilience to the system behavior."[10] In chaotic systems, many, many possible patterns open up, but no one can say if or when the system will settle on one. Complex systems, in contrast, provide a measure of stability against complete changes of system states by maintaining redundant subparts that do similar things. If failure or extreme stress in one part of the system appears, other interlinked systems can perhaps help maintain function.

COMPLEXITY IN ROSENAU'S TURBULENCE

Rosenau's *Turbulence in World Politics* goes a long way toward meeting the six characteristics of complex adaptive systems. Indeed, the subtitle of the book, "A Theory of Change and Continuity" intimates the potential his approach has for explaining emergent patterns. It already emphasizes micro-level behaviors. It is process dominant, in the sense that changes in one place can potentially influence others, but the history of the system constrains such change. "As perceived here, the parameters of a system are the wellsprings of continuity—the norms, procedures, and institutions evolved and tested through long experience that represent, as it were, 'history's dictates' and that thus exert pressure against any developments that might lead to fundamental transformations."[11] Rarely should we expect great turbulence, since the parameters with their variables of individuals, organizations, norms, and so forth ought to prevent shifts to alternate system states, such as the end of politics or, to use a much less radical version of a system shift, no territorial states. It is especially strong in showing how resiliency appears in world politics, because it highlights the many different mechanisms by which world politics transpire. Nevertheless, Rosenau emphasizes turbulence, not continuity.

The dynamics of change are also sometimes the dynamics of patterning. *Turbulence* relies heavily on patterns and this suggests how much transformation one can get through changes that are not turbulent. Organization appears at all scales in his theory. Organization here means orderliness—that a lively surface feeds on simple underlying rules. Orderliness, as mentioned before, does not mean stability; it means that ongoing processes will constantly present new opportunities for adaptation and failure. While Rosenau was most interested in exploring why disorder appears, the theory is at least as interesting for what it says or implies about how orderliness is sustained through nonparametric change. The orderliness in the theory does not come out clearly, however, because too little is made of local interactions and the history of the system he describes. Thus, critical features of his own system are not allowed to play out in *Turbulence*. Too little is made of the patterns he requires to build the theory and too much about discontinuity. Too much is based on recent snapshots, and too little on the shared history that moves initial conditions.

Parameters Change Variables and Variables Change Parameters

Normally, says Rosenau, variation within the parameters produces changes—but not transformation of the essential rules. On rare occasions, the variables that compose the three fundamental parameters of politics—micro, micro/macro (relational), and macro—eventually get so "beyond normal range" that they change the parameter itself. The parameter, for at least a bit, becomes a variable. Each parameter also interacts with the other two, at which point, Rosenau claims, the entire world political system goes into a turbulent period until the parameters re-equilibrate into a new system state. "These three parameters . . . are so intimately interrelated that if any one of them is disturbed by the dynamics of change, the other two become vulnerable as well, thereby increasing the likelihood that turbulence will overtake world politics."[12]

That parameters can become variables does not mean we choose variables and parameters willy-nilly. Rosenau argues we can avoid arbitrariness about what is a variable and what a parameter by emphasizing some aspects of a system as "more central to its functioning than others and as thus setting the conditions for the operation of the less central aspects."[13] This, in turn, means we could meaningfully compare a system over time and claim the one at point "B" is no longer behaving as it did at point "A." Rosenau looked at the world system today and compared it to earlier periods of the Westphalian system. What he saw suggested to him that old certainties about the dominance of states had faded; the central functioning of today's global system now included individuals and sovereignty-free actors (nonstate actors, for those less familiar with his term).

Another step used in *Turbulence* to determine whether a parameter has changed or whether variables have changed within the parameter requires an assessment of the abruptness of change. For Rosenau, abrupt, "breakpoint," change is nonlinear, evolutionary change is not. "[I]n evolutionary development parameter values shift systematically according to some constant additive or subtractive pattern, whereas in break point change parameter values pass beyond some threshold and shift exponentially."[14] This contention needs closer scrutiny.[15]

Parameters are parameters not because they are unchangingly stable (a point Rosenau well recognizes), but because they are continuous and remain recognizable over time.[16] Perhaps abrupt, "breakpoint" change is characteristic of chaotic systems, but complex adaptive ones rely on the surprises afforded by evolution and incrementalism. Fluctuations—even periods of chaotic behavior—will get "lost" over long periods of time: the further back one looks, the smoother patterns tend to get. It *is* worthwhile to remember that catastrophic change is possible; but, evolutionary processes can readily yield nonintuitive changes of considerable scale.

The evidence from nature both bolsters and weakens our respective claims about parameters and change. On the one hand, stability is a common feature of biological systems everywhere. On the other, change is a crucial feature for creating and maintaining that stability. Whether the change is so great that a new system has appeared—and how we would know while in the midst of it all—is quite troublesome. *Science*, the weekly journal of the American Association for the Advancement of Science, offers a ready place to see the problem of parameters versus variables, of turbulence versus complexity.

"Nothing is more constant about the nervous system than its ability to change."[17] The brain example represents constant change and reorganization. Some scientists in this area characterize the brain's processes as chaotic, and say one sign of brain disorder is often the arrival of regular, simple patterns. In the brain, simple signals may be a breakpoint sign of change. The healthy brain needs very short-term alterations in variables to maintain the stable parameters of the nervous system. This even includes constant physical reorganization of neural patterns. Change lies well within the parameters that set human (and other) behaviors.

Or consider the following examples of mass changes settling down around just a few main patterns and processes. Mammal species have changed over the last 65 million years in North America, but the number of genera, which has ranged from a high of 130 to a low of 60, has always returned to 90 and stayed there for millions of years.[18] "Life in the sea, with the exception of a brief creative frenzy half a billion years ago, has been in a rut." Six of the seven phyla now in the oceans appeared in the Cambrian—and the seventh showed up soon after. "If, as recent studies suggest, control 'isn't in the genome,' commented U.C. Berkeley scientist James Valentine, 'it must be in the ecosystem.' And if that is so, life's resilience in the face of mass extinctions also ensured 500 million years of monotony."[19]

The ancient fossil evidence seems to prove the "even-out" rule of long time; but, it also illustrates how utterly dependent the stability of parameters can be on where one sets them in analysis. Seven body types have stayed the course for half a billion years, even as genera and species and certainly phenotypes have come and gone by the thousands, if not millions. Just a handful of survivors of each phylum could repopulate the oceans after the total number of species were reduced 80–96 percent by the great mass extinction at the end of the Permian era (followed by other nearly as large catastrophes). Yet, if one focuses on the number of species, then the great extinctions represent massive parametric change. "As a result, 99.9 percent of all species that have ever lived are now extinct. As one statistical wag put it, 'To a first approximation all species are extinct.' "[20] A snapshot taken in the immediate aftermath of an extinction episode, might have prompted an observer to say life itself was on the verge of failure.

Taken from a different perspective, however, we find that extinctions certainly produced turbulence in many variables, but the parameters of life did not change. Put differently, a focus on species would suggest much breakpoint change at the level of variables, but not at the level of parameters. Species appearance, disappearance, and change are critical to life itself. The parameters of life *would* experience a shift to some alternate equilibrium, if either the *processes* of speciation ended or genetic information transfer (one of the speciation processes) failed. There is a parallelism between the extinctions of species and of political units. One could say that virtually all the territorially based political units that ever existed in human history have gone extinct, but the processes of politics—perhaps even world politics—have not. Thus, breakpoints may occur for species and empires and perhaps even for the modern state, but the evolutionary processes by which micro-level behaviors are aggregated may be quite stable.

Before claiming breakpoint change in parameters, we should, therefore, look first to see if political processes have changed notably. Some processes look familiar even over millennia: Territorial units constantly form themselves; political communities cycle between centralization and decentralization in their administration; individuals give and withdraw legitimacy. These processes may need much better explanation than political science now delivers, a point Rosenau acknowledges. "[M]ost of the diverse individuals that comprise a modern collectivity do not know each other, much less interact directly with each other, and yet somehow they acquire coherence and structure as a collective actor which develops, possesses, and uses resources on behalf of goals. That this occurs is self-evident, but to explain how it occurs is a stern challenge to our grasp of the human condition."[21] Aggregation processes, in sum, are where one might find parametric change.

Puzzling Patterns in Turbulence

Turbulence itself relies on lodes of coherence and preexisting organization. First, consider the puzzling presence of the multicentric world. This is organization on a vast scale, such scale, in fact, that it can successfully compete with the world of states—leading the bifurcation of the macro parameter into Rosenau's two worlds of world politics:

state- and multicentric. In a discipline that expends considerable energy on the behavior of states, the act of raising this other world of sovereignty-free actors coequal to states is at the very least a bold move. It might even suggest major change in world politics. But the fact that the multicentric world is there at all—it didn't come from a cabbage patch—suggests that change has been evolving between and within society and states for a long time. This evolutionary, complex view is evidenced by the fact Rosenau can list *rules* of interaction for sovereignty-bound actors in the state-centric world and the sovereignty-free actors of the multicentric world.[22] Rules would make little sense indeed unless typical patterns and strategies for working within them existed. Thus, while the situation for states and multi-centric actors alike may be more dynamic than it was, it remains orderly. Processes are at work that permit new patterns to emerge and often to persist for some time.

Second, there is the puzzle of more competent micro actors, who are better able to grasp how they can influence—or at least how they are influenced by—others, be they leaders, institutions, or the unfolding dynamics of a faraway decision. This, too, suggests discernible patterns, even as those patterns may be vulnerable to more precise actions by micro actors. What are they "seeing" and "expecting?" The answer seems to be something like this: "scenarios of the future begin to project across longer time spans and alternative explanations and perspectives begin to be acknowledged and considered more frequently."[23] Yet to do this, the micro actor must have *patterns in mind*. Rosenau's explanation of competent individuals, to work at all, entails assuming that individuals have knowledge of the impinging array of systems around them and in which they participate. Yet the turbulence he describes shows how increased micro capacities destabilize the other parameters. In that case, there would be a point where turbulence would have to stop, because micro knowledge of patterns would no longer be of use. How much use of a new path between what individuals want and the larger collectivities that can support that desire makes for a new patterned relationship? How much micro competence creates or preserves the path, and how much use of a path destroys it for others?

Exploring the Micro Parameter through the Habdaptive Function

For Rosenau the ultimate source for turbulence in world politics is the changed capacities of individuals.[24] "What is needed is a model organized around a central premise in which the form and direction of micro action is conceived to spring from a combination of habits that perpetuate continuity and orientations that allow for thoughtful estimates and are open to change. It is the shifting balance between rote behavior and adaptive learning that forms the conditions of postinternational politics"[25] He calls individuals who achieve an active balance between habit and adaptation, habdaptive actors. Thus, "[T]urbulence has engulfed world politics partly, even largely, because citizens and officials have moved away from the habit end of the learning continuum and towards the adaptive end."[26] Given the significance of individuals for his theory, considerable attention must be placed on how change within the micro parameter occurs and on how change there relates to the other parameters, if we are to constitute complexity from *Turbulence*.

The behavior of individuals in a complex adaptive system is constrained by the systems around them. This is because the individual elements in a complex adaptive system contain the information of the system. In complex (biological) systems, individual actors learn, they even anticipate the future. This does not seem to be the case in turbulent systems, where, randomly, a point in a system may suddenly find itself elsewhere in the system or subject to new systemic rules. Learning does not really work in a chaotic system, nor will habit. Since the habdaptive function marks an individual's place on a continuum between habit and adaptation, it is unlikely that chaotical dynamics originate here. The habdaptive function only exists in the realm of complex adaptive systems.

The nature of the continuum—what is habit and what is adaptation—is limited by the systems that support it. We can imagine settings where individuals are flung, suddenly, from one system to another. European arrival in the New World effectively did this for the indigenous peoples. The original inhabitants certainly tried to anticipate and understand the unfolding events around them; but, at least at first, the intersection of these two worlds was so discontinuous, that very little reasoning was useful. Through no fault of their own, indigenous peoples must have felt habit was no longer an option and adaptation must have seemed nearly random. The very stability of the habdaptive function depends on other systems.[27] The interaction of native individuals with the foreign systems destroyed elements of the habdaptive function, and with it the individual's command of the history of the system. As Chief Plenty Coups explained, "when the buffalo went away the hearts of my people fell to the ground, and they could not lift them up again. After this nothing happened."[28] Of course, his people, the Crow, continue to exist. They live, however, in someone else's world and in someone else's history. This is what it means for an individual to live in a chaotical, rather than in a complex adaptive system.

Rosenau argues that the habdaptive function, always engaged, becomes more plastic when learning is encouraged. Learning, "and the change that follows it, can occur in one or both of two ways: (1) when external stimuli are persistently and startlingly new; (2) when new skills and orientations develop within the actor."[29] A war, or its end, is an example of the former; the microelectronic revolution is an example of the latter. These distinctions are not actually so clear cut, since adding a computer to one's life can be a persistently and startlingly new stimulus, just as learning to use a bayonet during war develops new skills and orientations.

As systems evolve, individuals may adjust. The adjustment is not likely to be uniform, since the individual's connections to the assorted systems will be stronger or weaker, moving slowly or rapidly. Individuals shift along the continuum as the novel becomes mundane or the familiar disappears. Consider centenarians. They remember a world before W.W.I, a political world where the Austro-Hungarian and Ottoman empires still existed. They perhaps served in that awful war or grieved over the loved ones who died. Their homes may or may not have had electricity and certainly did not have radio or TV for decades after their birth. Horses were commoner than cars when they were young. In American politics, the federal government got the right to tax personal income only in 1913, and women got the right to vote in 1920. And yet, these centenarians raised families, went to war, bought radios, learned to drive cars, paid their taxes to Washington, and voted coed.

Rosenau says individuals have become more cognitively and emotionally competent due to changes since W.W.II in communications[30] and transportation technologies. As a consequence, their behaviors can no longer be taken for granted by elites. Individuals may be more willing to give and withdraw legitimacy to leaders, thus the relational parameter is weakened because individuals may emphasize subgroupism, nation, or supranational authorities; this in turn causes considerable tumult in the macro parameter. He says, as well, that citizens are applying a new standard to assess whether to continue allegiances to leaders or organizations: competence.

Are the revolutions in microelectronics and global transportation really important to explaining the extent and plasticity of the habdaptive function? To the degree the new technologies disrupt the systems that prop up the habdaptive function, they matter a great deal. Rosenau notes the way every fax machine in China was sent information on the Tiananmen Square demonstrations; that may have sustained the demonstrations longer than they might otherwise have lasted. Similarly, the widespread use of air express packages—or people taking themselves from place to place in a few hours—greatly complicates the problem of control, whether for trade, terrorism, or disease. A new virus found at the ragged edge between a virgin forest and urban sprawl can be spread everywhere in the world in twenty-four hours. "[T]he Boeing 747 has become the vector of the AIDS virus," commented one epidemiologist, semiseriously.[31] That, certainly, was not possible until recently.

Yet, technology may not matter as much for the adaptive capacities of people as Rosenau seems to think. The technological revolutions he notes as key exogenous factors contributing to the onset of turbulence only matter when they impinge on the relational, (micro-macro) parameter. Technology changes, per se, do not enlarge the habdaptive function, but they may bridge or connect subsystems, so that micro actions move with greater force. Local interaction rules in one domain may touch rules in another; thus, action gets redistributed through the subsystems. What makes these technological changes destabilizing is not an individual's ability or inability to adapt to them. What matters is the way once largely unconnected subsystems become connected by technologies, often on quite short time scales.

What about his claim that increased competence leads individuals to reallocate loyalties? Do individuals have any sense as to where they are redirecting them? Do individuals sense when they cross systems? These are empirical questions, and worth the effort of pursuit. Certainly elites and professionals engage in "forum shopping" to find the best level of governance for coping with a given problem. A manager with one of the many industry trade associations located in Washington, D.C. once complained to me about how Congress had moved some regulatory decisions from the national to the state level. He wanted at least national-level rules, but he would have prefered the rules be hammered out through discussions at the OECD level. But what about nonelites? Everyday citizens may take advantage of differing rules for some personal issues, like marriage and divorce, but do they ever think much about what mode of governance would help them achieve other goals?

Rosenau begins to answer this question by arguing that individuals use performance and proof criteria to judge leaders and collectivities. These criteria weaken the hold of leaders—or at least make retaining a hold a more costly affair. But these criteria also suggest a ready source of reorganization even as they may sustain turbulence in world politics.[32] For example, one of my graduate students told me of the time she worked in a midwest state agricultural office located in a county seat. Men in bib overalls and baseball caps would come by and talk about farming. She was struck by how much they talked about global warming. They were up on all the latest theories, which they then applied to local conditions in order to assess the merits of the theories. They speculated on the best policies to avert disaster on their own farms and globally; they even explored various roles for governments (at all levels) and private organizations. Their well-structured scenarios on cause and effects could lead to decisive behaviors and demands on governments, but these demands might increase the capacity of the governments to govern. These individuals might well resist policies that would worsen global warming, but they might reallocate it constructively toward government policies that would tackle the problem.

Rethinking the Relational Parameter

Turbulence, noted Rosenau, is a feature of flows. Complexity is a feature of local interactions; it is more network than flow.[33] The relational parameter in Rosenau's theory can accommodate either flows or networks. Yet, it seems to be underspecified, perhaps even misplaced. Rather than thinking of it as lying only between the micro and macro, it might be better to think of it as a "T" lying between the multicentric and state-centric worlds, as well as between the micro and macro parameters. This way, we could more readily imagine how information and actions between the micro and macro parameters flows, and also have a "space" in which the state-centric and multi-centric worlds network with each other. The outcome of these changing flows and networks is likely to be organization at many different scales, not turbulence. The emergence of complex orderliness begins here.

If, as argued earlier, the habdaptive function is strongly dependent on larger systems, it stands to reason that the habdaptive function operates relative to both the multi-centric and state-centric worlds. Some people are very creative at imagining how they can use opportunities in a firm or an organization dedicated to some cause to influence world events. Others can do the same with government, still others can patch strategies together using collectivities in both worlds.[34] When, through aggregations and cascades, the knowledge of systems imbricated in this function come together in different ways, new patterns and strategies may form. These may then serve to reshape the very relationships between and within the two worlds in the macro parameter.

Placing the relational parameter between the two worlds would make it easier to talk about what happens when the two worlds "meet" over an issue. Their interaction is not in either world, it is in the relational parameter. Results of the interactions, however, appear in both of the worlds, adapted appropriately for the collectivities involved. Thus it may be possible to take a given interaction and see results in two places at once. This might even help us untangle the nature of treaty-based international organizations. They are certainly not states, but they often act on behalf of or in lieu of states. On yet other occasions, they seem to behave quite independently of them. These behaviors could be parsed by their effects in the two worlds, thus yielding a better description of the effects and character of international organizations. The relational parameter, therefore, serves not just to transmit authoritative statements down or rejection of authority up, but also to channel, shape, speed, and slow interactions at all scales. It spreads action over time and space. This more clearly introduces the history of the system into the picture.

CONCLUSION

Turbulence in World Politics provides theorists powerful concepts and propositions with which to view the global scene. Its emphasis on the behavior of individuals liberates international relations theory by allowing it to study world politics in its many manifestations. It presses analysts to study the range of interactions that constitute world politics. Its attention to the possibility and sources of turbulence disciplines us to face the task of understanding the simple rules that underlie the commotion on the surface. Many of the concepts within the theory encourage us to understand better the sources of order in ways international relations theory rarely ever does.

The effort offered here was inspired by the challenging and useful ideas offered in *Turbulence*. This chapter's brief exploration of the complex systemic aspects of Rosenau's postinternational theory illustrates some of the ways the theory can be employed to understand the emergence of order. The more patterning a system has, the more likely it will be resilient and less susceptible to sudden changes. The less susceptible it is to sudden changes, the more likely it is patterns will form. By acknowledging that the range of behaviors of individuals is strongly limited by the systems on and in which individual knowledge depends, we can see how individuals can change the character of the other parameters—and be changed by them. By looking more carefully at the relational parameter, we can learn how organization appears, disappears, and spreads. Together, the dynamics of turbulence and complexity constitute the well springs of change and continuity in world politics.

NOTES

1. Michael Kammen, *A Machine That Would Go of Itself: The Constitution in American Culture* (New York: Knopf, 1986).

2. As quoted in James N. Rosenau, *Turbulence in World Politics* (Princeton, N.J.: Princeton University Press, 1990), p. 61, hereafter, *Turbulence*. Jack Snyder and Robert Jervis, eds. *Coping with Complexity in the International System* (Boulder, Colo.: Westview, 1993), also quote Simon on p. 9.

3. I would like to extend my thanks to Nazli Choucri, Political Science, MIT; Matthew J. Hoffmann, Political Science, George Washington University; and to Jiquan Chen, Forestry, Michigan Tech, for their cogent comments on these propositions as they evolved. None of them completely agree with my proposed list of characteristics, but all agree with parts. They are, themselves, in hot pursuit of the question, "what do systems do?"

4. This is typically thought of as the computational capacity of the individuals to cope with the environment.

5. It may be that chaotic systems merely have a past, which is more a description of the system than information used by the elements to respond to opportunities in the system.

6. Another way of thinking of history is that the system itself has a history that limits and opens options to individual parts. For a fascinating, clear, and readily accessible discussion of a decentralized system see Robert Axelrod, "The Dissemination of Culture: A Model with Local convergence and Global Polarization,"*Journal of Conflict Resolution* 41 (April 1997): pp. 203–26.

7. *The Federalist Papers*, ed. Clinton Rossiter (New York: Mentor, 1961), p. 322.

8. One name for it, although I use it advisedly as any social scientist should when using analogies from the physical and biological sciences, is "punctuated equilibrium," a term proposed in 1972 by Stephen Jay Gould and Niles Eldredge to describe this phenomenon. See Roger Lewin, *Complexity: Life at the Edge of Chaos* (New York: Macmillan, 1992), p. 100. In fluid flows, this behavior is called "intermittency" (ibid., p. 101). I watched a flock of geese landing and reached this hypothesis on my own, however.

9. For the impossibly curious, the list for endotherm temperature regulation includes: evaporative cooling, metabolic heat generation, regulation of blood flow, insulation, and habitat selection. We should, however, be cautious with *organismic* biology analogies. There is nothing in the social world equivalent to the integrity of a single biological organism and its interacting components. See Herbert Kaufman's *Time, Chance, and Organizations*, 2d ed. (Chatham,

N.J.: Chatham House, 1991), especially pp. 89–91. Ecosystem or landscape ecology analogies should not present these particular difficulties, since they are studies of communities.

10. C. S. Holling, "Engineering Resilience versus Ecological Resilience," pp. 31–43 in Peter C. Schulze, ed. *Engineering within Ecological Constraints* (Washington, D.C.: National Academy of Sciences Press, 1996), pp. 39–40.

11. Rosenau, *Turbulence*, p. 79.

12. Ibid., *Turbulence*, p. 88.

13. Ibid., *Turbulence*, p. 81.

14. Ibid., *Turbulence*, p. 82.

15. Jonathan Bendor and Thomas H. Hammond, "Rethinking Allison's Models," *American Political Science Review* 86, 2 (June 1992): 301–22. See pp. 301–11.

16. Personal correspondence from Matthew Hoffmann, 1997.

17. Marcia Barinaga, "Watching the Brain Remake Itself," *Science* 266 (December 2, 1994): 1475.

18. Elizabeth Culotta, "Ninety Ways to Be a Mammal," *Science* 266 (November 18, 1994): 1161.

19. Richard A. Kerr, "Crowding Innovation Out of Evolution," *Science* 266 (November 18, 1994): 1163.

20. Lewin, *Complexity*, p. 64.

21. Rosenau, p. 156.

22. Ibid., pp. 306, 308.

23. Ibid., p. 242.

24. Ibid., pp. 12–13.

25. Ibid., p. 228.

26. Ibid., p. 228.

27. In other words, it is socially constructed.

28. William Cronon, "A Place for Stories: Nature, History, and Narrative," *The Journal of American History* 78, 4 (March 1992): 1347–79, 1366.

29. Rosenau, *Turbulence*, p. 235.

30. A vast expansion like this took place with the printing press when it was invented in Europe (Koreans invented moveable type, elites of that society banned it).

31. Thomas Bass, "Virus Hunting on the Niger," in his *Camping with the Prince* (New York: Penguin, 1990), p. 243.

32. This is a point Rosenau acknowledges on p. 440 of *Turbulence*. "[T]he bases of cooperation may soon be no less prominent in global politics than are those of conflict."

33. Axelrod, "The Dissemination of Culture" illustrates a network, but it may also be a simulation of a cascade.

34. See Paul Wapner, *Environmental Activism and World Civic Politics* (Albany: State University of New York Press, 1996), especially, chaps. 3–5.

CHAPTER 9

An Intellectual Agenda for Students of Postinternational World Politics

Joseph Lepgold

There is little doubt that we live in politically, socially, and economically turbulent times. One need only follow world developments in the most cursory way to see that domestic and international structures are changing rapidly, in some heretofore uncharted directions, and with some novel results. There are more independent states than ever before, coupled with a reasonable likelihood that existing units will splinter into even more pieces. Yet despite the proliferation of sovereign jurisdictions, most violent conflict now occurs within states, not between them, and the proportion of international transactions controlled by states has declined dramatically. Within the societies of the European Union, confederal, national, and subnational authorities increasingly compete for legitimacy and rule-making authority within the same political space. Nearly everywhere, the lines between domestic politics and foreign policy in the traditional sense are ever harder to discern, and may at some point become as indistinct as they were in pre-Westphalian Europe. Moreover, as the degree, ways, and speed with which societies are linked have increased dramatically, globalization is rapidly altering the context in which politics and policy-making take place.

More than most scholars, James Rosenau has observed these developments attentively and tried to explain them in creative ways. In recent works, he suggests that a pervasive feature of contemporary world

I would like to thank Mary Durfee for her perceptive comments on an earlier version of this chapter.

political life is *turbulence*, and that what he calls *postinternationalism* is the most fruitful paradigm for analyzing the field. This argument is stimulating and offers many insights. Postinternationalism clarifies several points that Liberal models have traditionally obscured or ignored, and it offers the prospect of developing analytical connections between important micro- and macro-level political trends. If this argument were to be laid out precisely and systematically connected to related scholarly work, it could help scholars frame globalization processes and other important aspects of change in world politics. Over the years, few international relations scholars have been as intellectually daring as Jim or have asked questions that have been as consistently interesting. But postinternationalism suffers a weakness common to many international relations (IR) theories. It is framed too unconditionally: the prevailing empirical conditions that must obtain for the propositions to hold are imprecise or only implicitly laid out. As a result, Rosenau's work on postinternationalism cannot realize its intellectual potential: it encourages unproductive debates with opposing schools of thought and leads neither to a progressive research program nor a cumulative body of propositions and empirical evidence. Unless these problems are corrected, what is creative and useful about the argument could be lost.

In this chapter, I argue that advocates of a postinternationalist model or lens on world politics should take the argument seriously enough to help refine it. It deserves such attention. Postinternationalism makes a distinct argument about the sources and effects of system change. Specifying it more explicitly and precisely could therefore lay the basis for an interesting and sustained research agenda. For these reaons, it is useful to clarify postinternationalism's distinct contribution, highlight its limitations and suggest some solutions for them, and sketch out some ideas for a productive research agenda.

WHAT DOES THE POSTINTERNATIONALISM MODEL TELL US?

In *Turbulence in World Politics*, Rosenau claims that "global life may have entered a period of turbulence the likes of which it has not known for three hundred years and the outcomes of which are far from clear."[1] He sees five major shifts as responsible for this upheaval. Technologies have emerged that have dramatically heightened interdependence by making money, ideas, and information move qualitatively faster than before. This has been accompanied by the emergence of transnational issues that governments cannot control. National governments have weakened, in part because they cannot manage the resulting turbulence and in part because their citizens pay them less deference than before. At the same time, vibrant political and social organizations have emerged at lower levels, further weakening the state as an unchallenged political authority. Finally, these changes have induced the creation of new skills and affective orientations among individuals, making them more effective political actors.[2] Taken together, these developments have produced a "parametric change" in world politics unseen for centuries. The effect is what Rosenau calls "postinternational politics," in which interactions across state boundaries increasingly do not directly involve nations or states.[3]

Clearly, while all of these are important developments, none of them is new. For decades, Liberal observers of world politics have discussed the ways in which economic and social interdependence have affected policymakers' agendas and constrained their choices. This has long led Liberals to herald the obsolescence of state-centric perspectives. In three ways, however, Rosenau's postinternationalist perspective is a distinctive variation on traditional Liberal themes. First, it claims that threshold changes have occurred in the values of the variables just mentioned, producing qualitative kinds of changes in outcomes. Second, it claims that individuals' skills and beliefs are changing in unprecedented ways, and that these changes intensify the effects of the other variables. Third, it posits important feedback effects between changes in individuals and changes in their environments. Each of these merits discussion.

Rosenau posits a historically rare confluence of events that have produced threshold changes in the level, density, and effects of intersocietal interdepedence. To understand these changes, he argues that we need "a conception of turbulence that denotes the tensions and changes that ensue when the structures and processes that normally sustain world politics are unsettled and appear to be undergoing rearrangement."[4] In such situations, he contends that pattern maintenance is disrupted and disequilibrium sets in. Rosenau claims that under these conditions, the structures and processes of world politics lack "prior rules or boundaries" and that as a result, "anything can happen."[5]

In making this claim, Rosenau places his work within one of two Liberal approaches to understanding world political change. Some Liberals believe that change occurs incrementally, while others view change more nonincrementally. Commercial Liberalism and functionalism fall in the first category. These intellectual traditions depict a world in which scientific and technical progress facilitates international exchanges, the demand for which is rooted in people's desire for higher living standards. As exchanges grow in volume and value, interdependencies deepen and, in functionalism, produce problem-driven institutions to facilitate further (or more efficient) exchanges. These developments, in turn, feed back on the way people define their interests, leading governments to more cooperative behavior.[6] In the incremental versions of Liberalism, these processes are seen as evolutionary but essentially linear. One gets little sense from writers in this tradition that if interdependence reaches a certain volume or density, *qualitative changes* in preferences or governance structures will ensue that would not have occurred at other levels.

Other liberals, Rosenau among them, believe that major changes in people's values, preferences, and behavior can and do occur non-incrementally. One example of such an argument is the notion that democracies do not fight one another, however they behave toward states with nonpluralistic political systems. Here, a major aspect of foreign-policy behavior is seen as dichotomous, depending on unit-level characteristics, and it changes in step-level fashion when those characteristics change. Another example posits that all systems have finite capacities to sustain interactions that, if exceeded, produce system-level changes. For instance, when the volume or speed of interactions among states grows sufficiently high, these interactions could begin to override what are assumed to be the "deep structural" effects of anarchy, such as a desire to limit specialization, and thus dependencies on others. The result could be closer economic or even political integration than one would expect in a Hobbesian self-help system.[7] In Rosenau's version of this argument, threshold changes in the system's interaction capacity lead to intensified demands on governments, many of which are beyond their capacity to manage.[8]

Rosenau's attempts to draw out the dysfunctional effects of high interdependence is one way in which his turbulence and postinternationalism notions differ from most Liberal arguments. Liberals have always recognized the transformative and thus the destabilizing effects of economic change, but have tended not to explore the ways in which such change hurts as well as helps people. By contrast, as seen through Rosenau's lens, high levels of interdependence result not just in prosperity, and more interstate collaboration to achieve it, but also in such effects as system overload, escalating crises of authority, and perhaps serious conflict over how to respond to these challenges. This is *not* the largely benign Liberalism of David Mitrany, Michael Doyle, or John Mueller. A key difference is a sense that governments may lose control over the processes by which they facilitated greater intersocietal transactions in the first place. This implication is implicit in some versions of Liberalism, but has rarely been developed. In what Rosenau calls a "multicentric world," various substate actors and coalitions are empowered, and their preferences might not be the same as any existing government's. As compared with most other analytic lenses on world politics, this highlights the disruptive implications of globalization and related developments.

A second distinctive feature of Rosenau's argument is the emphasis on individuals' skills and affective orientations as a response to and then as a catalyst for other changes. Liberal analysts have tended not to locate major causal processes at the indivudual level of analysis. Yet doing so can be useful. As Rosenau points out, Liberal arguments often posit quite narrow utility functions: *homo economicus* is at the root of many functionalist conceptions. In this more standard view, changes in people's environments either enable or constrain them to pursue the same kinds of objectives, often quite habitually, that they pursued under other sets of conditions.[9] By contrast, in Rosenau's view, people are actively adaptive learners as well as habit-driven actors. People may learn new ideas or objectives when they encounter external stimuli that are "peristently and startlingly new," but learning is more profound when it is reinforced by the development of new skills and orientations within actors. For Rosenau, responses to the microelectronic revolution exemplify learning of the deeper type. It has catalyzed far-reaching change in many areas of life—education, employment, even the way people shop—changes that demand qualitatively new cognitive skills.[10] In this way, Rosenau is able to connect key kinds of environmental change to changes in the values and dispositions of ordinary actors.

A third distinctive feature of the argument is the way in which these changes in individuals are seen to feed back on social and political structures. As people's capabilities grow, so does their productivity. But in addition to these economic changes, people may also become more broadly confident and assertive, and thus less compliant as citizens. This will directly affect political relationships. Such a feedback loop allows Rosenau to suggest novel outcomes as a result of "startlingly high" levels of interdependence: major environmental change causes changes in individuals, who then may act on different preferences or habits than they did before. Traditional governance norms and structures may not be able to contain the new demands that result. In short, the development of more skillful, adaptive citizens is a destabilizing as well as a harmonizing force among collective actors in world politics.

ANALYTIC PROBLEMS AND SOME SUGGESTED SOLUTIONS

Rosenau recognizes that his notion of postinternationalism is at present not a systematic argument, but simply a metaphor for a number of trends in world politics.[11] As with many metaphors, it suggests analytic connections or empirical phenomena that might be worth further exploration. How might this proceed? I believe that the argument suffers two key weaknesses: it is not clearly enough linked to its intellectual precursors and is framed too imprecisely to foster sustained, cumulative scholarship. Correcting these problems would make it easier to develop and sustain a coherent research program around Rosenau's ideas.

One weakness in Rosenau's presentation is that the links between postinternationalism and other Liberal arguments are unclear. Clarifying one's intellectual debts makes it easier to understand the rationales for specific assertions and conclusions and facilitates comparison with other arguments.[12] Failure to do this makes it likely that key analytic assumptions will remain implicit. This, in turn, means that it will be hard for other scholars to work through the deductive logic of the argument on their own and that what *is* distinctive in the postinternationalist literature will not receive the attention it deserves.

Liberal international theorists make the following assumptions:

1. Individual people are the primary international actors. States are the most important collective actors at present, but they are pluralistic actors, in which preferences and policies are determined by internal bargaining.

2. The agenda of world politics is extensive, with no single dominant issue. The preferences and interests of individuals, groups, and states are a product of various international and domestic factors. As individuals' values or incentives and power relations among factions change over time, policy agendas will shift.

3. The relative impact of coercion on international outcomes has declined over time.[13]

Rosenau is clearly a Liberal, since he shares each of these assumptions. Clarifying the connections between his argument and the overall body of Liberal theory could help other analysts make his causal logic explicit where it is currently not so. In the process, his own contribution would be highlighted. For example, Rosenau contends that in politically turbulent situations, "the repercussions of the various participants' actions cascade through their networks of interdependence." This, he claims, is what induced negotiations to end wars during a short period in 1988 in conflicts as diverse as Afghanistan, Angola, Central America, Cambodia, the Western Sahara, and the Persian Gulf.[14] But what precisely is the causal mechanism at work here? What specific aspects of turbulence are responsible for such diffusion, and how do they produce that result? Does it have something to do with the ways policymakers' agendas were set in each of these cases before threshold effect was reached? Perhaps related to this, do turbulent conditions produce a reshuffling of internal policy coalitions, leading to the possibility of dramatic policy shifts? Do several of these mechanisms interact to reinforce turbulence? We do not know, because the reasoning is not spelled out.

Processes related to the three core Liberal assumptions might help us unpack Rosenau's argument. For example, a major feature of turbulent political conditions, as Rosenau understands them, seems to be that the "circuits" connecting individuals to societies and governments, and the "circuits" linking governments to one another become overloaded. Perhaps various diffusion and imitation mechanisms work their way through these circuits at some times or on some sorts of issues. This would not be surprising: sensitivity to one another's actions is a key aspect of interdependence. Such a development, in turn, might be expected to destabilize existing political and policy coalitions within states, producing cascade effects through a mechanism related to Liberal assumption no. 2. But to fairly and accurately evaluate such propositions, we need to be able to see each aspect of the larger mechanism at work. It would be surprising, given Rosenau's Liberal roots, if Liberal ideas were *not* helpful in separating out and then analyzing these effects. Careful process tracing could then be used to show whether hypothesized causes produced hypothesized effects at each stage of process.

A second weakness in Rosenau's presentation is that the assertions are too unconditional. This is a problem in much of the field. Even though virtually all social-science explanations are conditional, many scholars fail to identify clearly the empirical contingencies under which they apply. Theoretical statements require a set of scope conditions that describe when a relationship between two or more concepts applies.[15] In a turbulence argument, for instance, it may be the case that certain "sparks" or stimuli diffuse more quickly or easily through some policy-making systems than others, because the societies are especially closely linked in the sense of sensitivity interdependence and thus are less viscous as a group with respect to these stimuli than more disjoined units. Alternatively, because modern telecommunications technologies make it easy to notice and then fairly quickly imitate certain behaviors across units, what may really have changed is not the level or kind of intersocietal interactions so much as the degree of transparency across units. Of course, either or both processes *could* be at work; the point is that nothing in Rosenau's presentation helps us choose among the candidate explanations. This is because his argument now lacks a set of statements that specify what those catalysts might be or which aspects of interdependence lead most quickly to cascade effects.

One way to incorporate scope conditions explicitly into contingent generalizations is through judicious use of typologies.[16] A "type" is a group of cases in which the values of the variables are strongly related. A typology asserts that the relevant variables occur together in fairly few combinations. For example, small, highly industrialized states that have long been vigorously exposed to international competition may have economic sectors that are highly flexible as compared to those found in bigger, relatively more self-sufficient states. Consequently, states in the former group might be less apt to have their "circuits" overloaded by a significant increase in international transactions than those in the latter category.[17] Of course, this is just a possible example. But it suggests that carefully chosen typologies present a systematic way to be precise about mixes of explanatory and outcome variables.

What this could lead to is a set of typological propositions connecting various kinds of disturbance stimuli to various kinds of behavioral outcomes, operating perhaps through a set of related but distinct diffusion mechanisms. Researchers who follow this strategy seek to discover the conditions under which each distinctive type of causal pattern obtains.[18] Consider another example using the turbulence argument. It may be that currency crises and AIDS are phenomena that cascade through and across national systems especially quickly and explosively because the private actors who spread them interact (largely or essentially entirely) without government supervision. The diffusion process is unusually swift by historic standards because electronic transactions occur instantaneously and because those who have infectious diseases today are much more mobile than comparable individuals were even a few decades ago. By contrast, terrorism and drug trafficking cascade more slowly, since governments at least passively are involved in supporting or inhibiting these activities. As a result, conscious political choices need to be made for these processes to start up or continue.

This example illustrates a commonsensical point: the degree to which sovereign states try to regulate cross-national behavior, along with the technological and other environmental conditions Rosenau emphasizes, significantly affect how quickly turbulence spreads. These are just two of the empirical conditions that would need to be clarified in a well-specified argument. Because the postinternationalism and turbulence notions are relatively rich in implications, it would be easy to pull out many more such examples.

Specifying these kinds of empirical contingencies would have two salutary effects on a research program based upon Rosenau's work. First, and most important, it would make the argument easier to test, and perhaps encourage people to do so. Unless a community of scholars becomes engaged with a set of ideas and propositions, as we have seen in the Democratic Peace literature, the ideas in this work are likely to remain undeveloped. Yet Rosenau's argument is impossible to test if, as he says, "anything can happen" under conditions of turbulence.[19] As Rosenau has framed the argument, virtually no outcome is ruled out, since all of the parameters that have heretofore regulated social and political life have been broken. This is very unlikely to be the case in any literal sense. Surely *not every* social and political parameter has been broken, and surely some theoretically conceivable outcomes are extremely unlikely even in the presence of cascade effects that are unprecedented in their swiftness. A careful set of typological arguments about the conditions under which various turbulent processes work their way through national and international systems could, over time, provide evidence that some outcomes are rather likely, some are rather unlikely, and some almost never occur.

Second, a set of contingent generalizations about the causes and effects of turbulence would likely indicate that Rosenau is incorrect to say that because some important empirical conditions have changed, "theorizing must begin anew."[20] Unfortunately, such a view is common. For instance, Charles Kegley recently claimed that "theories must respond to changes in international behavior that erode faith in the prevalent paradigm's usefulness and provoke alternative approaches. There are fashions in everything; the study of international relations is no exception."[21] This view is unfortunate because theory is useful precisely when it has some distance from current developments. Of course, especially in international relations, one would expect a close comingling between conversations within a scholarly field (what Lakatos called a discipline's "internal history") and discussions of real-world events and issues that stimulate scholars' interest in various theoretical puzzles. Yet unless scholarly agendas and research traditions are sustained across the ebb and flow of external events, rather than closely mirroring them, the field's intellectual autonomy can become skewed.[22] A good international relations theory should identify and explain patterns that transcend issues, actors, and historical eras.[23] It offers little diagnostic or explanatory power if it must be reinvented each time these factors change.

Liberal arguments, moreover, do *not* need to be reinvented, even though our era surely is turbulent. By indicating where and in what sense his work builds upon Liberal theories, Rosenau would probably find that what has made the times turbulent is not a qualitatively new set of causal factors—which clearly *would* call for a new theory—but new and perhaps extreme values of some (or many?) of the variables in existing Liberal arguments. For example, under very high conditions of sensitivity interdependence, certain kinds of stimuli could produce unparalleled cascade effects. This follows quite directly from theories of information processing in organizations. When variables change in new, unpredicted ways, critical organizational dependencies are affected and policymakers may not know how to respond.[24] If so, what is new in Rosenau's recent work is not the causal logic at all. What is new and potentially valuable is a recognition that the value of key variables has significantly changed, leading to major step-level effects in outcomes. Simply recognizing this is a major accomplishment for any scholar; one need not reinvent the wheel to illuminate important world political issues.

SUGGESTIONS FOR A POSTINTERNATIONALIST RESEARCH AGENDA

The foregoing analysis suggests two related tasks that would be necessary to construct a coherent research agenda around the notion of postinternationalist world politics. First, the logic behind Rosenau's major assertions needs to be spelled out more explicitly and precisely. As I indicated above, one of his key contributions may be the notion that major increases in the kind or volume of interactions across units can have important threshold effects on politics. Relatively little serious scholarly literature seems to entertain or develop this idea. Yet in order to explore and test this contention systematically, we need to know why the catalytic variables Rosenau has identified produce their hypothesized effects. Any argument about major threshold effects in the values of the variables must, after all, identify the previously prevailing equilbrium situation and why certain factors rather than others are responsible for disrupting it. Unless scholars ask these more specific questions, we will be unable to understand why globalization and the skills revolution produce their political effects.

A research program that focused in part on such threshold changes could explore many interesting questions. For example, do new skills necessarily make people less compliant citizens, as Rosenau contends? If so, why? The literature that shows a strong association between high indicators of socioeconomic status and self-assurance about the ability to participate successfully in politics suggests that there may be such a connection, but Rosenau's more general version of this claim needs a firmer analytic foundation. A typological approach could provide a way to build more precise generalizations about it. This effect may turn out to be weak in cultures where positive changes in people's self-esteem tend to find outlets in business or other societally based pursuits rather than in politics. In any case, a sustained postinternationalist research agenda would likely take up this issue.

Spelling out the reasoning that supports Rosenau's conclusions could have other benefits as well. Theories have value not simply in answering questions identified early in a research program; they continue to have value when they provide a "positive heuristic" that directs scholars toward "new facts" or different puzzles, as distinct from those that animated earlier work. A set of propositions that carefully identified the empirical conditions under which disturbences produce turbulent effects would probably suggest new relationships that scholars would want to examine. It might be the case, for instance, that many turbulence outcomes hinge on how prepared organizations are to improvise in an unpredictable environment. If this were so, a new line of research linking organizational behavior and adaptation to external environmental conditions might be opened.

Second, much of what is now hard to follow in Rosenau's presentation stems from his tendency to conflate a number of distinct causal propositions into one generic argument. A set of more precisely specified contingent generalizations about various aspects of turbulent phenomena would help us disentangle various related but distinct processes. At bottom, Rosenau is concerned with what happens when high sensitivity interdependence takes new forms and produces results at what seems like unprecedented speed. Breaking out these mechanisms either by issue-area, by the way they affect organizations and people's decision making capacities, or by the degree to which states cannot control their effects would allow us to say a number of more precise—though no less interesting—things about these phenomena. Precisely because the phenomena at issue here are so turbulent, the way we try to understand them should be careful, patient, and precise.

NOTES

1. James N. Rosenau, *Turbulence in World Politics: A Theory of Change and Continuity* (Princeton, N.J.: Princeton University Press, 1990), p. 5.

2. Ibid., pp. 12–13.

3. Ibid., pp. 10, 6.

4. Ibid., p. 8.

5. Ibid.

6. Mark W. Zacher and Richard A. Matthew, "Liberal International Theory: Common Threads, Divergent Strands," in Charles W. Kegley, Jr., *Controversies in International Relations Theory: Realism and the Neoliberal Challenge* (New York: St. Martin's, 1995), p. 124.

7. Barry Buzan, Charles Jones, and Richard Little, *The Logic of Anarchy: Neorealism to Structural Realism* (New York: Columbia University Press, 1993), p. 78.

8. Rosenau, *Turbulence in World Politics*, p. 8.

9. Ibid., pp. 234–35.

10. Ibid.

11. Ibid., p. 9.

12. Zacher and Matthew, "Liberal International Theory," p. 118.

13. I have adapted this list, with minor modifications, from Zacher and Matthew, "Liberal International Theory," pp. 118–19.

14. Rosenau, *Turbulence in World Politics*, pp. 8–9. The quoted passage is on p. 8.

15. Paul Davidson Reynolds, *A Primer in Theory Construction* (Indianapolis, Ind.: Bobbs-Merrill, 1971), pp. 76–77; Abraham Kaplan, *The Conduct of Inquiry* (San Francisco: Chandler, 1964), p. 352.

16. For a more complete discussion, see Joseph Lepgold, "Is Anyone Listening? International Relations Theory and the Problem of Policy Relevance," *Political Science Quarterly* 113, 1 (spring 1998).

17. For an elaboration of this argument, see Peter J. Katzenstein, *Small States in World Markets: Industrial Policy in Europe* (Ithaca, N.Y.: Cornell University Press, 1985).

18. Alexander L. George, "Case Studies and Theory Development: The Method of Structured, Focused Comparison," in Paul Gordon Lauren, ed. *Diplomacy: New Approaches in History, Theory, and Policy* (New York: Free Press, 1979), pp. 59–60.

19. Rosenau, *Turbulence in World Politics*, p. 8.

20. Ibid., p. 5.

21. Charles W. Kegley Jr., "The Neoidealist Moment in International Studies? Realist Myths and the New International Realities," *International Studies Quarterly* 37, 2 (January 1993): 132.

22. Imre Lakatos, "The Problem of Appraising Scientific Theories: Three Approaches," in Imre Lakatos, *Mathematics, Science, and Epistemology*, Philosophical Papers Vol. 2, John Worrall and Greogry Currie, eds. (Cambridge: Cambridge University Press, 1978), pp. 115–16.

23. Alan C. Lamborn, "Theory and the Politics in World Politics," *International Studies Quarterly* 41, 2 (June 1997).

24. Jeffrey Pfeffer, *Organizational Design* (Arlington Heights, Ill.: AHM Publishers, 1978), p. 133.

CHAPTER TEN

Turbulence and Tradition in International Relations Theory: Prospects for a Postinternational Revolution

Ralph B. A. DiMuccio
and
Eric Drew Cooper

INTRODUCTION

The underlying structures and parameters of world politics appear to be changing dramatically. Authority structures are being challenged and uncertainty is increasing in cascading fashion. Amidst the apparent chaos, however, it is possible to perceive and delineate an underlying order. From diverse outcomes, a unified explanation can be derived based on the notion of "turbulence" in world politics.

These are among the major themes that underpin the focus of this volume: "The Postinternational Paradigm," "postinternationalism," or simply "turbulence theory." The putative genesis of turbulence theory is the book *Turbulence in World Politics*, published some ten years ago by James N. Rosenau.[1] As such, it serves as a useful point of reference in a broader discussion about turbulence theory and international theory in general. This book is ambitious (in that it attempts a "wholescale reformulation of international relations theory") and in many senses path breaking (since it rests upon a relatively underexplored set of causes for change and continuity in the world political system). Thus, the central arguments of the book—outlined briefly below—

169

constitute in many senses a direct challenge to what is widely considered to be the theoretical mainstream of the discipline.

Yet, despite what in important ways is a novel framework, turbulence theory can readily be placed within a larger theoretical and discursive context. This context, as we will attempt to establish in this essay, is well defined by the liberal tradition in international relations theory and by the epistemological positivism that underlies its neoliberal variant. This essay will identify some of the more distinctive properties of turbulence theory, while suggesting its direct and indirect linkages to other traditions within the discipline. It also seeks to uncover some of the possible factors, inherent in the diverse discourses of international relations that have contributed to the theory's content and approach. Finally, we conclude that despite notable signs to the contrary, such a postinternational revolution may be forthcoming in the field of international relations, albeit within the broader neoliberal movement that seems to be afoot in the field.

TURBULENCE THEORY IN BRIEF

Rosenau's postinternational paradigm is an amalgam of ideas and concepts that come together to form a complex, multilevel framework. The essays in this volume all attempt in one or another way to summarize turbulence theory, so the details need not be exhaustively covered here. For present purposes, we find three aspects of turbulence theory to be of particular note: (1) a focus on the variable and changing nature of world politics, (2) an acceptance of a degree of continuity, yielding an image of two competing and coexisting worlds of world politics, and (3) the central importance of the microlevel as a source of large-scale change. These serve both to distinguish and help contextualize Rosenau's approach.

As a work that focuses first and foremost on change, *Turbulence in World Politics* goes to great lengths to illustrate the extent to which the simplicities of the past have given way. That is, the well-established patterns that at one time successfully sustained the basic parameters of world politics have yielded to a state of high "complexity" and "dynamism." Such a condition is defined as that of "turbulence." Any international system is "turbulent" when its parameters (micro, macro, and micro-macro) undergo substantial increases in the number of actors, in the extent of dissimilarity among actors, and in the scope and depth of their interdependence (complexity), while at the same time there is a high degree of variability across time in terms of the goals and activities of such actors (dynamism).[2] With the onset of turbulence comes a high likelihood of fundamental change particularly at the micro-macro level and thereby at the macro level.

According to turbulence theory, there are five fundamental elements of change that underlie turbulence in world politics. The first and foremost of these elements is the shift from an industrial to postindustrial order. The focus here is on the dynamics of technology, and in particularly on the so-called microelectronic revolution that has "shortened social, economic and political distances, eased and hastened the movement of information and ideas, and increased the interdependence of diverse peoples and events." The second source of turbulence has been the emergence of inherently transnational or transsovereign issues, such as pollution, terrorism, drug trade, currency crises, AIDS, all of which, Rosenau argues, are the direct products of new technologies and interdependence. The inherently transnational character of such factors clearly distinguishes postinternational politics from traditional political issues.

The third engine of change is the central consequence of the first two: the reduced capabilities of states and governments to provide satisfactory solutions to the major issues on their political agendas. This is so partly because issues are increasingly transsovereign but also partly because the compliance of citizens can no longer be taken for granted. The reason for this latter condition is reflective of the fourth engine of change, "subgroupism." Subgroupism refers to the weakening of whole systems that has caused a corresponding strengthening of subgroups or micro-level actors. This tendency toward the increasing centrality of subgroups leads both to centralizing and decentralizing tendencies and toward shifts in people's political loyalties, both "inward" (toward subnational or transnational groups) and "outward" (toward extrastatal or supranational bodies).[3]

Finally, the feedback of all of the foregoing for the skills and orientations of the world's adults who make up the groups, states, and other collectivities, constitutes the fifth and most determinate engine of change according to turbulence theory. That is, "with their analytical skills enlarged and their orientations toward authority more self-conscious, today's persons-in-the-street are no longer as uninvolved, ignorant, and manipulable with respect to world affairs as were their forebears."[4] This change in micro-level loyalty/acquiescence patterns has, in turn, far-reaching implications for the macro-political patterns of world politics. Indeed, the distinctly micro-level skills factor has had comparatively the most important influence, "so much so as to be a requisite to the expansivity and intensity of the other four."[5] Thus, macro changes (postindustrialism, etc.) bring about micro changes (increased intellectual and cathectic capabilities) that serve both to reflect and accelerate turbulence in world politics. However, while changes at the macro level constitute necessary contributors of global turbulence, the micro-level changes provide the sufficient causes of such turbulence.

Turbulence is therefore both cause and effect, seen both in terms of change and continuity. At a broad level, turbulence is a direct cause and reflection of the disarray and uncertainty that characterize world politics today. More specifically, interdependence and the increased skills of individuals have translated into a "global authority crisis" and an increased questioning of the legitimacy of leaders at all levels of society. This authority crisis creates the disaggregation of old wholes and the aggregation of diverse subsystems either within whole systems, around certain issues, or between whole systems.[6]

But amidst the change, Rosenau argues, there is still much continuity; so much so that it is necessary to see world politics as being comprised of two distinct, coexisting, and largely mutually exclusive worlds. That is, while the pressures of turbulence have created novel relations and structures in world politics, the old structures persist in certain spheres. As a result of this observation, Rosenau argues that the domain of world politics has become bifurcated into a "state-centric" world representing the old order dominated by sovereignty-bound actors (states), and a "multi-centric world" representing a new order dominated by sovereignty-free (nonstate) actors.[7] Turbulence in world politics has weakened—as most of the book argues—many of the core assumptions implicit in the workings of the state-centric world, but it has not destroyed that world. Wars between states are still fought, there is still no supranational body to direct the foreign policies of such states, and power conceived as the military and economic capabilities of states to influence the course of affairs is still a crucial variable in explaining certain aspects of world politics. Nevertheless, the multi-centric world has become far too central to the dynamics of world politics to be ignored or trivialized in terms of its political importance and theoretical relevance.

CONTEXTUALIZING TURBULENCE THEORY

Turbulence and the "Rosenauian Tradition"

A key in reading "turbulence theory" as text is to recognize that the novel elements can easily overshadow those that should be familiar, thereby causing readers to misinterpret the underlying context. In the following sections, we attempt to locate turbulence theory within the available debates in the field, first through a brief biographical analysis of Rosenau and his work, and then through a discussion of the confluence of behavioral and liberal thought in international relations.

As a first contextual point, it must be pointed out that *Turbulence in World Politics* (including the turbulence theory that underlies it) is much more than merely a reaction to events such as those that occupy a prominent role on the book's front cover.[8] Rather this work must be seen as the culmination of a career-long effort on Rosenau's part to analyze critically the extent to which the rigid images of world politics as forwarded by a myriad of Western, primarily "realist" scholars have been an accurate reflection of world politics. For Rosenau, this compulsion has denoted the life-long study of transnational relations and the transnationalization of world politics. This aspect of Rosenau's intellectual "temperament" has manifested itself in a continual effort to locate the role of sub- and nonstate actors in the processes of foreign policy-making and world politics in general. In his brief intellectual autobiography,[9] Rosenau indicates that this "temperament" may have had its origins at least partly in his experiences as coeditor of the second volume of Franklin Roosevelt's personal letters.[10] This experience, along with his undergraduate training in history, impressed upon him the realization that "[contemporary] history [was] made by people who had set the world on its postwar course even as they also lived on farms, had families, saved their letters and coped with personal dilemmas."[11] The beginnings of Rosenau's interest in the relationship between the micro and macro levels are thus evident.

Accordingly, Rosenau's preoccupation with "things transnational," emerged early in his academic career and has remained consistent to the present. Among his first works were: a popular book on F. D. Roosevelt written on the basis of his work on the Roosevelt papers;[12] a doctoral dissertation on senatorial attitudes toward Secretary of State Dean Acheson;[13] a methodological treatise on public opinion and foreign policy;[14] several studies on national consensus and leadership in foreign policy;[15] and a number of works on the nexus between international relations and civil strife.[16] Later in the 1960s and into the 1970s and 1980s, Rosenau's work continued to focus on transnational politics,[17] while expanding to encompass ever broader aspects of transnationalization such as interdependence,[18] the domestic sources of foreign policy,[19] and political adaptation.[20] While Rosenau's interest in foreign policy analysis waned in the middle 1980s as he became more enamored with the study of the large-scale changes he saw occurring in the world, this shift did not undermine his continued passion for analyzing world politics from an explicitly transnational perspective, as is indicated by his continued work on habit-driven actors,[21] comparative foreign policy,[22] critiques of the state as a viable unit of analysis,[23] and leadership in U.S. foreign policy.[24] Thus, while turbulence theory is substantively rather far removed from the product of Rosenau's brief stint as a biographer, the lineage and continuity between them are clear.

In addition to a deep interest in the transnationalization of world politics, Rosenau's work has always displayed—as he states in the preface to *Turbulence*—a "preoccupation with the dynamics of change as they interplay with the statics of continuity."[25] In this sense as well, there is a continuity with earlier works, especially vis-à-vis those texts that have focused on the concept of interdependence. For example, in the first sentence in his collection of essays, *The Study of Global Interdependence: Essays on the Transnationalization of World Affairs*, Rosenau argues that "the essays in this volume focus on change in world affairs and . . . on how to study and comprehend such change."[26] More importantly, the *Interdependence* volume is highly reflective of many of the same driving assumptions that tend to give *Turbulence* its (in some ways) unique, yet (in other ways) predictable content. In *Interdependence*, Rosenau's aim was to demonstrate the processes whereby world affairs were becoming increasingly *transnationalized* and to delineate the ways in which dynamic change, initiated by technological innovation and sustained by continuing advances in communications and transportation, had brought about new associations into the political arena, which in turn served to intensify the dynamics of world affairs. For Rosenau, therefore, while some important aspects of the traditional nation-state system have remained intact, interdependence and transnationalization have caused the onset of fundamental changes in the basic structures of world affairs. This has been one of Rosenau's most enduring theses, and one that is central to turbulence theory. As Rosenau states in the introduction to *Turbulence in World Politics*,

> Taken together with the impact of modern technologies and the many other sources that are rendering the world ever more interdependent, the bifurcated structures [of the world] and the more [analytically and emotionally] skillful citizens are perceived to have fostered such a profound transformation in world politics that the lessons of history may no longer be very helpful. Theory must [therefore] begin anew and present premises and understandings of history's dynamics must be treated as conceptual jails from which an escape can be engineered only by allowing for the possibility that a breakpoint in human affairs is imminent, if not upon us, as the twentieth century comes to an end.[27]

It is plain, in short, that there has been a great deal of consistency in the development of Rosenau's thinking over time. This fact illustrates the difficulty of making simplistic conclusions about the sources of Rosenau's emphasis on transnational issues and change in *Turbulence in World Politics* simply by looking at the book's cover. In other words, since *Turbulence* represents the culmination of many years of coherent and largely cumulative thinking, we must look beyond the dramatic events of recent years to find the context of Rosenau's latest theoretical work.

Turbulence Theory as "Dynamic Behavioral Science"

Although orthodox approaches in international relations theory have focused largely on the (perceived) statics of world politics, there has of course been a strong tradition in the field of IR—a tradition in which Rosenau has been more than just a key player—that has taken a dynamic look at the changing nature of world politics and that which is "variable." Indeed, Rosenau played a critical role in propelling the field of international relations out of the traditionalist/realist dogma of the 1940s and 1950s and into the behavioralist consensus that guides the vast majority of international relations research today.[28] What is the tradition upon which this consensus has been built, and of what does it consist?

The "behavioralist" revolution in international relations can be explained as the confluence of two key epistemic developments in American social and political science in the 1950s and 1960s: (1) a general blossoming of technology and scientific methods as applied to the study of social phenomena; and (2) a growing perception that the approaches of the traditional, classical realists like Carr, Lippmann, Morgenthau, were static, dogmatic, and unsystematic. The former development is traceable, as Dougherty and Pfaltzgraff state, to

> the availability of quantitative methodologies and conceptual frameworks borrowed or adapted from other [scientific] disciplines. The advent of the computer and advanced technologies of information storage, retrieval and analysis [enhanced] the prospects for testing theory and allegedly furnish[ed] unprecedented opportunities for developing international relations theory. Since the conduct of research in international relations, as in other disciplines, has usually been strongly influenced by younger scholars impatient with the conventional wisdom of their elders, "credibility gaps," and "generation gaps" emerge periodically... [S]uch a gap [in international relations], by the 1970s, was based in part on a division... between

those who assigned greater or lesser importance to qualitative or quantitative techniques of research and analysis.[29]

Thus, although scholars have differed over specific modes of analysis (inductive vs. deductive theory), levels of analysis (state-centric vs. multicentric), and methods of analysis (game theory, vs. decision analysis), all behavioralists share "a commitment to some form of value neutral analytical empiricism as a philosophy of science, as exemplified in the data-making and hypothesis-testing procedures of contemporary polimetric practice." They also share "an emulative admiration of the mathematical and logical practices assumed to characterize the natural sciences, including the search for objective, timeless, universal laws,"[30] and the enlightenment idea "that all problems can be resolved, that the way to resolve them is to apply the scientific method—assumed to be value free—and to combine empirical investigation, hypothesis formation, and testing."[31]

Behavioral research in international relations has thus had from its beginning an intrinsic relation to a sort of "cult of the variable," in which analysis purports to begin with the observable variations in human behavior. For Rosenau, this general outlook on scholarship has produced at least three fundamental lessons of the scientific study of world politics: "always let your variables vary;" the idea of operationalizing variables so that one's findings, procedures, and interpretations can be checked-out or rendered "checkable-upable," and an obsession with the "arrogance of absolutist understanding and the virtues of probabilistic knowledge."[32] Indeed, James Rosenau was one of the leading figures in the effort to bolster scientific methods in International Relations (IR) and to discredit classical and other heavily normative, value-based, or otherwise "unscientific" approaches. This stage in Rosenau's career, exemplified by the oft-cited readers, *Contending Approaches to International Politics* and *The Scientific Study of Foreign Policy*, began as Rosenau himself puts it,

> a zealous phase in which I joined the ranks of the behavioral revolutionists and stormed the ramparts of traditional approaches. In articles and books, in class and outside lectures, I rattled away on behalf of science, arguing that it is possible, through theoretical and empirical explication, to assess knowledge independently of those who uncover it and that therein lay a route to understanding the deeper dynamics of world politics.[33]

The work of James Rosenau therefore both reflected and helped propel this new methodological and epistemological "route" to understanding in international relations.

However, as much as the behavioral revolution (and Rosenau's part in it) was occasioned by the introduction of scientific approaches to the study of the social and political world, it was the growing general perception of the "unrealism of realism" that had given structure and substantive shape to the emerging behavioral consensus in the field of international relations. Traditional theory, in other words, had been based on images of international relations "that differed fundamentally from the contemporary world" and could therefore not possibly provide an adequate basis for contemporary theory building.[34] In a world that was becoming increasingly multicentric, how could the analyst ignore all actors other than the state? In a world in which the state was increasingly under siege as a political and economic unit, how could the analyst even "save" the state as a legitimate unit of analysis? In a world in which more and more forms of organized and interdependent behavior could be observed, how could the analyst retain a sterile and simplistic assumption of international anarchy. In a world in which foreign policy was becoming increasingly political and subject to the influence of sub- and nonstate actors, how could the notion of the state-as-a-unit, be salvaged by analysts? In short, recognizing "reality" and the massive variation and complexity inherent in it could only render orthodox approaches both empirically and prescriptively obsolescent. Consequently, much behavioral research in the 1950s, 1960s, and 1970s sought to expose systematically the inaccuracy of realist imagery. Behavioralists expressed their general dissatisfaction with traditional theory by taking realist assumptions and subjecting them to systematic, behavioral analysis.[35] What emerged was a radically different image of the world from that of the traditional realists.

In practice, Rosenau's own pursuit of "checkable-upable" knowledge as a corrective to realist dogma manifested itself first in the comparative study of foreign policy; it focused thereafter on the broader processes of transnationalization and interdependence in world politics. As is the case with his general methodological approach, Rosenau's work on interdependence can be shown to be both cause and effect and therefore both novel and derivative.

Although the term, "interdependence" has become commonplace in the contemporary lexicon of international relations, the dominance of realism in the 1940s and 1950s assured that the concept would not begin to appear in the literature with any regularity until the early and mid-1970s. The apparent relative decline of U.S. hegemony, along with the great global economic turbulence during that period, brought about a growing tendency among scholars of international relations to see the world in terms of increasing global interdependence. These events served to focus substantial behavioralist scholarship on the specific ways in which realist assumptions were being undermined, and—in particular from the standpoint of economic interdependence—on the proliferation and growing importance of non-state actors, the decreasing fungibility of power, and a declining self-sufficiency of nation-states.

All of these notions are developed in Rosenau's work (initially) on interdependence and (later) on turbulence. As a result of dramatic events and developments in the late 1960s and 1970s (e.g., energy and dollar crises, oil embargoes, declining U.S. hegemony), scholars were faced with the task of explaining the conditions (perceived or real) of marked change in world politics, while at the same time having to account for the persistence of aspects of the "old order." A literature thus emerged that may be characterized as behavioralist as it both shows the manner in which world politics has departed from the assumptions of realism and employs the methods of positivist science. In general, it focuses on transformations in the nature and number of actors and issues, on the declining relevance of military power, on the increasing importance of economic issues, on the growth of norms and regimes that guide behavior under anarchy, on the expansion of global interdependence, on the complex processes of decision making, and on the impact of individuals and mass publics on the course of world affairs.

On these grounds, for example, Rosenau's notion of bifurcation can be located firmly within the liberal/behavioralist tradition, a tradition that without much of a conceptual stretch could be called the interdependence/bifurcationist school of international relations theory. Among the most significant of these works, Keohane and Nye point out in their edited volume, *Transnational Relations and World Politics*, and their co-authored book, *Power and Interdependence*, that while interdependence has pervaded world politics, the assumptions and predictions of structural realist approaches still apply under certain circumstances.[36] In this sense, the two worlds of "complex interdependence" and "structural realism" are bifurcated in a way that alludes to Rosenau's state-centric and multicentric worlds. Mansbach and Vasquez, in *In Search of Global Theory*, make a comparable argument aimed at predicting the circumstances under which the "globalist" or "realist" worlds (issues and actors) can be expected to appear on the world political agenda.[37] Finally, Rosecrance's dichotomy of the "trading world" versus the "military/territorial world" in *The Rise of the Trading State* closely resembles Rosenau's multicentric/state-centric framework and facilitates similar conclusions.[38]

In summary, the approaches and many of the key arguments embodied by the "Rosenauian tradition," including *Turbulence in World Politics*, are directly related to a rather dominant branch of thought in the behavioralist tradition of international relations. Much of the vernacular employed by Rosenau throughout his career, has been readily available in the lexicon of this behavioralist discourse in international relations.

Turbulence Theory as Enlightenment for the 1990s and Beyond

Despite the foregoing, it is clear that not all of the theoretical content of turbulence theory can be unproblematically located within the interdependence/behavioral discourse of the 1960s and 1970s. Clearly, the most challenging and novel element of the work is the critical role it accords the increasing intellectual and cathectic capabilities of individuals in causing change (and enabling continuity) in international relations. Though the turbulence model that Rosenau forwards is multilevel and provides for feedback among different levels, "skills" lie at the center of causality. Thus, *Turbulence in World Politics* is essentially a micro theory of macro change. Indeed, it is the "sheer craziness"[39] of this claim that makes it difficult for some to locate turbulence theory's contextual roots. One is hard-pressed to uncover other contemporary works in the field of IR that have forwarded an even remotely similar causal argument. Of course, many scholars have focused their attention on decision makers and their influence on particular foreign-policy outcomes. Biohistorians and their tendency toward "Great Man" explanations of major historical events, also bring to mind possible connections to the centrality of the micro level in turbulence theory. But to posit that a mass enhancement of the intellectual skills of the world's adults is a major cause of the structural changes occurring in world politics is clearly a significant leap from such analyses.

Notwithstanding, there are key linkages between Rosenau's body of work and the liberal tradition in Western political and social thought that offer clues into the origins of Rosenau's novel micro theory. In particular, the view of individuals and subgroups that is inherent in Rosenau's writings provides a strong connection between neoliberal and classical liberal approaches. Along these lines, one key strand of thought that is common to much liberal thought is the importance of individual reason and rationality. Rosenau's work bears clear evidence of such preoccupations both in the form of his model of research and in his explanatory thinking about the relationship between the micro and macro levels in international relations.

As argued above for example, Rosenau has consistently made clear his deep belief in the ability of scholars to sift through rhetoric and find truth—or at the very least, the *probable* truth. Science, in his view, has always been the only way to discover the underlying dynamics of foreign policy world politics. As a result, Rosenau's scholarship has been rooted in a firm belief in the rational abilities of the scientist to investigate dispassionately the subject of his/her curiosities and arrive at a detached evaluation of the evidence. In *Turbulence in World Politics*, it appears clear that Rosenau is simply extending this conviction from the exclusive domain of scholars, to all adults, and from there to the world political process.

Thus, we can justifiably draw an implicit connection between Rosenau's turbulence theory and the Western liberal tradition in political theory that would later become linked to the behavioralist revolution in the social sciences in the United States. Although contemporary liberals have displayed a tendency to focus their ideas about individual and collective rationality on political leaders, a small segment of that group (including Rosenau) has identified itself more closely with earlier generations of liberal scholars whose putative audience and analytical focus was the mass public. It is therefore possible to forward the proposition that Rosenau's faith in human reason bears an interesting resemblance to eighteenth-century Enlightenment philosophy.

At a broad level, Enlightenment philosophers sought to break the "intellectual bondage" imposed by dogmatic Christian doctrines, thereby setting the stage for a "freedom of thought." By conceiving of individual explanations of social processes without reference to the limitations of institutions and conventions, or any Christian eschatology, philosophers of the Enlightenment became philosophers of intellectual liberty. Such liberty, it was widely thought, could be seen as having the potential for much broader institutional and structural effects. As Zacher and Matthew note in their comprehensive review of liberal international theory, Enlightenment liberalism

> suggested that cognitive factors could have a decisive effect on the very nature of international relations. Locke and Rousseau wrote treatises on education aimed at improving the state from below by producing virtuous citizens, a strategy that would ultimately affect the nature of the international system.[40]

Furthermore, by the late nineteenth and early twentieth centuries, Zacher and Matthew point out, many prominent liberalist thinkers (such as Mill, Hobson, Zimmern, Markwell, and Toynbee) afforded education, individual reason, and knowledge a central role in their discussions of progress in international relations. Closely associated with this more "cognitive liberalism," according to Zacher and Matthew, is a "republican liberalism" of which one of the main aims was to expose the arbitrariness of political institutions and provide a rational basis for the mass criticism of ineffective, corrupt, and oppressive governments. Both the cognitive and republican forms of liberal thinking are evident in turbulence theory.

For Rosenau, if the abilities of individuals are being enhanced—in part by the advances of the microelectronic revolution—a decline in virulent patriotism and a corresponding spread of the "nascent norm" of performance criteria are likely to result. As performance criteria are increasingly used by individuals, the effectiveness of subgroups is strengthened in proportion to the weakening of national governments. Increased skills are therefore coterminous with decreased allegiance to state governments. In Rosenau's framework, the interdependence-caused ineffectiveness of governments is a fact that is abundantly clear to intellectually enhanced individuals. This leads to a widening of the range of bodies or institutions to which postindustrial adults will look for the satisfaction of their needs in the world of postinternational politics.

This notion of "performance criteria" described in *Turbulence* could easily be seen as an outgrowth of the implicit and explicit belief in the power of reason, which Rosenau has championed with much passion within the field of international relations over the course of four decades. According to this line of argument, individuals have the capacity for rational reason that enables knowledge. For the scientist, reason enables freedom from the kinds of values and beliefs that cloud analysis. For the adult citizen, reason enables freedom from obsolescent governments and opens up a nearly infinite range of sources for welfare and security as well as a potentially unlimited number of possible targets of loyalty and legitimacy.

Interestingly, similar arguments are central to the international relations and domestic theories of Enlightenment philosophers like Jean Jacques Rousseau.[41] Though he is often claimed by realists, Rousseau was among the first to comprehend the tension between individual reason, interdependence, and the sovereignty of nation-states in world politics. The essence of Rousseau's argument is that states tend to be inherently insecure, envious, and warlike for two fundamental reasons. First, the artificial nature of the state imbues it with instability and the inherent drive to define its (perceived) interests in terms of relative power. Because the state in an international state of nature is by definition a product of social innovation, it is from the beginning consumed by *amour propre*, or a competitive greed and need to compare itself to others. By contrast, individuals in a state of nature, because of their physical capacity for self-sufficiency, are dominated by *amour de soi*, or a healthy need for self preservation that combined with modesty and diffidence, creates in them a natural reason and peacefulness. Only when people join societies does their *amour de soi* degenerate into the *amour propre* that then pervades states from the first minute of their existence.

A second source of the state's war-proneness closely follows from the first in Rousseau's political philosophy. Though individuals in nature are content and secure, their entry into civil society insures the onset of corruption and depravity. This manifests itself in the social institutions of domestic society that place war firmly within the narrow interests of important sectors of the state's political machinery. In his critique of the Abbe de Saint Pierre's peace plan, Rousseau establishes a direct connection between the depravity of political elites and the tendency toward war between states. Elites needed war, Rousseau argued, to make themselves necessary. Wars were thus purely outgrowths of habit, institution, and convention, fought in pursuit of the leaders' *perceived interests* and in sharp contrast to the people's (and state's) *real interests*, which lay in achieving international cooperation and peace. Princes made at least as much war against their own people as they did against their foreign "enemies." War was merely a useful method for squelching domestic discontent and weakening the positions of unruly subjects by focusing their aggressions on largely manufactured security fears of the state. As states grew less and less capable of fulfilling their obligations to citizens (due to increasing interdependence), and as state elites continued to become involved in arbitrary wars, they increasingly lost their grasp on legitimate rule. For Rousseau and a host of other observers of the Enlightenment era, reason and legitimacy went hand in hand.

Writers of the Enlightenment, such as Rousseau, thus tended to harbor a distinct optimism toward mass publics while simultaneously viewing political elites with more than a small amount of skepticism. The same can be said for the later liberal writers of the early twentieth century. For this reason, the characterization of such writers as "idealists" or "optimists" can be quite misleading. It is true that many of the liberals of this period argued that warfare had become a fundamentally irrational endeavor. Norman Angell, for example, posited that because of interdependence, the business of conquering neighboring countries could only bring commercial and financial suicide. Thus, the growth of international interdependence had "brought an end to the idea that the wealth, prosperity and well-being of a nation depended on political power"; as a result, war had become "useless, even when completely victorious, as a means of securing those moral or material ends which represent the needs of modern, civilized peoples."[42]

Nevertheless, most of the well-known liberal theorists of the early twentieth century were not particularly sanguine about the possibility that decision makers would recognize the increasing futility and irrationality of war. Instead, it was a common perception that enough leaders would retain their anachronistic views so that war would continue to be an oft-used instrument of policy. The vocabulary of international political discourse would remain "a survival of conditions no longer existing;" although the world had entered a new era of interdependence, this new world was "threatened by chaos because it [had] not learnt how to adjust its institutions and traditions to the new conditions."[43] In the liberal viewpoint, then, interdependence has been characterized by a "continual, uneasy relationship between the conditions of interdependence and their acceptance or cognition" by political elites.[44]

In summary, neither Rosenau's acceptance of the possibility of a multitude of potential future world orders, nor his admission that skill enhancement can either lead to aggregation or disaggregation, war or peace, nor his belief that the state-centric and multicentric worlds can coexist, can exempt his ideas from inclusion in the long tradition of liberal political and international theory. On the basis of this argument, it is conceivable that "postinternationalism" could be seen as "Enlightenment for the 1990s and beyond" or at least an important data point in the "neoidealist movement" predicted by some.[45] This is emphatically not to say that turbulence theory is a mere rehashing of classic liberal thought, butthat there has arguably been a substantial continuity throughout the evolution of liberal thinking from the classical period to the contemporary era in which the work of James Rosenau has been so central. Turbulence theory in short is firmly entrenched in the liberal tradition of international political theory.

TURBULENCE, TRADITION, AND PROSPECTS FOR A POSTINTERNATIONAL REVOLUTION IN IR THEORY

What are the implications of the foregoing for the key questions being addressed in this volume? Having placed Rosenau's work within a historiographical context—as a part of the broad liberal tradition, as a part of the behavioral revolution in political science, and thus as both a derivative but also importantly novel approach to understanding international politics—the question naturally arises as to the place of postinternationalism within the contemporary milieu of international relations scholarship. Consequently, an assessment of the impact of Rosenau's work—both current and potential—on the field of international relations requires that the general state of theory in the field be examined; only in this way will it be possible to determine the prospects for a postinternational revolution in the field of international relations.

Such a task is not as simple as it may seem at first glance. The idea that the study of international relations is and has been dominated by the realist approach has achieved a sort of secular theodicy among observers of the field and thus is a claim that is widely and uncritically accepted. For example, in his recent text on international relations theory Kegley refers to a decade-old quotation to lament the continued dominance of realist thinking in the field. In looking at the field in the middle 1980s, Michael Banks estimated that the discipline had become "intellectually totalitarian, dominated by [the realist] school of thought," a field in which "such notions as reasons of state, balance of power and national security dominate our thinking."[46] In the same volume, Grieco's near ten-year-old view of the field as one that has been "dominated by realism since at least WW II" is also offered in unrevised and unqualified form as an accurate assessment of the state of the field in the middle 1990s.[47]

Nevertheless, there are increasing indications that both realism's applicability in the post–Cold War era and its place as a dominant approach in the academic discipline of international relations may be on the wane. As Kegley himself noted in his 1993 International Studies Association presidential address:

> Indicators abound that realism is losing its grip on the imagination of those writing in our field and on policy makers' thinking. Our professional journals now frequently take "neo-Wilsonian idealism," ... "idealpolitik," ... "neoidealism," ... and "neoliberalism," seriously, whereas attacks on the "poverty of realism," ... the 'poverty of neorealism,' and the dangers of realpolitik based policies have become a growth industry.[48]

For these reasons, Kegley suggests, "Realism ... is increasingly perceived to have become an anachronism that has lost much of its explanatory and prescriptive power."[49]

In short, despite the tendency for the realist paradigm to be considered dominant as a matter of course there is actually a considerable amount of debate—sometimes even ostensibly within the minds of individual observers—as to whether realism continues to dominate the field as it once likely did in the 1940s and 1950s. Clearly, further investigation into this question is required if we are to be able to assess the state of the field and thereby speculate on the existence (or not) of a broad basis for a general acceptance of turbulence theory.

Do realist analyses of international politics remain dominant in the field[50] or has realism lost its place of centrality to liberal analyses?[51] To provide the beginnings of an answer to this question and to initiate the process of moving beyond the realm of dogma and conjecture on this subject, we undertook to create a simple data set of publications in several major journals of international relations. The results obtained here, while not exhaustive, provide the basis for at least tentative conclusions about the current state of the discipline.[52] The results of our classification of recent publications in five major journals of international relations are provided in Table 10.1.

As is evident from Table 10.1, realist analyses were not predominant in any journal, the closest case occurring in International Security, which, because of its self-conscious focus on security issues, can be considered a "most likely case." In the other journals and overall, the

Table 10.1
Recent Publications in Selected International Relations Journals

	Realist/ Neorealist	Liberal/ Neoliberal	Marxist/ Neomarxist	Postmodern	Other	Total
International Security	34	40	0	0	16	90
	(37.8)	(44.4)	(0)	(0)	(17.8)	(100)
International Studies Quarterly	26	55	4	2	19	106
	(24.5)	(51.9)	(3.3)	(1.9)	(17.9)	(100)
Journal of Peace Research	14	40	1	3	36	94
	(14.9)	(42.5)	(1.1)	(3.2)	(38.3)	(100)
International Organization	15	71	3	3	12	104
	(14.4)	(68.3)	(2.4)	(2.9)	(11.5)	(100)
Millennium	0	30	2	13	3	48
	(0)	(62.5)	(4.2)	(27.1)	(6.2)	(100)
Total articles	89	236	10	21	86	442
	(20.1)	(53.4)	(2.3)	(4.7)	(19.5)	(100)

(Percentages in parenthesis)

amount of realist scholarship did not come close to plurality. In contrast, it appears evident from in Table 10.1 that the liberal perspective provides the theoretical underpinnings of most contemporary research in international relations. If realism had once been the dominant theoretical paradigm in international relations, this seems no longer to be the case.

Assuming that our claim is accurate—that the liberal perspective has replaced the realist perspective as the most influential at least in the five major journals analyzed—it is reasonable to inquire whether turbulence theory, as a part of the broader liberal perspective, has achieved an appreciable level of acceptance or impact in the field of international relations generally and within the liberal perspective specifically. An answer to these questions will lay a firm foundation for speculation as to the chances for a postinternational revolution in international theory.

Here again, the answer is less predictable than it may intuitively seem. That is, if the development of political and international theory and the historical development of world politics over the last two centuries have led inexorably to the birth of Rosenau's micro theory of macro change, as this essay has implied, then the *Turbulence* argument should be widely accepted in the discipline and especially within the liberal camp. One would therefore expect to see several works in the contemporary literature that seriously consider the kinds of micro-macro postulates forwarded by turbulence theory, and that this acceptance should have laid the foundation for a postinternational revolution in international relations theory.

In general, this does not appear to be the case. Though it is difficult to measure precisely the magnitude of impact of a given body of work (especially since turbulence theory has only recently been elaborated) preliminary indications have not been altogether promising. For instance, initial presentations of turbulence theory garnered reviews that were mixed at best.[53] In addition, *Turbulence in World Politics* itself was reviewed around the time of its publication with somewhat better, although not entirely favorable results.[54]

Furthermore, as a "potentially distinctive paradigm for the post–Cold War period," *Turbulence in World Politics* has yet to prove competitive. For all intents and purposes, *Turbulence in World Politics* and turbulence theory purport to be improvements on and potential replacements for the realist and neorealist paradigms that are presumed to be dominant in international relations theory. This being the case, one way to get a sense of the overall relative impact of turbulence theory versus realist/neorealist theory is to investigate the rate of citations to prominent works in each tradition as reported in the Social

Sciences Citation Index. As a point of comparison, it makes sense to use the volume that has served for nearly two decades as the definitive statement of the neorealist cause: *Theory of International Politics* by Kenneth Waltz. Of course, the fact that *Theory* was published in 1979 and *Turbulence* was published in 1990 renders this an inherently unfair comparison. Nevertheless, such a comparison can provide at least a tentative idea about the relative salience of neorealism and turbulence theory.

Between 1991 and 1996 *Theory of International Politics* was cited far more frequently, both overall and on an annual basis than *Turbulence in World Politics*, however, the ratio of citations of *Theory* to *Turbulence* has come down from about 9:1 in 1991 (this is predictable so soon after the publication of the book) to approximately 4:1 in more recent years. But what about more bold inferences? The turbulence-optimist would point out that relative to neorealism, turbulence theory is about twice as relevant today as it was in 1991, while the pessimist would argue that neorealism appears still to be four times as relevant as turbulence theory, despite a substantial campaign over the last decade or so to proclaim its demise. Leaving the ratios aside, the neorealists' claim to centrality in the debates of the field (at least as compared to turbulence theory) is bolstered by the sheer number of citations to Waltz, which has not declined at all in recent years, with an all-time high of close to 98 citations as recently as 1996. In short, the raw citation data indicate that turbulence theory has yet to pose a serious challenge to neorealism as the focal point for theoretical debate in the field.

Unfortunately this simple comparison of the number of citations to *Turbulence* and *Theory* provides only rather superficial information. It demonstrates that *Theory* continues to be cited more frequently than *Turbulence* but says little about the exact nature of those references or what they in fact mean. That is, the raw citation numbers tell us a great deal about relative "centrality" but not much if anything about relative acceptance or adherence. Therefore, the substance of those references should be examined in order to gain greater understanding of the relative acceptance of the central theses within international relations scholarship.

In order to evaluate the substance of such references, the Social Science Citation Index was again consulted. Specifically, the articles in which citations to either Rosenau or Waltz appeared were read and analyzed for content, approach, and—in particular—their view of the works (either Rosenau's or Waltz's) that they cited. On the basis of this reading, articles with citations to *Theory* or *Turbulence* were categorized as falling into one of four classifications. Each work cited was deemed either "favorable" or "unfavorable" within the general theoretical perspective of the work examined (liberal for Rosenau and realist for Waltz), as emanating from the "alternate perspective" and therefore most likely critical, or simply as being nonjudgmental or incidental; such citations are categorized as "other." The results of this examination are provided in Table 10.2.

Table 10.2 provides several indicators of the level of acceptance of *turbulence theory* in the literature. It demonstrates the importance of these works within their particular theoretical schools, highlighting the uses to which they have been put. It also allows us to judge the importance that has been placed upon each of these works by scholars working out of alternate perspectives even if it is as nothing more than a null hypothesis to be countered. Although this examination entails citations from only 1995, its findings are consistent with other indicators of the importance of these works within the body of international relations theory. For example, Table 10.1 demonstrated that the liberal perspective serves as the predominant arena for contemporary research. Postinternationalism's theoretical place within that liberal perspective has likewise been discussed. Given the prevalence of liberal research in international relations, there were surprisingly few references to *Turbulence* in 1995. In contrast, despite the apparent shift to the liberal from the realist perspective, *Theory* remains cited four times more than *Turbulence* during this time period. Therefore, although one can argue that liberalism has supplanted realism as predominant, the same cannot be said about the ideas of Rosenau versus those of Waltz. *Theory* continues to be the more influential work, both within its own perspective and within the whole of international relations literature.

Turning again to the results reported in Table 10.2, it is then interesting to note the uses to which *Theory* and *Turbulence* have been put within international relations scholarship. Rosenau's postinternational

Table 10.2

Analysis of 1995 Citations to *Turbulence* (Rosenau) and *Theory* (Waltz)

Author	Supportive from within the same perspective	Critical from within the same perspective	Alternate perspective	Neither realist or liberal	Articles not examined	Total
Rosenau	11	0	0	5	6	22
Waltz	21	11	35	11	10	88

theory seems to be dismissed as irrelevant by those scholars who have not embraced it, regardless of whether they are realist or liberal. Of the citations to *Turbulence* that were found, 69 percent were supportive whereas the remaining 31 percent made only incidental reference to it, or references that did not otherwise fit into the schema that we had developed. Neither realists nor liberals who appear to have disagreed with *Turbulence* saw any need to so much as address this work, even in counterargument. *Theory*, on the other hand, has been more frequently and broadly cited. Among the references examined, 27 percent were found in otherwise realist texts that endorsed Waltz's analysis, another 14 percent of which were realists who tended to disagree but still felt it necessary to address Waltz, while an additional 45 percent were liberalists who still deemed it necessary to argue against *Theory*. In short, the substantial importance and influence of Waltz within the whole of international relations scholarship relative to that of Rosenau is readily apparent.

In summary, the data presented in Table 10.1 demonstrate that it is within the liberal perspective that most recent scholarship has taken place. The data presented in Table 10.2 indicates that while the current relative importance of liberalism over realism is well established, no similar claim can be made that postinternationalism is more central to international relations theory than is neorealism. Put simply, postinternationalism appears to be languishing on the fringes of theoretical discourse. Clearly, the claim of postinternationalism to a status as "distinctive paradigm for the post–Cold War period" is not justified, at least on the basis of these preliminary studies. However, it is equally clear from the evidence reported above that the relative invisibility of Rosenau's turbulence theory exists despite an abundance of otherwise similar research and writing in the field. The vast majority of work done in the field—as evidenced by recent publication trends in the field's leading journals—adheres to a multi-actor, multichannel, multi-issue model of which Rosenau's most recent work is certainly exemplary. Thus, although the liberal/neoliberal approach appears to be well on its way to assuming a dominant role, turbulence theory does not appear to have benefited from neoliberalism's "coattails."

The question then arises as to what developments would need to take place in the discipline of international relations for this state of affairs to change. Here, common sense and the data agree: at minimum, postinternationalism must be viewed as important, if not definitive, by those favoring alternate explanatory theories or perspectives. But perhaps even more important, if postinternationalism is ever to achieve anything close to paradigmatic status, substantially more support for postinternationalism must be garnered from within the liberal perspective.

What are the chances for such developments? Of course, one can only speculate about future prospects on the basis of past patterns. As a brief case study, the recent edited volume *Bringing Transnational Relations Back In: Non-State Actors, Domestic Structures and International Institution* may provide some clues.[55] Indeed, this volume, essentially an attempt to refine and reinvigorate the study of how transnational actors affect world politics, is arguably a "most likely case" for present purposes and thus an especially helpful source of insights. That is, as a comprehensive work that seeks to "take a fresh look at the impact of non-state actors on world politics" this volume could reasonably be expected to include significant direct or indirect references to *Turbulence in World Politics*.

As it turns out, turbulence theory appears to have had little direct or indirect impact on the formulation of this book. In his broadly grounded introduction to the volume, Risse-Kappen makes only two rather insignificant references to *Turbulence in World Politics*.[56] Thus, although *Turbulence* offers numerous potential insights into the transnationalization of world politics—the most important of them from a unique, micro-level perspective—the work is nearly completely eschewed in a volume that could easily have paid rather close attention to it.

The final question that arises is, why might this be the case. In our view, it would seem that Rosenau has been among the very few who have remained true to some of the key philosophical and theoretical tenets of the liberal tradition and the scientific epistemology that underlies it: do not shy away from placing individual reason at the center of political/structural causality, and always let your variables vary. The structural (neorealist) and institutional (neoliberal) fixations that have pervaded much of the scholarly work in the field of IR in recent years may well have caused theorists to disregard the role of the individual. James Rosenau, on the other hand, by allowing his mind to wander and his variables to vary, has developed a model that anticipated the events surrounding the end of the Cold War, suggests a variety of future scenarios, and outlines the conditions under which each scenario might or might not ascend to a dominant position. The theory that underlies *Turbulence in World Politics* (whether it be called the Postinternational Paradigm, postinternationalism, or simply turbulence theory) follows and extends the behavioral and liberal traditions. This theoretical duality makes it a compelling set of ideas that deserves further critique and development along the lines suggested by the contributors to this volume. The fact that it has yet to be widely embraced within the international relations scholarly community renders it no less worthy of such treatment.

NOTES

1. J. N. Rosenau, *Turbulence in World Politics: A Theory of Change and Continuity* (Princeton, N.J.: Princeton University Press, 1990).

2. Ibid., pp. 62–63.

3. For an in-depth discussion of "inward" versus "outward" loyalty shifts, see R. B. A. DiMuccio and J. N. Rosenau, "Turbulence and Sovereignty in World Politics: Explaining the Relocation of legitimacy in the 1990s and Beyond," in Z. Mlinar, ed. *Globalization and Territorial Identities* (Aldershot: Avebury Press, 1992).

4. J. N. Rosenau, *Turbulence*, p. 13.

5. Ibid., pp. 13–15.

6. Ibid., pp. 159–73.

7. Ibid., pp. 249–52.

8. The two images on the cover of *Turbulence* are photos that have achieved a great degree of notoriety: one of several youths standing atop the Berlin Wall in the foreground of the Brandenburg Gate; and the other of a Chinese student standing in front of a column of government tanks at Tienanmen Square. As Rosenau notes in an addendum to the preface of the book, "the final draft was readied for publication in August 1989, just weeks before the upheavals that culminated in the onset of considerable turbulence in the Soviet Union and the rapid-fire collapse of communist regimes . . . " ("Turbulence and Sovereignty," p. xviii). Thus these events occurred only in the very latter stages of the development of turbulence theory.

9. J. N. Rosenau, "The Scholar as an Adaptive System," in *Journeys through World Politics*, ed. Joseph Kruzel and James Rosenau (Lexington: Lexington Press, 1988).

10. E. Roosevelt (assisted by J. N. Rosenau), eds., *FDR: His Personal Letters, 1905–28* (New York: Duell, Sloan & Pierce, 1949).

11. Rosenau, "The Scholar as an Apaptive System," p. 57.

12. J. N. Rosenau. ed., The Roosevelt Treasury (New York: Doubleday, 1951).

13. J. N. Rosenau, "The Senate and Dean Acheson: A Case Study in Legislative Attitudes" (Princeton University: Unpublished Ph.D. diss., 1957).

14. J. N. Rosenau, *Public Opinion and Foreign Policy: An Operational Formulation* (New York: Random House, 1961).

15. See for example, J. N. Rosenau, "Consensus, Leadership, and Foreign Policy." in *SAIS Review* 6 (1962): 3–10, and J. N. Rosenau, *National Leadership and Foreign Policy: A Case Study in the Mobilization of Public Support* (Princeton, N.J.: Princeton University Press, 1963).

16. J. N. Rosenau, ed., *International Aspects of Civil Strife* (Princeton, N.J.: Princeton University Press, 1964).

17. See J. N. Rosenau, "Private Preferences and Political Responsibilities: The Relative Potency of Individual and Role Variables in the Behavior of U.S. Senators," in *Quantitative International Relations: Insights and Evidence*, ed. J. D. Singer (New York: Free Press, 1968); or J. N. Rosenau, *Citizenship between Elections: An Inquiry into the Mobilizable American* (New York: Free Press, 1974).

18. See J. N. Rosenau, *The Study of Global Interdependence: Essays on the Transnationalization of World Affairs* (London: Frances Pinter, 1980); or J. N. Rosenau, "A Pre-Theory Revisited: World Politics in an Era of Cascading Interdependence," *International Studies Quarterly* 28 (1984): 245–305.

19. J. N. Rosenau, ed., *Linkage Politics: Essays on the Convergence of National and International Systems* New York: The Free Press, 1969).

20. See J. N. Rosenau, *The Adaptation of National Societies: A Theory of Political Behavior and Its Transformation* (New York: McCaleb-Seiler, 1970; and J. N. Rosenau, *The Study of Political Adaptation* (London: Frances Pinter, 1980).

21. See J. N. Rosenau, "Before Cooperation: Hegemons, Regimes and Habit-Driven Actors in World Politics," *International Organization* 40 (1986):884–86; and J. N. Rosenau, "Learning in East-West Relations: The Superpowers as Habit-Driven Actors," *Australian Outlook* 41 (1987): 141–50.

22. J. N. Rosenau, "New Directions and Recurrent Questions in the Comparative Study of Foreign Policy," in *New Directions in the Study of Foreign Policy*, ed. C. Hermann, C. Kegley, and J. N. Rosenau (Boston: Allen & Unwin, 1987).

23. J. N. Rosenau, "The State in an Era of Cascading Politics: Wavering Concept, Widening Competence, Withering Colossus, or Weathering Change," *Comparative Political Studies* 21 (1988): 13–44.

24. O. Holsti and J. N. Rosenau, "Foreign and Domestic Policy Systems among American Leaders," *Journal of Conflict Resolution* 32 (1988): 248–94.

25. J. N. Rosenau, *Turbulence*, p. xvi.

26. J. N. Rosenau, *The Scientific Study of Foreign Policy*, 2d ed., (London: Frances Pinter, 1980), p. 1.

27. Rosenau, *Turbulence*, pp. 5–6.

28. In addition to the citation and publication data that are presented below, the earlier arguments of S. Hoffmann, "An American Social Science: International Relations," *Daedalus* 106 (1977): 41–60; and H. Alker and T. Biersteker, "The Dialectics of World Order: Notes for a Future Archaeologist of International Savoir-Faire," *International Studies Quarterly* 28 (1984), provide compelling textual support for this point.

29. J. Dougherty and R. Pfaltzgraff, *Contending Theories of International Relations* (New York: HarperCollins Publishers, 1990), p. 537.

30. Alker and Biersteker, "Dialectics," pp. 126–27.

31. Hoffman, "An American Social Science," p. 45.

32. J. N. Rosenau, "The Scholar as an Adaptive System," p. 59.

33. Ibid., p. 63. See also K. Knorr and J. N. Rosenau, *Contending Approaches to International Politics* (Princeton, N.J.: Princeton University Press, 1969); and J. N. Rosenau, *The Scientific Study of Foreign Policy* (New York: Free Press, 1971).

34. Dougherty and Pfaltzgraff, *Contending Theories*, p. 536.

35. For some examples of this, one could cite decision analysis (e.g., Allison, *Essence of Decision: Explaining the Cuban Missile Crisis* [New York: Little, Brown, and Co., 1969]; J. Steinbruner, *The Cybernetic Theory of Decision* [Princeton, N.J.: Princeton University Press, 1974]; R. Jervis, *Perception and Misperception in International Politics* [Princeton, N.J.: Princeton University Press, 1976]); systems theory (e.g., O. Young, *Systems of Political Science* [Englewood Cliffs, N.J.: Prentice-Hall, 1968]; J. Burton, *Systems, States, Diplomacy, and Rules* [Cambridge: Cambridge University Press, 1968]; J. D. Singer, *A General Systems Taxonomy for Political Science* [New York: General Learning Press, 1971]); or regional integration theory (e.g., L. Lindberg, *The Political Dynamics of European Economic Integration* [Stanford, Ill.: Stanford University Press, 1963]; E. Haas, *The Uniting of Europe* [Stanford, Ill.: Stanford University Press, 1958]; A. Etzioni, *Political Unification* [New York: Holt, Rinehart and Winston, 1958]).

36. See R. Keohane and J. Nye, eds., *Transnational Relations and World Politics* (Cambridge: Harvard University Press, 1972); and R. Keohane and J. Nye, *Power and Interdependence: World Politics in Transition* (Boston: Little, Brown, Inc., 1977).

37. R. Mansbach and J. Vasquez, *In Search of Global Theory* (New York: Columbia University Press, 1981).

38. R. Rosecrance, *The Rise of the Trading State* (New York: Basic Books, 1986).

39. J.N. Rosenau, *Turbulence*, p. xviii.

40. M. Zacher and R. Matthew, "Liberal International Theory: Common Threads, Divergent Strands," in C. Kegley, ed., *Controversies in International Relations Theory: Realism and the Neoliberal Challenge* (New York: St. Martin's Press, 1995) pp. 129–30.

41. Rousseau's most notable works on international relations are found in his "Unfinished Manuscript on the 'State of War,' " and his "Summary and Critique of the Abbe de Saint Pierre's Plan for Perpetual Peace." The theoretical basis for his arguments in these works, though, is clearly evident in his *Discourses on the Origins of Inequality, Social Contract*, and his constitutional project for Poland. For an in-depth analysis of Rousseau's ideas about international relations, see DiMuccio, R.B.A, "Man, the State, and International Politics: A Reconsideration of Rousseau," *Journal of Public and International Affairs* (1992): 15–38.

42. N. Angell, *The Great Illusion: A Study of the Relation of Military Power to National Advantage* (London: Heineman, 1913), pp. v–13.

43. R. Muir, *The Interdependent World and its Problems* (London: Kennicat Press, 1925), p. vii.

44. J. de Wilde, *"Saved from Oblivion: Interdependence Theory in the First Half of the 20th Century"* (Ph.D. diss., University of Groningen, Netherlands, 1990), p. 55.

45. C. Kegley, "The Neoidealist Moment in International Studies? Realist Myths and the New International Realities," *International Studies Quarterly*, 37, 2 (June 1993): 131–46.

46. Quotation is from M. Banks, "The International Relations Discipline: Asset or Liability for Conflict Resolution?" in E Azar and J. Burton, eds., *International Conflict Resolution* (Boulder: Lynne Rienner, 1986), p. 11, as quoted by C. Kegley, *Controversies*, p. 2.

47. J. Grieco, "Anarchy and the Limits of Cooperation: A Realist Critique of the Newest Liberal Institutionalism," in C. Kegley, ed., *Controversies*, p. 151.

48. C. Kegley, "Neoidealist Moment," p. 134.

49. Ibid (citing O. Holsti, "International Systems, System Change, and Foreign Policy," *Diplomatic History* 15: 84).

50. C. Kegley, *Controversies*, p. 2.

51. C. Kegley, "Neoidealist Moment," p. 134.

52. Space does not permit a detailed description of our research procedure. The methodology used in scrutinizing these articles was based on subjective interpretations; no attempt was made to achieve "inter-coder reliability." In brief, we hypothesized that if realism were indeed the dominant approach in the field, at least a plurality of articles in several major journals should be classifiable as realist in character and content. To investigate this proposition, we chose to evaluate recent issues of *International Studies Quarterly* (March 1991–December 1995), *International Organization* (winter 1991–autumn 1995), *Journal of Peace Research* (February 1992–November 1995), *International Security* (spring 1991–spring 1995) and *Millennium* (spring 1994–spring 1995). Each article appearing in these journals was read and its predominant theoretical perspective was determined. Each article was categorized as being realist/neorealist, liberal/neoliberal, Marxist/neo-Marxist, or postmodern or feminist, using generally accepted notions of what each approach entails in terms of actors, issues, assumptions, and so forth.

53. As judged on the basis of the first author's own observations of the proceedings of a conference on "Change in the International System," University of Southern California, Institute for Transnational Studies, May 1988. Here, James Rosenau publicly presented for the first time his ideas on micro-level skills as a source of large-scale political change to a univerally unreceptive audience of prominent scholars of international relations.

54. Of the eight published (English-language) reviews that were found, only three were decidedly favorable (A. J. Pierre, review of *Turbulence in World Politics*, by James Rosenau, *Foreign Affairs* (winter 1991) 70: 183; H. Starr, review of *Turbulence in World Politics*, *The Journal of Politics*, 53, 3 [1991]; 924. R. A. Matthew, review of *Turbulence in World Politics*, *Canadian Journal of Political Science* 24 [1991]: 444–46), while the other five were substantially less sanguine about its prospects for lasting impact on the field (J. Sipila, review of *Turbulence in World Politics*, *Journal of Peace Research* 29 [1992]: 474–76; Government and Opposition, review of *Turbulence in World Politics*. *Government and Opposition*, 27: 523–26; M. Clarke. 1992. review of *Turbulence in World Politics*, *International Affairs* January 1992, v68, n1, p141(1); D. S. Sorenson, review of *Turbulence in World Politics*, *The Annals of the American Academy of Political and Social Science* 518; C. F. Hermann, review of *Turbulence in World Politics*, *American Political Science review* 85 [1991]: 1081–84).

55. T. Risse-Kappen, ed., *Bringing Transnational Back In: Non-State Actors, Domestic Structures, and International Institutions* (Cambridge: Cambridge University Press, 1995).

56. One refers to a somewhat obscure piece of data on the growth in the number of international nongovernmental organizations (Risse-Kappen, *Bringing Transnational*, p. 10); the other (misguidedly) cites *Turbulence* as an example of work on interdependence (Risse-Kappen, *Bringing Transnational*, 8).

CHAPTER 11

Postinternationalism and the Future of IR Theory

Yale Ferguson

This chapter[1] offers reflections, first, about James N. Rosenau's personality as it infuses his scholarship; second, about his ideas and especially postinternationalism as a theoretical perspective, contrasted with statist theory; and finally about the need for postinternational revolution, broadly conceived, in the international relations (IR) field today. Such a revolution, I shall argue, is already underway. Various strains of cutting-edge theoretical work all appear to be converging on a vision of global politics, reflecting "real-world" political trends, that is much less state-centric than traditional scholarship.

ROSENAU AND POSTINTERNATIONALISM

I have known Rosenau ever since the late 1960s when Richard Mansbach and I were assistant professors in the same graduate program at Rutgers for which Rosenau was graduate director. What struck me immediately was his enormous enthusiasm, inquisitiveness, energy, and inventiveness. For decades he has been a kid in a candy shop, which for him is a world of politics. He loves what he does and does it at breakneck pace, and for anyone around him his enthusiasm is as contagious as the ebola virus. He's a true pioneer, a genuinely original thinker, and today a firebreathing radical who makes extreme-relativist postmodernists seem mild by comparison. For them, nothing is ultimately "knowable," except that scholars talk past one another, while particular "discourses" provide whatever hierarchy and order prevail. Postmodernists challenge us to consider more carefully what we are saying, and why, which is a healthy exercise. However, by

197

contrast, imagine!, Rosenau actually believes that complexity is observable, comprehensible, and ultimately measurable!

Rosenau is the quintessential optimist, for whom hope springs eternal that the fountain of true understanding is just over the next hill. He is continually pushing ahead, asking (what he insists his students ask) "of what is this an instance?", classifying, identifying puzzles, and suggesting possible answers. "Pre-theory," as he has practiced it, is not just about comparative foreign policy, but a lifetime battlefield, now littered as far as the eye can see with abandoned or mutated concepts and partial metatheories—and a new battlezone is always opening up. Rosenau has more ideas in twenty-four hours than most of us do in a quarter century, which poses a problem. Pity the graduate student who tries to operationalize what Rosenau wrote in his latest theoretical salvo, only to discover that he has already critiqued his own work and moved on.

Rosenau has a rare capacity to admit he might have been on the wrong track, as he did, for example, when he distanced himself from strict science. He is far more interested in constructing than deconstructing or, for that matter, reconstructing. Those who have followed his work over the years have never found it dull and, regularly, a source of remarkable insight and inspiration. Of the work of how many of our IR colleagues can we make such a statement?

When Rosenau was a strict scientist and science was in vogue, he was one of those who defined the mainstream. Rosenau and the world of global politics moved on, strict science became much less fashionable, but the study of "international relations" in political science remained securely rooted in realism and its neorealist, institutionalist, and (more recently) neoliberal and statist-constructivist variants. Today, Rosenau is one of the larger whitewater tributaries that are defining the non-state-centric broad mainstream of tomorrow. Meanwhile, the price of all this originality, perhaps predictably, is that the present Mississippi mainstream of mediocrity (how's that for a Rosenau alliteration?) in the IR field can only try to ignore him. They have largely succeeded in this effort of late. When was the last time an article in a major U.S. journal really took Rosenau to task, engaging and refining his arguments? Most of our colleagues are enmeshed in a very narrow band of debates that have never ventured very far from their realism cave. Rosenau and they are literally living in different universes, his small-r real and theirs, a statist never-never land (more on this shortly).

In this collection, Mansbach has neatly summarized the progression of Rosenau's ideas over the years, so I shall only comment about the aspects of his work that impress me the most. He himself has both summarized and extended it, most recently, in two major volumes, *Turbulence in World Politics* and *Along The Domestic—Foreign Frontier*.[2] As Mansbach notes, Rosenau has always been interested in the relationship between domestic and international politics, and of wholes and parts in the political universe in general. *Linkage Politics*[3] had a great impact upon me personally, and my own favorite among his many books (with the possible exception of *Turbulence* and *Along the Domestic-Foreign Frontier*), is his *The Dramas of Politics*[4]. Perhaps more than any other, that book still captures his boundless enthusiasm, desire to communicate the excitement and plain fun of discovery, and—most significantly for me—the notion that politics extends from individuals in families and other groups all the way to global structures. The sovereign, inside/outside divide remains in his most recent work—a little more than I would wish—but the divide is so permeated and transcended that it almost vanishes and, in any event, is not one of the most important features of global politics. In this regard, postinternationalism is not essentially an extension of the old liberal/pluralist model. Certainly the state does not act as a gatekeeper, as it does in the much less radical model advanced by Robert D. Putnam's notion of two-level games.[5] In Rosenau's view, while the state (itself rarely if ever a unified actor) plays "its" games within and without, a wide variety of other actors and authorities are doing a host of equally or more interesting things with little regard for the governments or boundaries of sovereign states.

For Rosenau, the political universe is populated by a vast range of actors and authorities that are continually evolving and differentially engaged in countless issues. Governance involves much more than what we have traditionally regarded as "governments," let alone sovereign states. Hosts of outcomes are shaped not only by broad trends in the world that affect most issues but also, as chaos and complexity theorists remind us, sometimes by the smallest of actions and developments (the butterfly effect). Ferguson/Mansbach adopt a similarly complex view of the political universe, although not drawing on natural-science complexity theory per se. Yet Rosenau leaves us light-years behind in articulating and empirically addressing the micro level. We keep emphasizing the importance of the micro-level, but Rosenau is actually investigating it, trying to gather the data to support his generalizations. We sense that the engagement in an increasingly globalized world for elites and many ordinary citizens is having a profound effect on the way they think and behave. Elites are frequent travelers and ordinary individuals surf the net. To what effect(s)? Rosenau wants to know and is determinedly designing research strategies to find out.

Allow me to approach another point with a personal story. A long-time Rutgers colleague and former coeditor of mine, Walter Weiker, and I for decades had a genial argument about the relationship between my field of international relations, and his, comparative politics. He argued that IR was a mere branch of comparative politics, and I, of course, vice versa. Well, imagine my chagrin when I had to acknowledge a few years ago that he had been correct all along. I could not, however, resist adding that he had been wrong all along about what he thought comparative politics was! The Introduction to Comparative Politics course that my department and most others offer— comparing the "domestic" political systems of the United States, France, China, Mexico, and so on—misses the "outside" shaping politics "inside" (and the other way about).[6] Many such influences bypass the governments of states, although some impact directly thereon and within those governments; and most affect the fortunes of states one way or another. Rosenau has known these things for a very long time, despite his flirtation with state boxes in his early pre-theory work on comparative foreign policy. *Linkage Politics* bridged the outside/inside divide, and *Dramas* went further, to highlight the political in virtually every individual and human institution and situation. That is global or universal politics in its essence, and, as I see it, where the task of categorizing and comparison must begin.

Rosenau may have drifted away from his early role as a prophet of the strict-science revolution, but he is still an empiricist, who seeks data and continues to look to the natural sciences for helpful models. Ferguson/Mansbach have increasingly moved toward history and the humanities (although we remain empiricists), but Rosenau's bumper sticker still seems to read "I'd rather be doing science." His current interest is in the work of the Santa Fe Institute and others on complexity theory, and it will be important to observe what comes of all that. Is this just a new phase of Rosenau's "physics envy," or has he now found the very body of scientific theory that we need? Stay tuned. As Mary Durfee points out in her contribution to this volume, complexity theory and its close relative, chaos, present their own conceptual problems as well as opportunities. My own belief is that natural scientists with an interest in individuals and societies are more likely to learn from us social "scientists" than we are from them.

Natural-science models may help break us out of the habit-driven thought patterns in our disciplines, encourage the "conceptual jailbeaks" that Rosenau rightly thinks are required, and offer us useful metaphors for some of the phenomena and patterns we observe. But, apart from the problems inherent in various natural-science models, there is still no solid evidence that human behavior and social systems resemble natural-science systems in any but relatively superficial ways. I myself believe that it is more productive for social scientists to put both natural-science and traditional social-science models (that have had ample time to prove of limited worth) aside for a spell and "just" start describing what we seem to observe *actually happening* in the world of politics. To be sure, such an approach is "barefoot empiricism" (as Steve Smith, another IR theorist colleague, characterized it when I made the suggestion to him); and postmodernists would properly caution that we cannot avoid "seeing" through "the glasses inside our heads" whenever we look out at the world. Nonetheless, I must insist, we will not make adequate theoretical progress until we do ruthless ground clearing and start replanting new intellectual seedlings from the social-science nursery. In addition to his interest in the science of complexity, that is precisely what Rosenau seems to be doing in his own work and, as I shall explain shortly, what is occurring in various other promising approaches to global political theory as well.

Next, to Rosenau's supposed ahistoricism, about which I differ somewhat from Mansbach's assessment. To be sure, Rosenau is interested almost exclusively in the present. He suggests that the relevance of history is at least partly a matter of temperament, that some persons find continuities with the past while others are more keenly aware of the ways the present is different. Rosenau is decidedly one of the latter and, indeed, argues that the contemporary world is so different—because of the global revolutions in information, communication, and transportation, and their impact on the micro level—that it amounts to nothing less than a difference *in kind*. He contrasts, for example, the lingering demise of the Roman and British empires with the sudden collapse of the Soviet empire. Frankly, I have to admit that this line of argument is very persuasive. However. . . .

One day I shall write an article on the theoretical "nonissues" of global politics, which will be too long to publish, because most "great debates" in our field fall into that category. So does the debate about the relevance of history. Yes, on the one hand, Rosenau is entirely correct that the present is different from anything that came before and can be studied on its own terms. On the other hand, as Ferguson/Mansbach emphasize, a multitude of polities that ebb and flow has been the real norm in global politics for over five thousand years. As we demonstrate in *Polities,*[7] the past may give us clues about what to look for in the present—and even help us predict. Rosenau is correct that the sheer pace of change has speeded up, but that, too, can be overestimated: The mighty Assyrian empire collapsed in only thirty years, and the Aztecs' (with a little help from the Spanish) about as fast as the Soviets'. Chaos and complexity have been with us since the Big Bang, and there have been many eras of extreme instability. Some sources of instability are also strikingly different today from what they were, say, in ancient Egypt or the Roman Empire at its height, but many sources (e.g., nested polities and identities) are not different.

The bottom line is that Rosenau, as well as the rest of us, is obliged to specify the extent to which the present is different from the past but also similar. One thing is certain: the past is far more relevant to our understanding of the present and future than the state-centric Westphalian world of most of our IR colleagues. As Ferguson/Mansbach have argued repeatedly, it was the "Westphalian moment" in global politics that was exceptional. Global politics today resembles politics as it always was (and always will be?) more than that peculiar European-dominated era of sovereign states, only a few hundred years—itself punctuated by major changes and always involving many local variations—in the long train of human history. The Cold War period of the superpowers was dissimilar to that of Metternich. How shall we label the contemporary era? What Hedley Bull called "the new medievalism" (again a prominent theme in some literature) seems too Eurocentric a characterization, however accurately it points to overlapping political authorities and loyalties. Why not, simply, politics as usual? Ferguson/Mansbach entitled the second chapter of *Polities*, "The Subject is Politics"—and so global politics should be labeled and investigated.

"EMBEDDED STATISM" AND A WORLD OF POLITIES

There is an urgent need for a postinternational revolution in the study of global politics, broadly conceived as a take-no-prisoners campaign waged by all those from various disciplines who are non-state-centric and yet empirical in their approach(es). Some current approaches to the IR field are veritable monastic movements, having abandoned empirical analysis almost entirely for communal rites. The extreme relativists among postmodernists have their own liturgy but play games with the rest of language, while rational choice and formal theorists spin out equations that are the intellectual equivalent of Nintendo.[8] Realists, neorealists, institutionalists, neoliberals, statist constructivists, and others are to be commended for trying to analyze the world as it is, but their state-centric blinkers make it impossible for them to perceive the full spectrum of political reality. The glasses behind their eyes are focused on statist never-never land, a political universe that never existed in the form they think it did—not in 1648, not in 1815, not in 1945—and certainly does not today.

Consider the narrow band of "great debates" in the IR field that, along with rational choice and formal theories, currently fill the pages of mainstream journals: Will more democratic states mean a more peaceful world? (No matter that, historically, there is a very small *n* of democracies from which to generalize or that no one can seem to define "democracy" anyway. This debate at least keeps the war/peace contingent occupied on their familiar military security turf.) Are realism and neorealism still relevant in a post–Cold War world? Do international institutions merely reflect state interests, or do institutions shape states' perceptions of their interests and constrain state behavior? How do politics at the domestic level affect what states do in the international arena? (Thus far some two-level game institutionalists venture.) Are more autonomous international institutions virtually inevitable, given the demands of contemporary international society? Regardless of formal institutions, do rules routinely develop that considerably reduce genuine anarchy in global politics? (Thus far do neoliberals go.) Do states, in fact, perceive ("construct") their own reality, whatever the objective nature of the "real world"? (state-centric constructivists)

During the discussion session at the American Political Science Association panel that originally inspired this volume, Stephen Krasner (in the audience) asked whether—before looking for a revolution in the IR field—postinternationalists ought not first ponder why it is that some constructivists (e.g., Alexander Wendt) have received such a generally favorable reception, while postinternationalism as an approach has gained far fewer adherents. The plain answer is that state-centric constructivists offer something for everybody, which at the end of the day, it seems to me, involves only the most minimal sort of advance. Like institutionalism, this brand of constructivism is firmly rooted in a state-as-primary-actor political universe that realists and neorealists find entirely congenial. Partially convinced by postmodernist challenges? State-centric constructivists identify themselves as "critical theorists" and allow states to act on the basis of their perceptions. Never fear, however, there remains an objective reality that constrains state choices and can punish states that ignore it entirely.[9]

The shared intellectual conservatism (as the world has moved on, reactionary stance) of realists, neorealists, institutionalists, and state-centric constructivists has rarely been as clear as in a 1995 mini-symposium in *International Security*.[10] Robert O. Keohane and Lisa L. Martin acknowledge that neorealist John J. Mearsheimer "correctly asserts that liberal institutionalists treat states as rational egoists operating in a world in which agreements cannot be hierarchically enforced, and that institutionalists only expect interstate cooperation to occur if states have significant common interests."[11] For his part, Wendt groups postmodernists, constructivists, feminists, and others into a "family of theories" loosely classified as "critical IR theory." Yet he also says bluntly of his own brand of constructivism: "I share all five of Mearsheimer's 'realist' assumptions . . . : that international politics is anarchic, and that states have offensive capabilities, cannot be 100 percent certain about others' intentions, wish to survive, and are rational. We even share two more: a commitment to states as units of analysis, and to the importance of systemic or 'third image' theorizing." He adds: "All observation is theory-*laden* in the sense that what we see is mediated by our existing theories, and to that extent knowledge is inherently problematic. But this does not mean that observation, let alone reality, is theory-*determined*. The world is still out there constraining our beliefs, and may punish us for incorrect ones. Montezuma had a theory the Spanish were gods, but it was wrong, with disastrous consequences."[12]

In sum, as suggested earlier, the mainstream continues to count angels on the head of an essentially realist pin. Focus on the assumptions Wendt shares with neorealist John J. Mearsheimer. (1) International politics is anarchic. Well, OK, there's no world government. Isn't there more we need to say about actors, institutions, and processes? (2) States have offensive capabilities. Now that is really profound. (3) States cannot be 100 percent certain about others' intentions. Isn't that true for all actors? (4) States wish to survive. Right. East Germany? Canada? Do states wish upon a star, or how do they do it exactly? (5) States are rational. Any student of policy analysis would have grave problems with that assertion. Lastly, move on to theory versus reality. Accepted, and the Montezuma example is a brilliant one. Nevertheless, is the best we can do, theory-wise, a state-centric view, or does objective reality demand a more multidimensional analysis of global politics?

State-centric theory is so patently out of touch with reality that we might wonder how this contemporary equivalent of "the Spanish are gods" has managed to persist in the face of so much contradictory evidence? Political geographer Peter J. Taylor has reflected upon what he terms "embedded statism" in the social sciences.[13] The modern disciplines all emerged at the height of the state's prestige in the late nineteenth and twentieth centuries. Sovereign states with familiar boundaries on the world political map, which though "of obvious political significance," nevertheless came to be regarded "as much more than mere polities": "Nearly all social science has assumed that these political boundaries fix the limits of other key interactions." As for political science, its "comparative studies subfield" focused on the political systems of different states and had "little or nothing to offer by way of understanding globalization." Realism's sway especially among U.S. scholars resulted in "a concentration on questions of war and peace," a "security fetish" that reinforced a billiard ball model of a world of states. To be sure, a new subfield of international political economy gradually emerged, but that took the form, initially, of a new emphasis on the "interdependence" of states and then on "regimes" supposedly tailored by member states to serve their own state interests.

Although Taylor does not mention it, political science has also had a bedrock normative bias that has reinforced a state-centric vision. Most political scientists love "the state" because they tend to associate it with the public good as opposed to venal private interests. Political scientists as a profession are deeply suspicious of anything that smacks of "business" and, indeed, of any interest group that is not working for the "public interest." Political science tends to read history as a long climb of the sovereign state out of the segmented mire of the Middle Ages, the triumph of the popular will over religious fanatics, exploitative nobles, and so on. Even today, the privatization that is relentlessly taking place in most of the world's economies makes most political scientists profoundly uneasy. The very subject of their discipline appears to be withering away in a fashion utterly unforeseen by Marxists or anyone else. Likewise, the worldwide resurgence of "ethnicity" and the "failed state" phenomenon political scientists prefer to regard as a return to "tribalism"—something that the modern state was supposed to eradicate—rather than as a cultural phenomenon that is as perennial as it is fundamentally fictive and dangerous.

Mansbach and I have our own explanations for the continued strength of the image of neat state boxes on the global political map. We have attributed much of the problem to Eurocentrism and concomitant ahistoricism. A legalistic bias is one important aspect of the European tradition. Legalistic reasoning holds that the only true "authorities" are those that are enshrined in law, and states are the only legal sovereigns. Analysts are prone to forget that "sovereignty" was never more than a *claim* to authority, which has been achieved by individual state polities in a practical sense only to a greater or lesser degree over particular realms of social life. Possessing sovereignty has never meant having absolute control, an effective government, all that much legitimacy in the eyes of citizens, or even a Weberian monopoly of the legitimate use of violence.

Since sovereignty is essentially a legal status, all the speculation in the regime literature about its somehow being increasingly "divided" is misleading. Effective control or influence over specific issues has always been divided, and any number of genuinely sovereign entities have very little to show for that supposedly exhalted status. Even when a state's scope of authority is substantial, its government may be so paralyzed by bureaucratic infighting or legislative gridlock that it is incapable of acting; or certainly, except on the rarest occasion, of acting in anything like a unified fashion—and in this sense, "the state" hardly seems like a "real" actor at all. When policies emerge from the state, the result often seems little more than the triumph of parochial bureaucratic interests or a reflection of powerful private-interest groups.

Any survey of the world's nearly two hundred states reveals that the differences among them are far greater and more important than the similarities. Moreover, millennia of human history—as well as a closer look at the contemporary world—amply illustrates the existence of an enormous number of different types of political authorities that coexist, conflict, and cooperate and also overlap, layer, and nest. Political boundaries have not been immutable; rather they have shifted, sometimes rapidly and sometimes incrementally, throughout history. Polities are always "becoming." This is the essence of the "polities" model of global politics that Ferguson/Mansbach have advanced.

As we have repeatedly emphasized, the question is not whether sovereign states exist and "matter" in some respects, for, of course, they do. The questions are how do they matter? how do they not? how are they changing?—and especially what other polities exercise control or effective influence over some of the same and additional domains of social life? What does the sovereign-state model of global politics fail to tell us that is important, or, worse, what does that model severely distort or obscure? What are the patterns of change in political authorities, identities, and ideologies, and the factors shaping those patterns? Taylor observes that "the three orthodox social sciences have been largely caught out by globlization": "Their spatial ontology has been so severely undermined that reform, even where seriously attempted, is unable to cope with contemporary social change."[14] In fact, traditional scholarship has been caught out by a great deal more than globalization.

The end of the Cold War, perhaps more than any other development, reminded us that change is sweeping global politics. The overall pattern is one of two simultaneous and interrelated processes that we have termed fusion and fission, and Rosenau calls "fragmegration."[15] States are challenged by a variety of transnational forces as well as discontent and disintegration within. The increasing globalization of business and finance has amply demonstrated that there are vast areas with crucial impact on the welfare of citizens that most governments do not control or even influence to any major degree. Wrote the late Susan Strange: "Politicians everywhere talk as though they have the answers to economic and social problems, as if they really are in charge of their country's destiny. People no longer believe them."[16]

In failed or failing states—and in others better off in some respects—governments find it extremely difficult or impossible to maintain a modicum of public order. Some of these and numerous other states face rising mini-nationalist, ethnic, or regional demands for independence or autonomy. Cities and organized crime are also establishing global networks. In the historical heartland of nation-states, Europe—a veritable case study in fragmegration—the state faces strong challenges both from the European Union (EU) in its varied manifestations and from resurgent regions like Northern Italy, the Rhône-Alpes, and Catalonia (not to mention Basques and Corsicans, ambitious cities, the Italian mafia, and German *länder*).[17] Even in parts of the world where genuine political progress appears to have been made, as in the democratization (at least compared with the past) of much of Latin America and the former Soviet bloc, there remains a profound sense of malaise based on the conviction that government is hopelessly corrupt and/or in any event cannot deliver the goods. For example, Jorge I. Domínguez observes of Latin America that "a persistent fear haunts the region, what the economist Albert Hirschman once called *fracasomanía* or an obsession with failure." "Many still believe that economic success is ephemeral and that democracy's worst enemies are the politicians who claim to speak in its name."[18]

Susan Strange highlighted three basic paradoxes related to her "retreat of the state" thesis.[19] The first paradox is that, while overall state power declines in many national societies, the intervention of the state and its agencies in citizens' lives (often to their intense annoyance) seems to be increasing. Government regulations keep certain chemicals off the market, establish high-occupancy traffic lanes, force persons to wear seat belts, create affirmative-action quotas, and so on. However, national governments are "less effective on those basic matters that the market, left to itself, has never been able to provide—security against violence, stable money for trade and investment, a clear system of law and the means to enforce it, and a sufficiency of public goods like drains, water supplies, infrastructures for transport and communications." "Little wonder that it is less respected and lacks legitimacy."

Strange's second paradox, which Ferguson/Mansbach have also addressed, is the growing "queue" of various groups who want to have their own state. Die-hard realists like to seize on this pattern to insist that the state is doing fine, thank you, and even spawning new ones. In fact, the queue is a little shorter than it might first appear because a number of the more prominent movements, like the Catalonians, have made it clear that their goal is autonomy rather than legal independence. Where statehood is indeed the goal, such campaigns are likely to go on causing big trouble for established states. And when and if independence results, the result may only be a "facade of statehood" or "pyrrhic victory."

The third paradox is the relative success of the Asian state model. Are not detractors of "the state" themselves being Eurocentric by not paying more attention to successes in Asia? One might respond that admirers of the Asian model ignore the extent to which the private sector controls the state (e.g., "Japan Inc."). Be that as it may, Strange believed Asian "exceptionalism" to have been the product of special conditions that are now being eroded and will not be repeated, mainly post–World War II development aid and technology from the West, coupled with a dispensation to pursue closed-market policies. As Asian governments now face greater pressures to adopt nondiscriminatory policies on trade and investment, Strange predicted: "[T]here will be contests for control over the institutions and agencies of governments in most of the Asian countries. There will be contests between factions of political parties, between vested interests both in the private sectors and in the public sector. There will be power struggles between branches of the state bureaucracy. Both the unity and authority of governments is bound to suffer."[20] As for China, it remains to be seen whether a strong state can long coexist with increasingly privatized firms and markets. The national government is already having difficulty countering military influence and regional and local insubordination.

Rosenau, Strange, and others believe that the revolutions in transportation and especially information and communication, combined with educational progress in many parts of the world, is having a profound impact at the micro level (at least among elites and middle classes). In sum, an increasing number of people are getting harder to fool, and an irreverent investigative news media is giving them the "facts" that the national government is often incompetent, definitely expensive, and sometimes corrupt—and unable to do as much as they think it should for them in any case. The proverbial person on the street, reading and listening to today's news, may indeed be more equipped to understand the small-r reality of global politics than national politicians who still believe they are in charge. Moreover, amen to Strange's observation that "the commonsense of common people is a better guide to understanding than most of the academic theories being taught in universities."[21] Blinkered IR theorists are doubtless going to be among the last to wake up and recognize that everything of importance does not begin and end with the state. There are truly global issues like environmental degradation, rapid population growth, and infectious disease. There are also matters of concern to individuals, families, towns, professions, firms, single-interest groups, regions, globalized cities, ethnicities, churches, and so on and on.

What the world is facing is an accelerating and interrelated proliferation of polities and identities, which raises two fundamental questions that by their very nature are never going to be fully resolved. One of the questions is the global equivalent of the sort of situation currently both making controversy and opening opportunities in the European community. By which polity(ies) are certain functions best governed? For we are, indeed, in a "turbulent" era when patterns of governance, which have always been more diverse than mainstream IR theory has recognized, are nonetheless shifting at an extremely rapid pace. As Jessica T. Mathews expresses it: "The end of the Cold War has brought no mere adjustment among states but a novel redistribution of power among states, markets and civil societies. National governments are not simply losing autonomy in a globalizing economy. They are sharing powers—including political, social, and security roles at the core of sovereignty—with businesses, with international organizations, and with a multitude of citizens groups should be."[22] Her list of polities where authority is migrating could, in fact, have been much longer.

The second question is what Strange memorably labeled "Pinocchio's problem." Once Pinocchio became a real boy, he no longer had his puppet strings to guide him. Once those that tie us to the nation-state are loosed, what authorities have us in their sway? Strange closed her last book by underlining our dilemma: "[W]e have now, not a system of global governance by any stretch of the imagination, but rather a ramshackle assembly of conflicting sources of authority. . . . Where do allegiance, loyalty, identity lie? Not always, obviously in the same direction. Sometimes with the government of a state. But other times, with a firm, or with a social movement operating across territorial frontiers. Sometimes with a family or a generation; sometimes with fellow-members of an occupation or a profession. . . . [T]here is a new absence of absolutes. In a world of multiple, diffused authority, each of us shares Pinocchio's problem; our individual consciences are our only guide."[23] Perhaps, not quite. However much we are increasingly empowered at the micro-level, each of us as individuals is still tied up in old identities and loyalties and the choices we make for the future will not be strictly voluntaristic ones. Competing authorities are bidding for our allegiance, but they are also simultaneously establishing their control and influence over us—and are our only hope for advancing the values we cherish.

TOWARD A POSTINTERNATIONALIST REVOLUTION

Thus far I have sketched a fairly bleak contrast between an increasingly complex global politics and a Mississippi mainstream in IR theory that is less able to analyze that world than the person on the street. State-centrism is deeply embedded in the traditional disciplines, as we have seen, and mainstream U.S. academic journals. There is much more of potential theoretical relevance in *Foreign Affairs, Foreign Policy,* and *International Affairs. Global Governance* has the right subject but doesn't publish much theory, and the normative/"critical"/postmodern orientation of *Alternatives* has limited its appeal. Our European colleagues—except for some who have been attracted to institutionalism and state constructivism or have embraced postmodernism in protest—continue to be bewildered by the crazy Americans and are steadily improving their own journals to a point where they are far better than their U.S. counterparts: *Review of International Studies, European Journal of International Affairs,* and *Millennium.* Some of the most important IR work is also being done by political/historical sociologists, political economists, and political geographers rather than political scientists.

I have indeed offered a bleak description of the IR field generally, but it is not a complete description. A number of whitewater tributaries are already contributing to what I hope and trust will become tomorrow's broad mainstream. Front and center, of course, is Rosenau's postinternationalism, and for obvious reasons I am also especially fond of the Ferguson/Mansbach polities model. However, in concluding this essay, I shall simply list a few of the most promising theoretical developments emanating from various disciplinary and interdisciplinary quarters that seem to me to be converging on a much less state-centric map of global politics.

Although Kenneth Waltz firmly grounded his neorealist focus on a distribution of capabilities in the international system on realist assumptions about states as the primary actors in world politics, other efforts to do system-level analyses have been more imaginative. For instance, Barry Buzan and Richard Little have argued that Waltz's conception of structure is so parsimonious as to obscure a host of equally significant actors, institutions, and processes, which they are attempting to analyze. Their approach is promising partly because its historical perspective starts before the Westphalian era in Europe, although they do perhaps give the sovereign state too much credit (once it came along) for establishing its dominance over other actors.[24] Other, more familiar systems-level approaches are world-systems theory, associated with Immanuel Wallerstein (also admired by Peter Taylor, among many others), and world history.[25] The former has traditionally suffered from its definition of international structure as the distribution of economic capabilities, sort of a neo-Marxist Waltzianism. World history, by contrast, appears better able to accommodate more variables and especially matters of culture.

International political economists, as the very name of the subfield suggests, operate at the nexus of political science and economics, and many IPE specialists (though not those of a neorealist or institutionalist bent) are steadily pushing both disciplines in a less state-centric direction. Susan Strange's work is a case in point, although ironically she began her foray into markets partly to remind the leaders of states that they need to be more aware of globalizing forces, the better to exercise regulatory constraint. Over time, she grew less sanguine about the possibility of their doing so. For his part, another prominent IPE specialist, R. J. Barry Jones, remarks: "The complexities and indeterminacy of the current developments require a 'social science' that is open, cautious, and methodologically careful. There is clearly little place . . . for 'disciplinary divisions', if the more serious intellectual challenges are to be met." Warning against dismissing the continuing importance of states, he nonetheless acknowledges that "[g]lobalization has . . . dislodged territorial boundaries from their cosy status as givens and relocated them amongst the central problematics of the contemporary condition."[26]

Yet another promising approach in contemporary IR theory might be loosely classified as non-state-centric constructivism. Anthony Giddens's writings on "structuration" theory raised what Wendt and others defined as the agent/structure problem and applied it to the IR field. Although Wendt has subsequently focused nearly all of his analyses on states as supposedly primary agents, there is no inherent reason why asking such questions as who or what are the agents and structures in global politics, and how do they interact, shouldn't result in a vision of a much more complex world. Exploring just such a world is the task that a number of pioneering scholars have set for themselves, distinguishing themselves from less-venturesome neoliberals. Nicholas J. Onuf (see Chapter 6 in this volume) has been in the forefront of those who emphasize the "rules" that help structure social relationships at all levels,[27] along with Friedrich Kratochwil, whose intellectual roots are in international law and political theory rather than sociology.[28] Kratochwil and Yosef Lapid have also reminded the IR field of the continuing importance of culture and identity.[29] On a related front, Thomas J. Biersteker and Cynthia Weber treat state sovereignty as a "social construct," whose "meaning is negotiated out of interactions within intersubjectively identifiable communities." In their view, "practices construct, reproduce, reconstruct, and deconstruct both state and sovereignty."[30]

No survey of cutting-edge IR theory should overlook historical sociology and, in particular, the work of Michael Mann (which Ronnie Lipschutz explores in Chapter 5). Mann spent much of his early career explaining how the "autonomous power of the state" evolved, especially through connections with war and capitalism.[31] However, the historical reach of his famous triology *The Origins of Social Power*[32] extended to ancient Mesopotamia, encompassing a much wider range of social actors than the modern state. More recently, he has been probing the tension between nation-states and globalism, with particular attention to relationships and institutions that are essentially neither. He writes: "To endorse 'globalism' would be to repeat the mistake of 'nation-statism'. We must reject any view of societies as singular bounded systems." "[S]ocieties have never been unitary. They have been composed of a multiplicity of networks of interaction, many with differing, if overlapping and intersecting, boundaries. This has been true of all prehistoric and historic periods, . . . It remains true today." Mann, in fact, distinguishes five "sociospatial levels of social interaction": local, national, international, transnational, and global. All five, as he sees it, are "entwined yet partially autonomous."[33]

Finally, we come to the political geographers. The refreshing contribution of John Agnew, Stuart Corbridge, Peter Taylor, and others has been to invite us to think of the world as simply "political space" and proceed to fill that space, in our theories, with the things that appear to us to be most significant. One might well complain that that is really saying very little, but that, if I read them correctly, is precisely the point. They are using political space as a means out of what Agnew and Corbridge term "the territorial trap," inviting us to sweep away all the theoretical ties that bind, and reconceptualize the subject we are studying in more small-r realistic and imaginative ways. Nothing could be closer to the "conceptual jailbreak" strategy that Rosenau keeps urging upon us, and that he, himself, relentlessly pursues.

My wife, who has written about the physicist Stephen Hawking, is fond of quoting him on the point that some theories have been dead for fifty years but many theorists haven't read the obituary. Despite all the turbulence in contemporary global politics, many of our IR colleagues have similarly failed to read the papers and continue to insist that nothing much has fundamentally changed. One is reminded of Adlai Stevenson's old joke that when he was U.S. Ambassador at the UN, he was scheduled to speak right after a particularly brilliant orator and was wondering how he was going to match that performance. When Adlai got up to the podium, he saw that his predecessor had accidentally left a copy of his speech, with notes in the margin. One sentence was highlighted in yellow and the margin instruction read, "Weak point. Shout!" Unfortunately, there's a lot of that defensive bluster going on in our field, hiding mounting evidence that state-centric thinking is going the way of the dinosaur.

Nonetheless, those of us who are not state-centric in our approaches can take comfort from the fact that, in the language of sci-fi, we are not alone. My sense is that there are numerous scholars "out there" in various disciplines, as well as many practitioners, who are keenly aware that the brave new world (with links to a much older world) we are experiencing requires new modes of thought. They would be overjoyed—and more importantly, eager to contribute—if a suitably eclectic postinternational offensive could be organized. So let us organize it.

I suggest the following: Define postinternationalism broadly enough to include all those from all disciplines who are not state-centric in their approach and are willing to engage global politics in an empirical fashion, or who at least believe that meaningful general statements about the nature of global politics can be made (which might leave out some of the extreme relativists). Of course, as the realists would surely agree, at the end of the day, the success of ideas depends not only upon their inherent correctness but also upon power. I am talking war, for the present and future of IR theory. We need a postinternational section of the ISA, panels at professional meetings worldwide, officers in every professional association, a newsletter, and one or more journals.

The unassailable truth is that we are living in a postinternational world, and we should have mainstream scholarship in the field of global politics that accurately reflects that fact. Whatever happens, I am certain that Rosenau will continue to be in the thick of it, probably several steps ahead. I can picture him well into the next millennia, striding vigorously into an International Studies Association plenary, greeting some of the rest of us who (in contrast to himself) are in wheelchairs, and talking enthusiastically about his latest book. I do hope and expect that the speech from the podium on that occasion will be on a postinternational theme, with no shouting required.

NOTES

1. I am grateful to the Norwegian Nobel Institute for its support. Initial research for this essay was done in the Institute's library while I was Senior Fellow there from January–June, 1996.

2. James N. Rosenau, *Turbulence in World Politics: A Theory of Change and Continuity* (Princeton, N.J.: Princeton University Press, 1990); and *Along the Domestic-Foreign Frontier: Exploring Governance in a Turbulent World* (Cambridge: Cambridge University Press, 1997).

3. James N. Rosenau, *Linkage Politics* (New York: The Free Press, 1969).

4. James N. Rosenau, *The Dramas of Politics: An Introduction to the Joys of Inquiry* (Boston: Little, Brown, 1973).

5. Robert D. Putnam, "Diplomacy and Domestic Politics: The Logic of Two-Level Games," *International Organization* 43, 3 (autumn 1988): 427–60.

6. To be fair, the field of comparative politics is also changing these days, not least because of the obvious need for analysts of "domestic" political systems in Europe to include an EU dimension.

7. Yale H. Ferguson and Richard W. Mansbach, *Polities: Authority, Identities, and Change* (Columbia University of South Carolina Press, 1996). See also our "History's Revenge and Future Shock," in Martin Hewson and Timothy J. Sinclair, eds., *Approaches to Global Governance Theory* (Albany, N.Y.: State University of New York Press, 1999), pp. 197–238.

8. For a brilliant (much more sympathetic) critique of rational choice and discussion of prospect theory as an alternative, see Jack S. Levy, "Prospect Theory, Rational Choice, and International Relations," *International Studies Quarterly* 41, 1 (March 1997) 87–112.

9. *Cf.* Alexander Wendt, "Constructing International Politics," *International Security* 20, 1 (summer 1995): 71–81.

10. *International Security* 20, 1 (summer 1995).

11. Robert O. Keohane and Lisa Martin, "The Promise of Institutionalist Theory," *International Security* 20, 1 (summer 1995): 39.

12. Wendt, "Constructing International Politics," pp. 71–75.

13. P. J. Taylor, "Embedded Statism and the Social Sciences: Opening Up to New Spaces," *Environment and Planning* 28, 11 (November 1966): 1919–25. See also John Agnew and Stuart Corbridge, *Mastering Space: Hegemony, Territory and International Political Economy* (New York: Routledge, 1995), especially chapter 4 on "The Territorial Trap."

14. Taylor, "embedded Statism," p. 1925.

15. James N. Rosenau, "New Dimensions of Security: The Interaction of Globalizing and Localizing Dynamics," *Security Dialogue* 25, 3 (September 1994): 255–81.

16. Susan Strange, *The Retreat of the State: The Diffusion of Power in the World Economy* (Cambridge: Cambridge University Press, 1996), p. 3.

17. *Cf.* John Newhouse, "Europe's Rising Regionalism," *Foreign Affairs* 76, 1 (January/February 1997): 67–84.

18. Jorge I. Domínguez, "Latin America's Crisis of Representation," *Foreign Affairs* 76, 1 (January/February 1997): 101.

19. Strange, *The Retreat of the State*, pp. 4–7.

20. Ibid., p. 7.

21. *Ibid.*, pp. 3–4.

22. Jessica T. Mathews, "Power Shift," *Foreign Affairs*, 76,1 (January/February 1997): 50.

23. Strange, *The Retreat of the State*, pp. 198–99.

24. Barry Buzan, Charles Jones, and Richard Little, *The Logic of Anarchy: NeoRealism to Structural Realism* (New York: Columbia University Press, 1993). See also Barry Buzan and Richard Little, "Reconceptualizing Anarchy: Structural Realism Meets World History," *European Journal of International Relations* 2, 4 (December 1996): 403–38.

25. *Cf.* Lauren Benton, "From the World-Systems Perspective to Institutional World History: Culture and Economy in Global Theory," *Journal of World History* 7, 2 (1996), 261–95.

26. R. J. Barry Jones, "Social Science, Globalization, and the Problem of the State," *Environment and Planning* 28, 11 (1996): 1953.

27. See Nicholas J. Onuf, "Levels," *European Journal of International Relations* 1, 1 (March 1995): 35–58. Also his *World of Our Making: Rules and Rule in Social Theory and International Relations* (Columbia: University of South Carolina Press, 1989); and "Rules, Agents, Institutions: A Constructivist Approach," in Vendulka Kubálková, Nicholas Onuf, and Paul Kowert, eds., *International Relations in a Constructed World* (Armonik, NY: M.E. Sharpe, 1998).

28. See especially Friedrich Kratochwil, *Rules, Norms, and Decisions: On the Conditions of Practical and Legal Reasoning in International Relations and Domestic Affairs* (Cambridge: Cambridge University Press, 1989).

29. Yosef Lapid and Friedrich Kratochwil, *The Return of Culture and Identity in IR Theory* (Boulder, Colo.: Lynne Rienner, 1996).

30. Thomas J. Biersteker and Cynthia Weber, eds., *State Sovereignty as a Social Construct* (Cambridge: Cambridge University Press, 1996).

31. *Cf.* Michael Mann, *States, War, and Capitalism: Essays in Political Sociology* (Oxford, U.K.: Blackwell, 1988).

32. See especially Michael Mann, *The Sources of Social Power: A History of Power from the Beginning to A.D. 1760*, vol. 1 (Cambridge: Cambridge University Press, 1986).

33. M. Mann, "Neither Nation-State nor Globalism," *Environment and Planning* 28, 11 (1996): 1960.

PART 4

A Postinternationalist's Response

CHAPTER 12

Beyond Postinternationalism

James N. Rosenau

This is a coherent, good, and provocative collection of essays. It is coherent because it is organized around common themes. But it is good and provocative *not* because the themes derive from the corpus of my writing over the last five decades; rather, its quality is high because it probes big ideas and explores huge gaps that are central to the study of international relations (IR) as the world enters a new millennium. Indeed, throughout the essays there are a number of points at which issue is taken with my formulations, thus serving to highlight substantive and theoretical questions that are quite independent of my having originally authored them. More than that, I welcome the criticism, seeing in them vindication of a long-standing conviction that it is important to err importantly, that such errors facilitate the identification and clarification of where a field may have gone astray and where its future potentials lie.

Thus relieved of the embarrassment of appearing to be the focus for a coherent set of essays, here I shall address the criticisms only briefly in the course of exploring both the substantive and methodological problems of anticipating where postinternationalism is headed in the decades ahead. Questions abound: Will the dynamics of turbulence continue to roil global politics? Or will institutions evolve that manage to absorb or otherwise cope with the challenges of a bifurcated world sustained by pervasive authority crises and a continuing, even accelerating, skill revolution? Will the pace of change, in other

I am grateful to Hongying Wang for her helpful reactions to an earlier draft of this chapter.

219

words, slow to the point where it is possible to bring closure to what one observer calls the study of "transitology"?[1] Will new global equilibria develop that stabilize and moderate challenges to authority and heightened capacities to engage in collective action? And irrespective of whether world affairs are marked by turbulence or stability, will its essential structures be sufficiently patterned to signify the emergence of a new epoch and an end to the ambiguities and tentativeness inherent in the notion that for a decade we have been living in a period that is "post"—post the Cold War and post a unipolar international system? If it is the case, as Karns notes, that "the very term postinternational connotes its temporariness," ought we not develop a new, more substantive label for all the complexity and contradictions that seem to sustain the course of events? Or is it conceivable that when and if the dynamics of present-day turbulence settle into stable patterns, these will once again be founded on the predominance of the state system, thus necessitating abandoning the term postinternational in favor of a return to a reinvigorated international label?

And beyond substance and its nomenclature lie crucial questions of methodology: If the dynamics of change are as deep and pervasive as the postinternational model contends, how do we break with old analytic habits and evolve new ones suited to probing the complex, nonlinear dynamics through which actors, structures, and processes sustain the emergent epoch? Given extensive transformations, does it make sense to rely on the lessons of history, as at least five of the preceding essays argue, in efforts to elaborate the model and comprehend the global scene? Are there other methodologies that can be tailored to the task of probing a world in flux? Or are the key variables too numerous and too wide in their fluctuations to allow for the rigorous and systematic inquiries that our discipline has long demanded? Can methods be developed that allow for testing Peterson's assertion that while the postinternational model is not overtly antifeminist, embedded deep in its text are "masculinist" premises?

AN EMERGENT EPOCH

For all the insufficiencies of the postinternational model noted in the previous chapters, it does serve to highlight the emergence of what I regard as a new epoch in human affairs. The structures and processes of global life strike me as so different from those that have prevailed in the past that it is reasonable to presume an epochal transformation is underway in every corner of every country and continent. Not only have the underlying dynamics of turbulence—the skill revolution, the crises of authority, and the bifurcation of global structures[2]—undermined the conventional modes through which public affairs have been conducted, but they have also fostered still other dynamics that have intensified and widened the repercussions of change and the development of new orientations and practices that appear to be so recurrent as to trace the outlines of a new ontology—a new, widely shared common sense of how the world works.[3] Put differently, my analytic antennae tell me that when the new epoch settles fully into place sometime in the next fifty or hundred years, people then will look back and say, "Go back to the late twentieth century, for that is when it all began, that's when the seeds of transformation started to flower and yield both the fruits and poisons of our current circumstances."

In other words, my overall response to the substantive questions noted above is that yes, the dynamics of turbulence are likely to continue to roil global politics in the decades ahead, but that in the long run new global institutions and equilibria are likely to evolve that infuse stability into the conduct of world affairs. It is doubtful, however, whether the newly patterned equilibria will involve a restoration of the historic international system. Rather, it is possible to anticipate an eventual stability because, indeed, the outlines of the essential structures of a new epoch can already be discerned, an epoch that bears little resemblance to the anarchical world that has long been dominated by states.

Nine Transformative Dynamics

While the onset of a postinternational politics may have been precipitated by transformations of the three primary parameters specified by the turbulence model, now it seems appropriate to identify six other dynamics that, interactively, are also driving the emergence of a new epoch. One of these involves an intensification of the readiness of people to form and join associations, a transformation I call the "organizational explosion" wherein staggering numbers of new organizations, some tightly hierarchical and some more loosely structured, have sprung up in and across all the world's communities. A second consists of the vast movement of people from every country and corner of the world to other countries and corners, what might be called the "travel upheaval." A third dynamic focuses on the myriad processes of globalization through which goods, services, money, ideas, and norms are transgressing national boundaries and lessening the salience of territory. The fourth, fifth, and sixth dynamics are the obverse of the third, namely, the weakening of states, the erosion of sovereignty, and the decentralization of governments that are partly a reaction to globalization and partly a response to the skill revolution, the onset of authority crises, and the bifurcation of global structures. The complexity of these interactive dynamics is even greater than it seems when allowance is made for the fact that the pace at which each of them operates and unfolds varies in different parts of the world, with the result that the emergent epoch is sustained by uneven processes that shape each other through feedback mechanisms in uneven ways with uneven consequences.

Space limitations do not permit an elaboration of these several dynamics.[4] One of the least appreciated feedback mechanisms, however, can usefully be noted. It involves an expansion of the skill revolution to include not only enlarged capacities for analysis and for focusing emotion, but also a freeing up of peoples' imaginations. Due to the organizational explosion, the travel upheaval, and the advent of new and cheaper electronic and transportational technologies, more and more people are now able to envision alternative futures, lifestyles, and circumstances for themselves, their families, and their cherished associations. Besides their electronic connections and their personal travel, moreover, their friends and family abroad, their ethnic ties, and their professional contacts all serve to stimulate notions of different— and often preferred—ways of living. Whether the stimuli are provided by global television, soap operas, relatives working as maids in Hong Kong, cousins who find employment in Saudi Arabia, or children who marry foreign spouses, the materials for wide-ranging imaginative musings are abundantly available. These stimuli are especially relevant for peoples in developing countries whose circumstances have previously prevented contacts with other cultures and alternative lifestyles. Indeed, from the perspective of those who have long been hemmed in by the realities of life on or below the poverty line, the freeing up of imaginative capacities is among the most powerful forces at work in the emergent epoch. The imagination sharpens generational differences, divides families, undermines cultural affinities, and otherwise disturbs the routines and relations of individuals and communities.[5]

Tracing Essential Structures

But how is it possible, one can reasonably ask, for a world in which nine dynamics are considered structures essential to the routines and upheavals of global life to settle into recurrent and stable patterns? That is surely too much complexity, this line of reasoning would stress, for orderly patterns to emerge out of the welter of events, much less for analysts to comprehend the underpinnings and trajectories of such patterns. In positing the centrality of no less than nine interactive dynamics, in other words, are we not depriving ourselves of the capacity to trace the essential structures of the emergent epoch and then to anticipate its likely evolution in the future? Would it not be preferable to proceed parsimoniously by ranking the causal potential of the nine dynamics and focusing only on those with the highest rankings, thereby holding the lower ranked ones constant and sacrificing deep understanding in favor of partial but more reliable explanations?

To accept positive answers to these questions is, in my judgment, to abandon the search for comprehension. To ignore any of the dynamics by holding the lowest ranked ones constant is to presume a linear world in which each dynamic interacts with only one or two others. Such a presumption, however, is profoundly erroneous. Our world is marked by nonlinear processes, by contradictory patterns, by ambiguous causal chains, with the result that the nine dynamics cannot be ranked because each initiates feedback loops that shape the others. In other words, precisely because the emergent epoch is so complex we need to relax the criteria of parsimony to which we have long been accustomed and, instead, devise approaches that enable us to allow for the multiple dynamics and the feedback processes that link them together.[6]

Two approaches come to mind in this regard. One involves the application of complexity theory, an approach still so much in its infancy that it will be some time before meaningful applications to world affairs can be employed and the problems posed by the theory can be overcome.[7] Durfee's essay in this volume suggests, however, that eventually complexity theory may offer ways to probe the contradictions and ambiguities that arise when so many dynamics are interactive in nonlinear sequences.[8]

A second approach, one that I have been exploring for some time now, is to organize the dynamism of the emergent epoch in the context of a dialectic process that underlies and helps sustain the diverse feedback loops through which the emergent epoch is configured. The overriding dialectic concerns the interaction between the globalizing and localizing forces at work in the world, between those fostering fragmentation and those generating integration, between the centralizing and decentralizing dynamics. These three dialectics differ in some respects, but they involve essentially the same process in which the causal chain moves back and forth between expansions and contractions of the scope of political authority, as if each increment in one direction gives rise to a comparable increment in the opposite direction. In this sense it is a singular dialectic, one that is at work in and across community everywhere in the world, thus helping to orient our analytic eyes on all nine of the aforementioned dynamics and allowing us to begin to trace their operations by positing them as embedded in causal processes that move in one or the other opposite direction.

Indeed, since this dialectic appears to be operative at all times in all places, it lies at the very core of the emergent epoch. Admittedly, such a dialectic marks all of human history: some people and communities have always reacted against the expansion or contraction of their circumstances. Unlike earlier epochs, however, when it took weeks, months, and years for word of the expansions or contractions to reach those who reacted against them, today such information is received in milliseconds, minutes, and hours, thus evoking reactions that are virtually concomitant with its transmission. What distinguishes the emergent epoch, in other words, is that the dialectic unfolds so rapidly as to be characterized by simultaneity, by sequences of interaction in which there are few pauses for reflection that can lead to acceptable syntheses wherein the opposing forces accommodate each other. As a result, the emergent epoch is marked by pervasive contradictions, ambiguities, and uncertainties that nonetheless exhibit structured patterns that are traceable through the dialectic processes that sustain them.

It is not difficult to demonstrate the large extent to which the lack of acceptable syntheses have become patterned, even institutionalized, as a multiplicity of opposites: Territory and boundaries are still important, but attachments to them are weakening. Domestic and foreign affairs still stem like separate domains, but the line between them is transgressed with increasing frequency.[9] The international system is less commanding, but it is still powerful. States are changing, but they are not disappearing. State sovereignty has eroded, but it is still vigorously asserted. Governments are weaker, but they still possess considerable resources and they can still throw their weight around. Company profits are soaring and wages are stagnant. Scenes of unspeakable horror and genocide flicker on our TV screens even as humanitarian organizations mobilize and undertake heroic remedial actions. The United Nations is asked to take on more assignments and not supplied with the funds to carry them out. Defense establishments acknowledge that their roles have drastically altered and continue to adhere to traditional strategies. At times publics are more demanding, but at other times they are also more pliable. Citizens are both more active and more cynical. Borders still keep out intruders, but they are also increasingly porous. In sum, we have come to know that we live in a world that is deteriorating in some areas, remaining fixed in others, and thriving in still others—which is another way of concluding that both order and disorder simultaneously sustain global structures.

An incisive empirical example of the contradictions that pervade the emergent epoch is evident in this account of a recent period in the Israeli-Palestinian conflict:

> What ails the peace process is not just a crisis of confidence. It's a crisis of logic. It's not only that each side doesn't trust the other; it's that nothing makes sense. Opposite causes produce the same effect: There are suicide bombers when the peace process moves ahead and suicide bombers when the process is stuck. And the same causes produce opposite effects: Mr. Netanyahu strikes a Hebron deal one day and undermines it the next by building in Har Homa; Mr. Arafat exposes a cell of Palestinian suicide bombers in Beit Sahur one day and kisses the leader of Hamas the next. Closure of the territories increases Israel's security and decreases Israel's security. Everything that happens, for good or ill, seems utterly random. Oslo is no longer a peace process. It's a Tolstoy novel.[10]

Stated more generally, where people came to expect the Soviet-American rivalry to shape the course of events in the Cold War era, and where they became used to the ways in which U.S. hegemony shaped outcomes in the brief post–Cold War period, today they appear to be adjusting to the realization that outcomes stem from multiple sources, that the outcomes are transitory and ever subject to reversal, and that what happens at one level of community can unexpectedly cascade across other levels. For the most part, in other words, officials and publics alike have come to understand intersubjectively that their lives are intertwined in crazy-quilt ways that may often be enhancing and just as often denigrating. And intuitively they seem to know, too, that the skill revolution, the organizational explosion, the travel upheaval, the globalization of national economies, the weakening of states, the erosion of sovereignty, the decentralization of governments, and many other features of the emergent epoch are sources of new opportunities as well as serious threats.

Labeling the Emergent Epoch

For some time attempts to summarize the many changes that are generating a new stage in human history have followed three lines of reasoning and resulted in three labels for the emergent epoch. The three approaches differ greatly in several respects—one being pragmatic and framed by politicians and journalists, a second is philosophical and has evolved among diverse intellectuals, and a third is social scientific and used by IR specialists—but they share a lack of specificity about the essential underpinnings and nature of world affairs at the outset of a new millennium. The pragmatic line of reasoning acknowledges that present-day patterns and institutions are quite different from those of prior eras, but it does not seek to evaluate, much less synthesize, the differences or their long-run implications. Rather, it is a perspective that simply assumes that the end of the superpower rivalry between the United States and the USSR unleashed diverse processes that are altering the practices through which the political, economic, and social life of communities, nations, and the world are sustained. Lacking specificity, the pragmatic approach tends to treat every development, whether it be familiar or unusual, as expressive of the new historical epoch and thus it uses a nomenclature, the "post–Cold War" era, which hints at changes and differences without indicating what these might be. Indeed, by employing such a label pragmatists conclude that the present is a congeries of unsystematic, even unrelated, forces that are propelling the world into an uncertain future. Or perhaps more accurately, by positing conditions as "post" an earlier era, the pragmatic perspective implies that it is a transitional period, as if new historical developments have to evolve and generate new global structures before the world can settle once again into stable circumstances such as marked the Cold War era of 1945–1990, the interwar period of 1918–1939, or the Industrial Age of the nineteenth century.

The more philosophical response to the dynamics that are transforming the present-day world is more precise in terms of specifying what has changed, but it too is murky about what sustains the changes and where they may be taking the world. And thus it too uses the "post" prefix as part of its nomenclature for the epoch, thereby also suggesting that a congeries of diverse and unstructured forces are at work that offer no hint as to what the world's future may be like. In this case the label is that of "postmodernism," a school of thought that has different meanings for different postmodernists[11] who nonetheless share the conviction that basic changes have moved the world beyond modernity or, at least, into "late modernity." Whether the era is seen as "post" or "late," adherents of the various postmodernisms also share the belief that modernity has run its course because the notions of science and rationality that distinguish it have proven to be ill founded. After all, one wing of postmodernism asserts, two devastating world wars, a deep economic depression, and the hydrogen bomb mark the age of science and rationality—hardly a recommendation for a modernist perspective. For all their criticisms of modernity, however, postmodernists do not offer an understanding of where the world is today and where it is likely to be tomorrow. Indeed, many of them argue that speculation about future developments is wasted effort, that any scenarios depicting paths into the future are hidden political moves designed to advance the agenda of the scenarioist.

Much the same can be said about the nomenclature of postinternationalism. Having coined the label to denote a bifurcated world that was no longer dominated by the international system of states, I have come to appreciate that it too is a "post," that it is vague about the new arrangements and underlying structures that are in the process of evolving as the Cold War recedes into history. Like the contributors to this volume, those IR specialists who see value in the postinternational perspective share a view that long-established paradigms such as realism and liberalism no longer account adequately for the course of events, but their restlessness over the insufficiencies of conventional approaches has not led them to fix on a label that at least hints at the emergent shape of world affairs.

If the insight that pervasive contradictions and ambiguities have come to dominate world affairs is essentially correct, then the absence of any hints as to the nature and structure of the emergent epoch on the part of the post–Cold War, the postmodern, and postinternational labels is especially glaring. What is needed is a designation that points to the underlying dialectic that links globalizing and localizing forces. The dialectic can be framed in a number of ways and variously labeled, but a nomenclature that takes note of it does serve to focus attention on substantive phenomena that lie at the heart of the emergent epoch. And in doing so it encourages reflection on the dynamics whereby social and geographic distances have shrunk to a point where everything in a person's or community's environment is both distant and proximate. As already noted, the skill revolution, the organizational explosion, the travel upheaval, and the several aforementioned structural features of the emergent epoch come into focus as direct derivatives of this dialectical perspective.

In sum, it seems appropriate to develop a label for the emergent epoch that is more suggestive than calling it the post–Cold War, postmodern, or postinternational era, one that highlights the tensions between those dynamics promoting the fragmentation of societies and those conducing to their integration, thereby immediately conveying the essential nature of the epochal transformation. Several labels have been offered to serve this need. One is "glocalization," which joins globalizing and localizing dynamics into a unified whole;[12] another is "chaord," which highlights the tensions between chaos and order.[13] For a variety of reasons, my own preference is to use a label that combines the pervasive links between fragmentation and integration into a single word—"fragmegration," admittedly a bit awkward and grating, but in its very ungainliness a constant reminder that the world has moved beyond the condition of being "post" its predecessor to an era in which the foundations of daily life have settled into new and unique rhythms of their own. Put more succinctly, and as I have argued elsewhere, there is considerable understanding to be had by treating any situation in global life as founded on the fragmegrative dialectic.[14] To assert that we live in a fragmentative epoch is to say that we have become accustomed to the contradictions, ambiguities, and uncertainties that have replaced the regularities of prior eras. Comprised of nonlinear processes in which every effect is a cause of yet another outcome in a complex and endless array of feedback loops, these contradictions, ambiguities, and uncertainties are, in effect, the regularities of our age of fragmegration.

PROBLEMS OF METHOD, THEORY, AND PUBLIC RELATIONS

As already indicated, myriad problems attach to any model founded on numerous variables that interact through nonlinear processes. In the case of the postinternational model, some of these problems are methodological, others are theoretical and philosophical, and still others are matters of nuance and public relations. Indeed, it can be reasonably argued that the postinternational model has not, as Ferguson notes in chapter 11, attracted many adherents precisely because it presents mind-boggling methodological and theoretical dilemmas that are further confounded in the absence of nuanced formulations. For example, the original model sought to offer a way out of the methodological dilemmas by contending that analysts had to concentrate on "just noticeable differences" (JNDs),[15] but this is hardly a cogent methodology. Indeed, in some respects it is more misleading than it is helpful. As Onuf observes in chapter 6, the model does not specify how one determines when a difference is just noticeable and when it is not.

It follows that much thought needs to be devoted to developing a methodology appropriate to empirical explanations of the dynamics that configure and sustain the age of fragmegration. More accurately, the different dynamics may require different methodologies, a task that may have to be undertaken by a number of analysts who special-ize in the diverse dimensions of the model.[16] Clearly, this is not the place to confront, or even identify, all the methodological challenges that arise. Several of the theoretical/philosophical challenges, how-ever, are so fundamental that they can usefully be briefly amplified here. One is the challenge of change; a second concerns the treatment of historical phenomena, and a third is posed by the question of dis-cerning subtexts, especially those that may be rooted in antifeminist biases.

But the failure of the postinternational model to move from a tributary to the mainstream involves one nuanced distinction that can also be noted because it greatly hinders fair readings of the model. It is, in effect, a public-relations problem that I have not been able to solve: namely, how to stress that the authority of the state has eroded without being interpreted as asserting that states are weak and headed for oblivion?

The Challenge of Historical Comparisons

A criticism that recurs throughout the preceding chapters is that the postinternational model is ahistorical, that the turbulent dynamics that are posited as having driven world affairs since the 1950s may not be as unique as claimed, that the onset of turbulence was less a historical breakpoint and more a recurrence of familiar processes in new guises. The criticism is certainly understandable. The model explicitly treats history as susceptible to historical breakpoints, and the advent of tur-bulence on a worldwide scale is explicitly viewed as such a develop-ment.[17] Whether or not it is accurate, the criticism suffers from two flaws. The less important is that the model posits a continuing tension between change and continuity, which is another way of saying that the past does serve—to use a play on words—as brakes on breakpoints. People are deeply ensconced in long-standing habits, organizations are deeply mired in inertia, leaders are deeply committed to prece-dents, cultures are rooted in deep-seated practices—all of which tend to slow the pace at which change occurs in the absence of major sys-temic shocks (and even then the breakpoints may be moderated by the pervasive tendency wherein processes regress to the mean). However, despite the continuities—and for a theoretical reason elaborated be-low—I am still persuaded that the onset of present-day turbulence was a genuine breakpoint, that a new historical sequence was initiated in which habits, inertia, precedents, and cultures got reconfigured by transformative dynamics.

The second flaw in the criticism is that it lacks theoretical and philosophical foundations. To assert that there are lessons to be learned from historical comparisons, that the present is filled with developments comparable to those of the past, or that the course of events is often marked by cyclical patterns, is not to indicate or even suggest which of history's lessons are relevant, what earlier sequences may be comparable to current circumstances, or when a recurrent cycle is underway. To arrive at such conclusions one needs a theory of history, a philosophy of how historical sequences get compiled out of unique factors and recurrent imperatives, of when unexpected, contingent, or random events make a difference and when they do not, of what conditions allow societies and their institutions to absorb new challenges and what conditions overwhelm them, of when, where, and why the choices made by individuals and their organizations are predetermined and when, where, and why they are freely made. Admittedly, the original turbulence model is also flawed in this respect. It offered no theoretical underpinnings for ascertaining how a historical breakpoint evolves. It is only in pondering the presumption that eventually the fragmegrative epoch is likely to settle into established patterns and possibly be followed by yet another breakpoint and epoch that I have developed the outlines of a theory of historical sequences.

Following the lead of a philosophical formulation derived from complexity theory,[18] the onset and subsequent moderation of turbulence sequences are conceived as progressing through two major stages: in the first, early stage, the three basic parameters experience systemic shock that results in high degrees of uncertainty, contradiction, fluctuation, and unpredictability that border on chaos and thus accentuate the degree to which contingencies can underlie the actions of individuals and collectivities; then in the later stage, with the passage of enough time for habits and orderly patterns to evolve, the parameters begin to settle as fixed boundary conditions develop that reduce the degree to which contingencies can alter any sequence's trajectory. Once the world passes through a threshold from the previous epoch, in other words, high degrees of complexity and dynamism—the definition of turbulence[19]—set in and last for an indeterminate length of time wherein the lessons of history have little relevance for the course of events. Whenever this first stage gives way to lesser degrees of complexity and dynamism—and the time involved here can be variable but is likely to be measured in decades—the pattern of events begins to resemble prior sequences and the lessons of history can once again be pondered to good effect. Put differently, the change in historical sequences from the early to the later stages is gradual and occurs when and where the uncertainties, contradictions, and fluctuations induced by the complexities and dynamism of turbulence begin to yield to imperatives that cannot be readily ignored. As a result, the choices open to individuals and collectivities are much greater in the earlier than in the later stages of historical sequences.

From this theory of historical sequences follows the foregoing assumption that eventually—perhaps in the next fifty or one hundred years—the age of fragmegration will be fully established as the common sense of the prevailing epoch. At that distant time people will have become so accustomed to the contradictions, ambiguities, and uncertainties that, in effect, they will no longer be contradictory, ambiguous, and uncertain. Rather, they will have become regularities, stable patterns in which the skill revolution becomes commonplace, authority structures become institutionalized, and the processes of bifurcation become routinized. At that point, of course, the epoch enters a period of stasis that renders it increasingly vulnerable to the kind of systemic shocks that may induce the onset of yet another period of turbulence.

In sum, there is validity in both the claim of the postinternational model that historical breakpoints occur and the contention that prior circumstances are relevant. From this broad perspective, the analytic challenge is to comprehend the dynamics whereby shifts occur that move the historical sequence from its early to its later stage.

The Challenge of Change

Closely related to, but no less complicated than, the challenges of historical comparison are the problems inherent in the challenges of analyzing the dynamics of change. How do we know change when we see it? How to measure it? How to distinguish between slow, evolutionary change and breakpoint transformations? And perhaps most important, how to differentiate between changes that lead to differences in degree from those that result in differences in kind? Questions such as these proliferate the more one elaborates a dynamic, nonlinear model. But developing consensuses around answers to them is bound to be problematic. For at some level, assessments of change derive from temperamental differences among analysts that cannot be bridged no matter how extensive and compelling a conceptual formulation and its supporting data may be. These temperamental differences underlie our paradigmatic orientations and are thus central to our intellectual stances. Where one observer sees change, another sees the recurrence of age-old patterns; where one interprets the advent of nuclear weapons as a change in kind, another sees it as just another instance of the differences in degree that mark the long-term processes of technological advances that produced the gun, the tank, and the bomber; where one discerns complex processes, another discerns regression toward a long-standing mean; where one perceives the operation of a dialectic, another perceives independent processes; where one analyst cites evidence of the emergence of new institutions, another demonstrates that the evidence merely reflects the adaptation of old institutions; where one treats governments as paralyzed by the growing complexity of globalized space, another points to the stalemates as products of classic bureaucratic infighting; where one regards globalizing and localizing dynamics inextricably linked in deep dialectic processes, another presumes that localization derives from cultural origins unique to those who share a common locale.[20]

But the challenge of interpreting change cannot be dismissed simply by citing temperamental differences. Measurement problems remain in the case of the many observers with similar temperaments. Even under these circumstances agreed-upon criteria of difference need to be developed. In the case of the postinternationalist's concern with the distinction between differences in kind and degree, the criteria involve differences in the number scale, scope, and rapidity of the processes through which the affairs of collectivities are conducted. When agreed-upon measurements of the differences along these dimensions are regarded as huge and unmistakable, transformative changes in kind are deemed to have taken place. Lesser shifts along these dimensions—differences in degree—may eventually cumulate to differences in kind, but until they do the routines of politics are likely to be carried out in familiar ways.

It is the differences in kind that pose the most severe challenges to those who seek to grasp the course of events. For present purposes (i.e., in the absence of precise measurement criteria), the distinction between differences in degree and kind can be illustrated by pondering the dynamics of organizational decision making, societal mobilization, and intersocietal relationships in the present and previous eras to appreciate that the differences are not trivial, that they are so substantial as to be far more than merely updated repetitions of earlier patterns. Or, to use a more specific example, a comparison of the collapse of the Roman Empire across centuries and of the British empire across decades with that of the Soviet empire across weeks and months will highlight how modern technologies have fostered differences in kind rather than degree.[21]

Keeping the State In and Predominant

Difficult as the problems of interpreting the relevance of history and the dynamics of change may be, they often seem minimal when compared with the task of being understood about the role of the state in a fragmegrative model. For all the postinternational model's emphasis on the coexistence of the state-centric and multicentric world and the insistence that thus the state continues to play a vital role in the course of events, many observers somehow manage to ignore this nuanced formulation and regard it as consigning the state to the dustbin of history. It is almost as if their analytic habits are such that they need to insist on the commanding position of the state before they will begin to consider the activities of other collectivities. More than that, they need to insist that when "push comes to shove"[22] the state will prevail, as if the fact that push rarely comes to shove is analytically irrelevant. The analytic insight that states are pressed by the course of events to reflect the larger, more powerful forces inherent in the dynamics of fragmegration is, consequently, not considered and states are thus elevated to levels of competence that the postinternational model treats as empirically exaggerated. In effect, many analysts not only want to bring the state back in—to cite an oft-quoted phrase[23]— but they want to keep it in as the predominant and preeminent global actor. Usually the litany goes like this: only the state sets the rules; only the state provides sufficient resources; only the state can enforce the rules; only the state can alter the rules; and so on through an endless array of competencies that appear to leave little room for outcomes other than those imposed by the state. Yes, this line of reasoning concludes, nongovernmental organizations (NGOs) make inputs into policy-making processes and, yes, epistemic communities may help shape deliberations and, yes, different state officials may represent antagonistic interests and, yes, external circumstances may narrow policy alternatives or even dictate the decisions made and, yes, there are issues where the state appears peripheral and, yes, public pressures can be intense and, yes, forthcoming elections can further narrow the range of choices available to state officials; but no matter, the state is autonomous and has the ultimate authority to resort to force and exercise its right to use shove when situations need a push.

I confess to having failed to moderate or counter this perspective. Efforts to introduce nuances that more adequately reflect the complexities of global life invariably seem to fall on deaf ears when the nuances involve a possible erosion in the role of the state. The result is a stark choice: either one concedes that states are paramount and facilitates an ensuing discussion in which other actors are presumed to be secondary, or one clings to a nuanced formulation and fails to encourage inclinations to explore whether a revision of mainstream premises is in order. There may be something to be said, in other words, for generating audiences when none can otherwise exist by capitulating and saying what people want to hear before introducing any ambiguities, contradictions, or nuances. In the absence of such a strategy, conceivably the postinternational model runs the risk of eventually becoming extinct for want of concessions to the mainstream.

The Challenge of Subtexts

As one long committed to empirical as well as theoretical analysis, I must also confess to being perplexed by the feminist critique that underlying the postinternational model is a masculinist perspective. In her essay Peterson expresses pleasure that the model breaks with the tendency to cast analysis in dichotomous terms, but criticizes it for nonetheless adhering to two dichotomies that, she claims, are too fundamental to be ignored. One is the public-private dichotomy and the other is the male-female dichotomy. Furthermore, if I understand her argument correctly, the two dichotomies are closely linked because the failure to differentiate among public and private actions underlies the readiness to ignore the relevance of females for world affairs inasmuch as a preponderance of their activities are relegated to the private realm. More accurately, Peterson faults the model's treatment of these dichotomies not because they are explicitly advanced, but because of a failure to explicate them.

This criticism poses what I regard as a serious methodological problem. As an empiricist, I do not understand how she knows that a masculinist perspective underlies the model. I am perfectly willing to admit that such a perspective might be operative, that unbeknownst to myself the model may rest on an extensive gender bias, that by failing to differentiate between the public and private worlds I unknowingly downplay female roles in world affairs. In short, all of us should acknowledge that texts and subtexts may be at work in our writings without our being aware of them. On the other hand, perhaps they are not at work. Surely there is no wording, no formulation, built into the model's conception of turbulent dynamics that excludes the private realm or precludes the presence and active participation of women and other actors in that realm. If this is so, then we face a huge challenge: how do we discern, analyze, and assess texts and subtexts that are not explicated? How do we document, affirm, or disconfirm

Peterson's assertion that the postinternational model's "multicentric world of sovereignty-free actors looks suspiciously like male-bonding practices familiar from conventional states"?

Put differently, postmodernist and feminist models are said to uncover and give voice to groups whose treatment in political analyses are marked by silence. In so doing they undoubtedly serve the knowledge-building cause well. The oppressed or otherwise silent groups do need to be both heard and heeded, and their roles do need to be explicated so they can be fully evaluated. To acknowledge these needs, however, is a far cry from equating their omission from an abstract model with an imposed silence. No model can exhaustively embrace all variables, so that if particular variables or dichotomies are omitted, it may be because their relevance is presumed by the model rather than because gender biases are at work.

CONCLUSION

Given the problems posed by tracing the relevance of history, change, states, and implicit texts, it is clear that postinternationalism and its successor, the fragmegration model, must still confront severe tests if their utility as a means of comprehending world politics is to be more securely established. Challenges of this sort, however, are what make the intellectual enterprise so exhilarating. Accordingly, I for one intend to go on trying to fathom and surmount the dilemmas inherent in a complex and turbulent world while always recognizing that the importance of erring importantly runs the risk of failing to compensate for the important errors.

NOTES

1. John Mueller, "Democracy, Capitalism, and the End of Transition," in Michael Mandelbaum, ed., *Postcommunism: Four Perspectives* (New York: Council on Foreign Relations, 1996), p. 103.

2. These are the three key parameters that are posited as undergoing transformation by the postinternational model. Cf. James N. Rosenau, *Turbulence in World Politics: A Theory of Change and Continuity* (Princeton, N.J.: Princeton University Press, 1997), pp. 100–104.

3. Robert W. Cox, "Critical Political Economy," in Bjorn Hettne, ed., *International Political Economy: Understanding Global Disorder* (London: Zed Books, 1995), p. 34.

4. For an amplification of the several dynamics, see James N. Rosenau, *Along the Domestic-Foreign Frontier: Exploring Governance in a Turbulent World* (Cambridge: Cambridge University Press, 1997), chap. 4.

5. For a compelling elaboration of the ways in which unleashed imaginations are serving as change dynamics, see Arjun Appadurai, *Modernity at Large: Cultural Dimensions of Globalization* (Minneapolis: University of Minnesota Press, 1996).

6. Cf. Gary King, Robert O. Keohane, and Sidney Verba, *Designing Social Inquiry: Scientific Inquiry in Qualitative Research* (Princeton, N.J.: Princeton University Press, 1994), p. 20.

7. James N. Rosenau, "Many Damn Things Simultaneously: Complexity Theory and World Affairs," in David S. Alberts and Thomas J. Czerwinski, eds., *Complexity, Global Politics, and National Security* (Washington, D.C.: National Defense University, 1997), pp. 73–100.

8. For another effort to explicate the potential utility of complexity theory, see Matt Hoffman and David Johnson, "Change and Process in a Complex World: Using Complexity Theory to Understand World Politics," (paper presented at the ISA-Midwest Meeting, Cleveland, Ohio: October 3–5, 1997).

9. This is the central theme in Rosenau, *Along the Domestic-Foreign Frontier*.

10. Thomas Friedman, "The Physics of Mideast Peace," *New York Times*, September 15, 1997, p. A15.

11. Cf. Pauline Marie Rosenau, *Post-Modernism and the Social Sciences: Insights, Inroads, and Intrusions* (Princeton, N.J.: Princeton University Press, 1992), esp. pp. 14–17.

12. Roland Robertson, "Glocalization: Time-Space and Homogeneity-Heterogeneity," in Mike Featherstone, Scott Lash, and Roland Robertson, eds., *Global Modernities* (Thousand Oaks, Calif.: Sage Publications, 1995), pp. 25–44.

13. Dee W. Hock, "Institutions in the Age of Mindcrafting," a paper presented at the Bionomics Annual Conference, San Francisco, Calif., xerox, October 22, 1994), pp. 1–2.

14. This concept was first developed in James N. Rosenau, "'Fragmegrative' Challenges to National Security," in Terry Heyns, ed., *Understanding U.S. Strategy: A Reader* (Washington, D.C.: National Defense University, 1983), pp. 65–82. For a more recent and elaborate formulation, see James N. Rosenau, "New Dimensions of Security: The Interaction of Globalizing and Localizing Dynamics," *Security Dialogue* 25 (September 1994): 255–82.

15. Rosenau, *Turbulence in World Politics*, pp. 32–33.

16. For one effort to develop a methodology for probing the skill revolution see, James N. Rosenau and W. Michael Fagen, "Increasingly Skillful Citizens: A New Dynamism in World Politics?" *International Studies Quarterly*, 41 (December 1997), pp. 655–86.

17. Rosenau, *Turbulence in World Politics*, pp. 104–13.

18. Michael Shermer, "The Crooked Timber of History," *Complexity* 2, 6 (1997): pp. 23–29.

19. Rosenau, *Turbulence in World Politics*, p. 78.

20. For a cogent discussion illustrative of how different observers can interpret the same phenomena as reflective of highly discrepant degrees of

change, see Steve Lohr, "The Future Came Faster in the Old Days," *New York Times,* October 5, 1997, sec. 4, p. 1.

21. For an amusing fantasy that captures these differences by imagining King George III in 1776 tuned into CNN and possessing fiber optic phone lines, a pocket beeper, and access to the World Wide Web as he copes with a rebellious colony in America—with the result that "had the communications miracle been granted us earlier, there would be no Washington, D.C., for our politicians to blame for everything that annoys their constituents"—see Russell Baker, "Beep Beep King," *New York Times,* July 2, 1996, p. A15.

22. The use of this phrase can be found in Kenneth N. Waltz, *Theory of International Politics* (Reading, Mass.: Addison-Wesley, 1979), p. 94.

23. See the various essays in Peter B. Evans, Dietrich Rueschemeyer, and Theda Skocpol, eds., *Bringing the State Back In* (Cambridge: Cambridge University Press, 1985), as well as B. Guy Peters, "Bringing the State Back in—Again," (paper presented at the Seminar on Theories of Governance, Gartocharn, Scotland, October 10–11, 1997).

ABOUT THE AUTHORS

Eric Drew Cooper is a Ph.D. candidate in the Department of Political Science at the University of Florida. His current dissertation work focuses on Western Sahara as an example of international organizations processes and the resolution of civil conflict.

Ralph B.A. DiMuccio received his Ph.D. in International Relations from the School of International Relations at the University of Southern California in 1994. He headed the International Relations program in the Department of Political Science at the University of Florida until 1998. Currently, he is a Senior Analyst in the Corporate Development Group of Alta Vista, an Internet portal company.

Mary Durfee is Associate Professor of Political Science in the Social Sciences Department at Michigan Technological University. She is coauthor (with James N. Rosenau) of *Thinking Theory Thoroughly* and recently completed a new book manuscript, *Ecosystem Governance for the Great Lakes.*

Yale H. Ferguson is Professor of Political Science, department chair, and Faculty Associate of the Center for Global Change and Governance at Rutgers University-Newark. His books include *Contemporary Inter-American Relations; Continuing Issues in International Politics;* and with Richard W. Mansbach, *The Web of World Politics; The Elusive Quest: Theory and International Politics; The State, Conceptual Chaos, and the Future of International Relations Theory;* and *Polities: Authority, Identities, and Change.*

Heidi H. Hobbs is currently a Visiting Assistant Professor of Political Science and Public Administration at North Carolina State University, having previously served on the faculties of Florida International University and Illinois State University. She is the author of *City Hall Goes Abroad: The Foreign Policy of Local Politics.*

Ole R. Holsti is George V. Allen Professor of International Affairs Emeritus in the Department of Political Science at Duke University. Since 1975 he has collaborated with Jim Rosenau on surveys of American opinion leaders. His most recent book is *Public Opinion and American Foreign Policy*, and he is an associate editor of *The Encyclopedia of U.S. Foreign Relations*.

Margaret P. Karns is Professor of Political Science at the University of Dayton. She is coauthor with Karen A. Mingst of *The United Nations in the Post–Cold War Era, 2nd ed.* and *The United States and Multilateral Institutions*, as well as numerous articles.

Joseph Lepgold is Associate Professor in the School of Foreign Service and The Department of Government at Georgetown University. His recent publications include *Collective Conflict Management and Changing World Politics*, edited with Thomas G. Weiss, and an article in *Political Science Quarterly* on policy relevance and international relations theory, and an article in *International Security* on NATO's Post–Cold War Collective Action Problem.

Ronnie D. Lipschutz is Associate Professor of Politics and Associate Director of the Center for Global, International, and Regional Studies at the University of California at Santa Cruz. He is editor of *On Security* and author of *Global Civil Society and Global Environmental Governance* and *After Authority: War, Peace and Global Politics in the 21st Century.*

Richard W. Mansbach is currently Professor of Political Science at Iowa State University, where he has served as chair of the department. He has written or edited ten books. His most recent publications include *The Global Puzzle: Issues and Actors in World Politics*, and the coauthored *Polities: Authority, Identities and Change* with Yale H. Ferguson.

Dario V. Moreno is Associate Professor of Political Science at Florida International University. He is the author of *U.S. Policy in Central America: The Endless Debate* and *The Struggle for Peace in Central America.*

Nicholas Onuf is currently Professor of International Relations at Florida International University. He previously taught at Georgetown and American University, the latter for twenty-four years, and has held a number of visiting, exchange, and adjunct positions. He is the author of *World of Our Making, The Republican Legacy in International Thought*, and many other works.

V. Spike Peterson is Associate Professor in the Department of Political Science at the University of Arizona, with courtesy affiliations in Women's Studies, International Studies, and Comparative Cultural and Literary Studies. She edited and contributed to *Gendered States: Feminist (Re)Visions of International Relations Theory* and is the coauthor (with Anne Sisson Runyan) of *Global Gender Issues, 2nd edition.*

James N. Rosenau is University Professor of International Affairs at George Washington University, having previously been on the faculties of Rutgers University, Ohio State University, and the University of Southern California. His recent writings include *Turbulence in World Politics: A Theory of Change and Continuity; Along the Domestic-Foreign Frontier: Exploring Turbulence in a Turbulent World;* and coauthorship with Mary Durfee of *Thinking Theory Thoroughly: Coherent Approaches to an Incoherent World.*

INDEX

Abrams, Elliot, 35
Action: choices about, 140;
collective, 14; direct, 130;
freedom of, 29–30; individual, 9;
legitimacy and, 92; political, 91,
118, 130; possibility of, 141;
private, 140; public, 66, 69, 140;
sensitivity to others,' 161
Actors: collective, 160; diversity of,
29, 170; economic, 84; goals of,
141; growth of, 1; habdaptive, 65,
100, 104, 106, 109, 148, 159;
historically informed, 141;
increases in number of, 170;
individual, 81, 157, 160; interactions among, 39; international, 18,
160; macro, 12; micro, 140, 141,
147; private, 41, 162; proliferation
of, 28; public, 41; range of, 48;
rational, 100; readiness to learn by,
101; self-motivated, 9; sovereignty-
based, 15, 30, 39, 49, 96n21;
sovereignty-free, 27, 30, 31, 32,
33, 39, 41, 48, 49, 66, 70, 71, 85,
96n21, 108, 147, 172, 173, 178;
subnational/supranational, 65;
substate, 159, 173; transnational, 32
Adaptation, 1, 2
Aggregation, participation in, 13
Agnew, John, 212
Agraria, 18
Ahistoricism, 205, 229
Albania, 130
Almond, Gabriel, 120, 126–127
Amnesty International, 27, 49
Amour de soi, 182
Amour propre, 182

Angell, Norman, 182
Anomie, 17
Antarctica, 46
Asian state model, 208
Australia, 52
Authority, 206; adaptive learning
and, 107; colonial, 16; competition for, 27, 155, 210; conflicting
sources of, 209; constructions of,
71; crisis of, 14, 16, 25, 27, 158,
172, 221; demands for, 47;
dislocation of, 107; divisions of,
69, 72; expansion of, 16; habit
and, 107; jurisdictional, 91; legal,
205; legitimate, 26; local, 47, 91;
new forms of, 92; political, 35,
71, 206; regional, 91; rejection of,
16; relations, 29; relocation of, 28;
resistance to, 27; semisovereign,
97n32; sovereign, 41, 97n32; state,
26, 34; structures, 14, 15; supranational, 149; transfer of, 27, 91;
weakening of, 26
Autonomy: demands for, 207; loss
of, 209

Bailey, Thomas, 120
Banks, Michael, 184
Bartelson, Jens, 33–34
Behavior, 110; changes in, 158;
cooperative, 158; cross-national,
162; governance, 17; individual,
148; "intermittency," 153n8;
international, 163; micro-level,
143; regulation of, 162, 163;
repetitive, 111; rote, 148; social,
110; of states, 2, 8, 31